Mary Withall

DICTIONARY
of
MUSIC

First published 1992
© 1992 Geddes & Grosset Ltd,
New Lanark, Scotland.

Cover design by Cameron Graphics Ltd,
Glasgow, Scotland.

ISBN 1 85534 096 8

Printed and bound in Great Britain.

Dictionary
of
MUSIC

Peter Brooke-Ball

GEDDES&
GROSSET

Abbreviations

Abbrev.	abbreviation
c.	*circa* (about)
cent.	century
cents.	centuries
d.	died
D.B.E.	Dame Order of the British Empire
e.g.	*exempli gratia* (for example)
Fr.	France/French
Gk.	Greece/Greek
i.e.	*id est* (that is)
Is.	Israel/Israeli
It.	Italy/Italian
Lat.	Latin
no.	number
op.	opus
Port.	Portugal/ Portuguese
Russ.	Russia/Russian
Sp.	Spain/Spanish
St	saint
US	United States
USA	United States of America

A

A The sixth note of the scale of C; it is the note to which instruments of an orchestra are usually tuned.

Abbado, Claudio (1933–) Italian conductor who became musical director of *La* SCALA in 1971, principal conductor of the London Symphony Orchestra in 1979, and of the Berlin Philharmonic Orchestra in 1989. His speciality is 19th and 20th-cent. music.

abbandono (It.) 'Passionately'.

Abel, Carl Friedrich (1723–87) German composer and noted player of the VIOLA DA GAMBA. He wrote pieces specifically for the viola da gamba in addition to other types of chamber music.

Abendlied (Ger.) An 'evening song', often of religious significance.

Abendmusik (Ger.) An 'evening performance of music', particularly those performances of mainly religious music given at the Protestant church of Lübeck in Germany between 1673 and 1810.

absolute music Instumental music that exists purely as music and does not attempt to relate to a story or image. It is the opposite of PROGRAMME MUSIC.

absolute pitch (perfect pitch) The sense by which some people can exactly identify any note they hear.

abstract music *see* absolute music

Academic Festival Overture The name given to an orchestral piece (Op. 80) by BRAHMS. It was written

5

after Brahms had received an honorary degree from the University of Breslau, and was first performed in 1881.

a cappella (It.) Literally, 'in the chapel style'; it is a term that has come to mean unaccompanied choral singing.

accelerando (It.) 'Quickening'; a term used to indicate a gradual speeding up of pace. Abbrev.: *accel.*

accent The emphasis given to specific notes to indicate the RHYTHM of a piece of music.

acciaccatura (It.) An ornamental or auxiliary note, normally the semitone below, played just before, or at the same time as, a regular note. An *acciaccatura* is written in small type before the regular note and has a stroke through its tail. From the Italian *acciacciare*, to crush.

accidental A note in a piece of music that departs by one or two semitones from the KEY SIGNATURE. It is indicated by a SHARP, FLAT or NATURAL sign before it. An accidental holds good throughout a BAR unless contradicted.

accompaniment Support music supplied to a soloist or choir. An accompaniment may be provided by an orchestra, organ or, most usually, a piano.

accordion A portable REED ORGAN which was invented in Germany in the early 19th cent. Air is forced through the reeds by means of bellows which are operated by the player's arms, and notes and chords are played by pressing buttons. The *piano accordion*, has a keyboard (operated by the right hand) for playing melody notes, and buttons (operated by the left hand) for simple chords. The accordion is associated with informal or folk music and has only rarely been used by serious composers.

Acis and Galatea A MASQUE by HANDEL which was first performed in about 1718. The libretto was by John GAY (from Ovid and with additions by Pope, Dryden and Hughes) and tells the story of two lovers and Polyphemus, a jealous, one-eyed giant.

Acis et Galatée An opera by LULLY with a libretto by J.G. de Campistron which was first performed in 1686. HAYDN, too, wrote an opera on the same subject. *See* Acis and Galatea.

acoustic guitar *see* guitar.

acoustics 1 A branch of physics which is concerned with sound. The main characteristics of a sound are its pitch, intensity, resonance and quality. **2** The characteristics of a hall or auditorium that enable speech and music to be heard without the sounds being distorted. In a concert hall with good acoustics, sounds from the stage can be heard clearly in all quarters.

action 1 The mechanism of a keyboard instrument that links the keyboard to the strings or, in the case of an organ, to the pipes and stops. **2** The gap between the strings and fingerboard of a stringed instrument as dictated by the height of the BRIDGE.

act tune (curtain music) An instrumental piece of music that is played between the acts of a play while the curtain is down. It is usually associated with 17th and 18th-cent. music. *See* entr'acte; intermezzo.

adagietto (It.) **1** 'Slow', but not as slow as ADAGIO. **2** A short composition in an adagio tempo.

adagio (It.) **1** Literally, 'at ease', i.e. at a slow tempo. **2** A slow movement.

adagissimo (It.) 'Very slow'.

added sixth A frequently used chord created by adding the sixth note from the root to a major or minor TRIAD; for example, in the key of C major, A is added above the triad of C–E–G.

additional accompaniments New or revised parts for extra instruments written by later composers and added to 17th and 18th-cent. works in order to increase fullness. In many cases the additions did not match the quality of the original music; but MOZART once wrote additional music for HANDEL'S MESSIAH when an organ was not available.

ad libitum (Lat.) Literally, 'at pleasure' and usually abbreviated to *ad lib.* In music, the term is used to indicate that, when playing a piece, a performer can (*a*) alter the tempo or rhythm, (*b*) choose an alternative passage by the composer, (*c*) improvise a CADENZA, and (*d*) include or omit a passage if he so chooses.

à deux cordes (Fr.) *see* a due corde.

a due corde (It.) 'On two strings'. When applied to music for stringed instruments, the term means that a piece should be played on two strings, not just on one.

Aeolian harp A type of ZITHER which has strings of similar length but of different thickness. The instrument is not actually played but left outside to catch the wind; different chords are sounded according to the speed of the wind, which makes the strings vibrate faster or slower. The name is derived from Aeolus, who was the Greek god of the wind.

Aeolian mode A MODE which, on the piano, uses the white notes from A to A.

aeolina A type of HARMONICA.

aeoline A soft organ stop that imitates the sound of the AEOLIAN HARP.

aerophone Any instrument in which movement of air causes sound; for example, organ, oboe, trumpet, flute etc.

Affektenlehre (Ger.) A musical theory formulated in Germany during the 18th cent. which held that music should be judged by the way in which it arouses certain emotions, such as sorrow, happiness etc.

affettuoso (It.) Literally, 'tender' or 'affectionate', i.e. an indication that a piece of music should be played with tender feeling.

agiatamente (It.) Literally, 'comfortably', i.e. an indication that a piece should be played with a certain amount of liberty. Not to be confused with AGITATAMENTE.

agitato, agitatamente (It.) Literally, 'agitated', 'agitatedly', i.e. an indication that a piece should be played restlessly or wildly.

Agnus Dei (Lat.) 'O Lamb of God'; the concluding part of the Latin mass. Numerous musical settings have been written for the Agnus Dei.

agogic A note that is made to stand out by being lingered on rather than by being played more loudly. It may be the first note of a phrase, or an important high or discordant note.

Aida A tragic opera by VERDI to a four-act libretto by Ghislanzoni. First performed in the Italian Theatre, Cairo, in 1871, the opera was commissioned by Ismail Pasha (Khedive of Egypt). The story is set in ancient Egypt and concerns a warrior, Ramades, and an Ethiopian slave, Aida, who loves him. Ultimately, the two lovers are entombed together.

air 1 A simple tune or song. **2** A melodious BAROQUE composition.

Air on the G String The name given to August Wilhemj's arrangement for violin and accompaniment of the 2nd movement of BACH's Suite no. 3 in D. The transposed violin part is played on the lowest (G) string.

Albéniz, Isaac (1860–1909) A Spanish pianist and composer who was a child prodigy and went on to write operas, orchestral pieces and songs. He is best known for his piano suite *Iberia*, comprising 12 technically demanding pieces. He has had a lasting influence on Spanish music.

Albert Hall *see* Royal Albert Hall.

Albert Herring A comic chamber opera by BRITTEN (Op. 39) to a three-act libretto by Eric Crozier. It was first performed at GLYNDEBOURNE in 1947. The story concerns Albert, a shopkeeper, who is elected King of the May. He subsequently gets drunk and manages to rid himself from the clutches of his mother.

Alberti, Domenico (1710–40) An Italian singer, composer and harpsichordist who wrote many unremarkable works and is largely remembered for his use of 'broken' chords in his pieces for harpsichord.

Alberti bass A simple accompaniment to a melody consisting of 'broken' or spread chords arranged in a rhythmic pattern. It is so called because Domenico ALBERTI used it in his keyboard sonatas.

Albinoni, Tommaso (1671–1750) A prolific Italian composer, among the earliest to write concertos for solo violin. He wrote more than 40 operas. BACH composed fugues on themes by Albinoni.

alborada (Sp.) Literally, 'morning song'; a form of popular Spanish music for bagpipes and side drum.

Albumblatt (Ger.) Literally, 'album leaf'; a popular title given by 19th-cent. composers to short, instrumental compositions (often for the piano) and of a personal nature.

Alceste A three-act opera by GLUCK with a libretto by R. Calzabigi; the original, Italian version (1767) was revised by Gluck into a French version (1776) to a libretto by du Roullet. The story is based on a tale by Euripides: Alcestis gives up her life to save her husband, Admetus, and is rewarded by being restored to life. Other operas by the same name were composed by LULLY (1674) and HANDEL (1734), among others.

Aldeburgh Festival An annual music festival founded by Benjamin BRITTEN at Aldeburgh, Suffolk, in 1948. It maintains its strong association with Britten, many of whose works were first performed there.

aleatory music Music which contains unpredictable or chance elements so no two performances of a piece are ever similar. It is a form explored by composers such as CAGE and STOCKHAUSEN since 1945.

Alkan, Charles Henri Valentin (the pseudonym of Morhange, Charles Henri Valentin) (1813–88). A French composer and pianist who was a close friend of LISZT and CHOPIN. One of the foremost piano teachers of his day, he wrote many piano pieces of great complexity, often using ideas ahead of their time.

alla breve (It.) **1** An instruction that a piece of music should be performed twice as fast as the notation would suggest. **2** 2/2 time.

allargando (It.) Literally, 'getting broader', i.e. an indication that a piece should be played grandly whilst at the same time getting slower.

alla tedesca (It.) An abbreviation of *alla danza tedesca,* meaning 'in the style of a German dance'. *See* allemande.

alla turca (It.) Literally, 'in the Turkish style'.

alla zingarese (It.) Literally, 'in the style of gypsy music'.

alla zoppa (It.) Literally, 'in a limping way', i.e. in a syncopated rhythm.

allegretto (It.) A term indicating light and moderately quick movement, but not as fast as ALLEGRO.

allegro (It.) Literally, 'lively', i.e. in a quick tempo. The term is often used as the title of a bright composition or movement.

allemande (Fr.) An abbreviation of *danse allemande* or 'German dance', of which there are two forms. **1** A moderately slow dance used by 17th and 18th-cent. composers as the first movement of a suite of four contrasting dances. **2** A brisk dance of the 18th and 19th cents., similar to the WALTZ.

allentando (It.) 'Slowing down', i.e. a term used to indicate that the tempo of a piece of music should be slowed down.

all' ongarese (It.) Literally, 'in the style of Hungarian (gypsy) music'.

alphorn A primitive type of horn, with no valves, that is traditionally played by Swiss herdsmen to call in their cattle in the evening. Made from wood and bark, alphorns usually have an upturned bell which rests on the ground, and they can be up to 3 m (10 ft) long. Various composers, including MAHLER, have used the alphorn in their compositions.

al segno (It.) Literally, 'to the sign' (i.e. to a standard symbol used in musical notation, see Appendix). The term is used in two ways: it can instruct the player either to go *back* to the sign and start again, or to *continue* until the sign is reached.

Also sprach Zarathustra (Ger.) (Thus spake Zoroaster) A tone-poem by Richard STRAUSS (Op.30) which was inspired by Nietzsche's poem of the same name. It was first performed in Frankfurt in 1896, but found a new and appreciative audience when it was used as incidental music in the Stanley Kubrick's film *2001: A Space Odyssey*.

alt An abbreviation of the Latin phrase *in alto*, which means 'high'. It is used for the notes in the octave rising from G above the treble clef; the notes in the octave above that are said to be *in altissimo*.

alto (It.) 'High'. **1** The highest adult male voice, which is now used only in male-voice choirs. **2** An addition to the name of an instrument to indicate that it is one size

13

larger than the soprano member of the family; for example alto CLARINET. **3** A low female voice that has a greater compass than the male alto voice (usually, and more properly, called CONTRALTO).

Amati The name of a famous family of violin makers who worked in Cremona, Italy, in the 16th and 17th cents. The most famous member of the family is Nicolo Amati (1596–1684), who taught Antonio STRADIVARI.

Ambrosian chants A collection of chants, used in Milan Cathedral, which are named after St Ambrose (*c*. 340–97), Bishop of Milan, who greatly influenced church singing. Despite bearing his name, the earliest surviving chants were composed long after his death.

America the Beautiful The poem which has become the national song of the USA. The first version of the poem was written in 1893 by Katharine Lee Bates but she simplified it some 10 years later. More than 60 tunes have been written for the poem, but those by Will C. Macfarlane and S.A Ward are the most famous.

American in Paris, An A descriptive piece for orchestra by GERSHWIN (1928) in which, amongst other unusual instruments, four taxi horns are played. The incidental music for a film (1951) of the same name was based on Gershwin's original.

American organ (cabinet organ) A reed organ, similar to a HARMONIUM except that air is sucked through the reeds instead of being blown through them.

American Quartet The string quartet in F (Op. 96) by

DVORAK, which he wrote in 1893 and which was largely inspired by Black American melodies. For a time it was known as the Nigger Quartet but this title has been abandoned as insulting.

Amor brujo, El (Love, the Magician) A ballet in one act with music by FALLA and a scenario by Martinez (based on an Andalusian gypsy tale). It was first performed in Madrid in 1915 and is unusual in that the ballerina has to sing as well as dance.

amoroso (It.) Literally, 'lovingly', indicating that a piece should be played with warm affection.

amplifier any device, particularly an electric one, which renders a sound louder.

anacrusis An unstressed note or grouping of notes at the beginning of a musical phrase; it can also mean an unstressed syllable at the beginning of a song.

ancora (It.) Literally, 'yet' or 'still', as in *ancora forte* meaning 'still loud' and *ancora più forte* meaning 'yet louder'.

andante (It.) Literally, 'going' or 'moving', it is usually used to indicate a moderate tempo or a walking pace. *Più andante* means 'moving more' or slightly faster. Andante is sometimes used as a title for a moderately slow piece of music.

andantino (It.) Less slow (i.e. slightly faster) than ANDANTE.

Anfang (Ger.) Literally, the 'beginning'; *Anfangs* means 'from the beginning'.

anglaise (Fr.) Short for *danse anglaise* or 'English dance', i.e. a lively dance in quick time, such as a HORNPIPE.

Anglican chant A characteristically English way of setting to music prose, psalms and canticles, in which the number of syllables per line can vary. To accommodate this irregularity, the first note of each musical phrase is a RECITING NOTE which is timeless and is used to sing as many syllables as necessary before moving on to notes which are sung in time and which normally carry one syllable each. In many respects, it is a simple form of GREGORIAN CHANT.

anima (It.) Literally, 'soul', as in *con anima*, which means that a piece should be played 'with soul' or 'with emotion'.

animato (It.) Literally, 'animated'.

animo (It.) Literally, 'spirit', so *con animo* indicates that a piece should be performed 'with spirit'.

animoso (It.) 'Spirited'.

answer The second entry of the main subject (theme) of a FUGUE which is played a fifth higher or lower than the first entry. In a *real answer*, the subject and answer are identical; in a *tonal answer*, the intervals in the answer are changed.

Antheil, George (1900–59) An American composer and pianist of Polish descent who gained notoriety by incorporating the sounds of motor horns, door bells and aeroplane engines in some of his compositions, most notably his *Ballet mécanique* which was first performed in Paris in 1926. He also composed operas, piano sonatas, symphonies and film scores.

anthem The Anglican equivalent to the Roman Catholic MOTET. An anthem is usually an elaborate musical setting of non-liturgical words sung by a church choir without the congregation; solo parts are common and accompaniment by an organ is usual. PURCELL and WESLEY composed popular anthems.

anticipation The sounding of a note (or notes) of a chord before the rest of the chord is played.

antiphon The sacred words, sung in PLAINSONG by two choirs, before and after a psalm or canticle in a Roman Catholic service. *Antiphonal* is an adjective applied to the musical effect achieved by two choirs (or groups of instruments) which are positioned in different parts of a hall and sing (or play) alternately, one 'answering' the other.

anvil A percussion instrument consisting of steel bars which are struck with a wooden or metal mallet. It is meant to sound like a blacksmith's anvil being struck with a hammer and was used by both VERDI and WAGNER.

a piacere (It.) Literally, 'at pleasure', meaning that the performer of a piece of music is permitted to take a certain amount of liberty, particularly with tempo, while playing it. *See* ad libitum.

Appalachian Spring A ballet by COPLAND which was written for the ballerina and choreographer Martha Graham, and was inspired by Hart Crane's poem about country marriage. It was first performed in New York in 1945.

appassionato, appassionata (It.) Literally, 'impassioned', hence the title *Sonata appassionata* which was given to BEETHOVEN's piano sonata in F minor (Op. 57).

appoggiando (It.) Literally 'leaning'; when applied to

musical notes, this implies that they should pass very smoothly from one to the next.

appoggiatura (It.) A term for a 'leaning' note (*see* appoggiando), indicated in the score. **1** A *long appoggiatura* is a note of varying length that is different from the harmony note. **2** A *short appoggiatura* is a very short note of indefinite length, sometimes accented, sometimes not. **3** A *passing appoggiatura*, as used in the 18th cent., normally occurs when the principal notes of a melody form a sequence of thirds and it is played before the beat.

après-midi d'un faune, Prélude à l' (Prelude to the 'Afternoon of a Faun') An orchestral tone-poem by DEBUSSY written in 1892–4 and first performed in Paris in 1894. Debussy originally intended to write a set of three pieces to illustrate the poem by Mallarmé (*Prélude*, *Interlude*, and *Paraphrase finale*), but only finished the first part. In 1912 the Russian dancer Nijinsky based a ballet on the music.

arabesque 1 A florid treatment of thematic music. **2** A lyrical piece of music that employs an exaggerated and elaborate style, as used by SCHUMANN and DEBUSSY.

arabeske (Ger.) *see* arabesque.

Archduke Trio The nickname given to the piano trio in B flat (Op. 97) by BEETHOVEN, composed in 1811 and dedicated to Archduke Rudolph of Austria.

archet (Fr.) A bow, such as is used to play a stringed instrument.

archi (It.) Literally 'bows'; a term that refers to all stringed instruments played with a bow.

arco (It.) The singular of ARCHI. It is the usual

instruction to play with the bow after playing PIZZICATO.

Arensky, Anton Stepanovich (1861–1906) A Russian composer who studied under RIMSKY-KORSAKOV. He wrote three operas as well as symphonies, cantatas, church and chamber music, and incidental music to Shakespeare's *The Tempest*. However, his best known works are his piano pieces, especially his piano trio in D minor (Op. 32).

aria (It.) **1** A song or air. Originally the term was used for any song for one or more voices but it has come to be used exclusively for a long, solo song as found in oratorio and opera.

Ariadne auf Naxos (Ariadne on Naxos) An opera in two acts with music by Richard STRAUSS and a libretto by Hofmannsthal. Two versions were written. The first version (first performed in Stuttgart, 1912) was designed to follow Molière's play, *Le Bourgeois Gentilhomme* but was not successful. In the second version (first performed in Vienna, 1916), an operatic prologue was substituted for the play, and proved more successful. The story is the mythological tale of Ariadne being abandoned by her lover Theseus on the island of Naxos, where she is consoled by Bacchus. From time to time there are comic interruptions.

arioso (It.) Literally, 'like an aria'. **1** A melodious and song-like RECITATIVE. **2** A short air in an opera or oratorio. **3** An instrumental piece that follows the style of a vocal arioso.

Armida The name of operas by several composers including LULLY, GLUCK, HAYDN, ROSSINI, DVORAK.

The inspiration for these operas was the poem *La Gerusalemme liberata* (Jerusalem Delivered) by Tasso, which is about the Crusades.

Armstrong, Louis (1900–71) Black American jazz trumpeter and singer who remains one of the greatest figures in jazz history. He was born into poverty in New Orleans but started playing the trumpet at the age of 12. In 1922 he migrated to Chicago and later to New York. With his bands he made numerous recordings of such tunes as *Willie the Weeper* and *West End Blues*. After 1946 he concentrated on being an all-round entertainer but he never lost his worldwide popularity. He delighted in his nickname 'Satchmo', meaning 'satchel mouth'.

Arne, Michael (1740–86) An English singer and composer who was the illegitimate son of Thomas ARNE. His best works were for the stage and he worked with the great impresario, David Garrick.

Arne, Thomas Augustine (1710–78) A prolific English composer of operas, oratorios and instrumental pieces. His operas include *Artaxerxes* and *Thomas and Sally* but his best known work is his masque *Alfred* which contains the famous song RULE BRITANNIA.

Arnold, Malcolm (1921–) An English composer, trumpeter and conductor. His innovative compositions include seven symphonies, ballet music, numerous concertos for various instruments, as well as chamber and choral pieces. To the public at large, he is best known for his film score to the film, *The Bridge on the River Kwai* (1957).

arpeggiare (It.) Literally 'to play the harp', i.e. to play chords 'spread out' as they are on the harp. *See* arpeggio.

arpeggio (It.) 'Harp-wise', i.e. an indication that the notes of a chord should be played in rapid succession, as they are on a harp, and not simultaneously.

arpeggione An obsolete instrument invented in 1823, which is a cross between a VIOLONCELLO (cello) and a GUITAR, with six strings played with a bow, and a fretted keyboard. SCHUBERT wrote a sonata for arpeggione.

arrangement An adaptation of a piece of music for a medium different from that for which it was originally composed.

Arrau, Claudio (1903–91) An influential Chilean pianist who opened his own piano school in Santiago, Chile and taught in Berlin from 1925–40. He was recognized as one of the greatest interpreters of works by BEETHOVEN, and is also admired for his playing of CHOPIN, LISZT, BRAHMS and SCHUMANN.

Ars antiqua (Lat.) The 'old art', i.e. music of the 12th and 13th cents. as opposed to *Ars nova*, the new style of music that evolved in the 14th cent.

Ars nova (Lat.) *see* Ars antiqua.

Art of Fugue, The A keyboard work by Johann Sebastian BACH comprising 13 fugues and 4 canons that demonstrates virtually all possible contrapuntal treatments of a solitary theme. It was written in 1749 and published a year later.

assai (It.) 'Very', as in *allegro assai*, 'very fast'.

assez (Fr.) 'Moderately', as in *assez vite*, 'moderately quick'.

a tempo (It.) 'In time'; a term that indicates that a piece should revert to its normal tempo after a change of speed.

athematic music Music that does not have any themes or tunes as such; it is concerned with exploring the unconventional possibilities of sounds.

atonal music Music that is not in any KEY. Atonal music is particularly associated with the works of SCHOENBERG, although he preferred to use the word *pantonality*, meaning a synthesis of all the keys.

attacca (It.) 'Attack', i.e. start the next movement without a pause.

Attwood, Thomas (1765–1838) An English composer who was organist at St Paul's Cathedral, London. He was a pupil of MOZART in Vienna and became a close friend to MENDELSSOHN. He wrote anthems for the coronations of George IV and William IV.

aubade (Fr.) 'Morning music', as opposed to a SERENADE or evening music.

Auber, Daniel François Esprit (1782–1871) A French composer who wrote some 45 operas, including *La Muette de Portici* (1828) and *Fra Diavolo* (1830).

augmentation The lengthening of the time values of notes in melodic parts with the result that they sound more impressive and grand. The opposite of augmentation is DIMINUTION.

augmented interval The INTERVAL formed by increasing any perfect or major interval by a SEMITONE.

augmented sixth A chord based on the flattened SUBMEDIANT that contains the augmented sixth INTERVAL.

augmented triad A TRIAD of which the fifth is augmented.

a una corda (It.) 'On one string' (*compare* a due corde). In the context of a piano, it means left-hand pedal, i.e. reducing the volume.

Auric, Georges (1899–1983) A French composer and the youngest member of *Les* SIX. His compositions include operas, piano and chamber pieces, as well as music for films and ballets, the most notable of which is *Les Matelots*.

autoharp A type of ZITHER in which chords are produced by pressing down keys that dampen some of the strings but let others vibrate freely. The instrument was invented in the late 19th cent. and was popular with American folk musicians.

avant-garde (Fr.) Literally, 'vanguard', a term applied to music (or any other art) that is considered to break new ground in style or structure.

Ave Maria (Lat.) 'Hail Mary', a prayer to the Virgin Mary used in the Roman Catholic Church. It has been set to music by numerous composers including SCHUBERT, and LISZT, and GOUNOD in particular. •

Avison, Charles (1709–70) An English organist and composer, and the author of the controversial treatise *An Essay on Musical Expression*, which provides valuable evidence of the musical tastes of the time.

B

B 1 The seventh note of the scale of C major.
2 Abbrev. for bass or for Bachelor (as in *B. Mus.*, Bachelor of Music).

Babbitt, Milton (1916–) An American composer and mathematician whose early works were influenced by WEBERN and SCHOENBERG and who later turned to electronic devices such as synthesizers and tape recorders. His compositions include several orchestral and choral pieces as well as *Composition for Synthesizer* and *Vision and Prayer*, which had words by Dylan Thomas to a tape accompaniment.

baby grand The smallest size of grand PIANO.

Bach, Carl Philipp Emanuel (1714–88) A German composer who was the second son and pupil of Johann Sebastian BACH. He was a famous harpsichordist and was particularly well known for his skill at improvising. His compositions include 2 oratorios, 50 keyboard concertos and many songs, but his great claim to fame is that he is credited with developing the SONATA FORM. His treatise *An Essay on the proper method of playing keyboard instruments* provides an invaluable insight into the techniques and playing styles of his era.

Bach, Johann (John) Christian (1735–82) A German composer and the youngest son of Johann Sebastian BACH by his second wife. He studied under his father but moved to Italy in 1756 and then to London in 1762, where he settled (which is why he is sometimes referred to as the 'English' Bach). He befriended

MOZART when the eight-year-old prodigy visited London and was an early influence on the young Austrian's style, especially with regard to piano concertos. His compositions include 13 operas (such as *Amadis de Gaule*), an oratorio, and many piano concertos and symphonic pieces. As well as leaving a lasting impression on Mozart, his subtle way with melody also influenced HAYDN and BEETHOVEN.

Bach, Johann Christoph (1642–1703) A German organist and composer who was the cousin of Johann Sebastian BACH's father. He composed several choral and instrumental pieces of which *Ich lasse dich nicht* is the best known.

Bach, Johann Christoph Friedrich (1732–95) A German composer who was the eldest surviving son of Johann Sebastian BACH's marriage to his second wife. He was taught by his father and subsequently wrote a broad variety of music, including oratorios, concertos, sonatas and chamber music.

Bach, Johann Michael (1648–94) A German organist and composer who was the son of Johann Sebastian BACH's great-uncle and the father of the great composer's first wife, Maria Barbara. His output includes motets and some organ music.

Bach, Johann Sebastian (1685–1750) A German composer who was one of the most influential in history. He was orphaned at the age of 10 and consequently went to live with his elder brother, Johann Christoph, who was his first keyboard teacher. In 1700 he became a chorister and he may have learned from the resident organist at St Michael's Church, Lüneburg. In 1703 he became a violinist in the Weimar court orchestra and then the organist at Arnstadt. In 1707 he was organist at Mühlhausen and married his cousin, Maria Barbara. He went back to Weimar in 1708 to become court organist and it is during this period that he composed most of his organ music. In 1717 he became director of music (*Kapellmeister*) to Prince Leopold at the court of Anhalt-Köthen and concentrated on composing secular works including the BRANDENBURG CONCERTOS. His wife died in 1720 and the following year he married Anna Magdalena Wilcken. He was appointed cantor of St Thomas's in Leipzig in 1723 and that is where he spent the rest of his years. During this phase of his life he composed religious pieces such as his ST MATTHEW PASSION. In 1740 he began to have trouble with his eyesight and by the time he died he was completely blind. He had 20 children, but only 10 survived infancy.

During his lifetime, Bach had an unparalleled reputation as an organist but his compositions were considered old-fashioned and were only accepted by a minority. He had little time for opera, but his most powerful works express an unsurpassed dramatic and emotional force. Bach's profundity enriched every type of music that he was required to produce, and his music has influenced succeeding generations of composers. WAGNER said of Bach's work that it was 'the most stupendous miracle in all music'.

Bach's principal works include: ST JOHN PASSION, ST MATTHEW PASSION, CHRISTMAS ORATORIO, and the six Brandenburg Concertos. He also wrote numerous cantatas and pieces for the harpsichord and organ, as well as many pieces of chamber music.

Bach, Wilhelm Friedemann (1710–84) A German composer and organist who was the eldest of Johann Sebastian BACH's sons. He was taught by his father (who may have written *The Well-Tempered Klavier* for him) and became a reputable freelance organist. However, he struggled to make a living and ultimately died in poverty; at one time he passed off some of his father's works as his own. Ironically, many of his organ compositions proved popular after his death and are frequently played today.

Bach trumpet A 19th-cent. valved trumpet which was designed to make it easier play the high-pitched parts which were originally composed by Bach and his contemporaries for a natural (unvalved) trumpet.

badinage or **badinerie** (Fr.) Literally, 'frolic'; a term for fast, frivolous music.

badinerie (Fr.) *see* badinage.

bagatelle (Fr.) 'Trifle'; a short, light piece of music, usually for piano, e.g. BEETHOVEN'S FÜR ELISE.

bagpipes A reed instrument in which air is supplied to the pipe or pipes from an inflated bag. Bagpipes are known to have existed for 3000 years or more and hundreds of different types are found today. The best known form of bagpipe is played in Scotland and consists of a *bag* which is inflated through a pipe and is held under the arm; a *chanter* (a reed pipe with finger holes) on which the melody is played; and several *drone* pipes, each of which is tuned to a different note. Air is rhythmically squeezed from the bag by the arm (and is then replenished with more breath) and is forced out through the chanter and drone pipes.

Baker, Janet (1933–) An English mezzo-soprano (formerly a contralto) of international repute. She was famed for her dramatic roles (e.g. Dido in PURCELL'S DIDO AND AENEAS) but was equally capable of singing comic parts. As a concert hall singer, she is especially remembered for her renditions of some of MAHLER's works. She was made a D.B.E. in 1976.

Balakirev, Mily Alexeyevich (1837–1910) A Russian composer, famed for his leadership of a group of nationalistic composers known as 'The FIVE' or 'The Mighty Handful'. After a turbulent life in which he had numerous jobs, not all linked to music, he became the director of the Court Chapel in 1883. He was a fine pianist and his virtuoso piano piece *Islamey* proves his talent as a composer as well. His other works include 2 symphonies, 2 symphonic poems (*Russia* and *Tamara*), an overture (*King Lear*), and a piano sonata.

balalaika (Russ.) A Russian folk-instrument of the GUITAR family, with a triangular body. It is of Tartar origin and usually has just three strings and a fretted fingerboard. Balalaikas are made in several sizes and are often played in concert with one another.

Balfe, Michael William (1808–70) An Irish composer, baritone singer and violinist. Amongst his most noted roles as a singer were Figaro in *The* BARBER OF SEVILLE and Papageno in *The* MAGIC FLUTE. He wrote 29 operas of which *The Bohemian Girl* (1843) is the best known.

ballabile (It.) 'In a dancing style'.

ballad 1 A simple, easy-to-sing song, for solo voice; such songs, which frequently dealt with contemporary events, were printed on broadsheets and sold at public functions and fairs between the 16th and 19th cents. **2** A sentimental 'drawing-room' song of the late 19th cent., sometimes referred to as a 'Shop Ballad' to differentiate it from the type of songs that were sold by street vendors. **3** A narrative song or operatic ARIA.

ballade (Fr.) **1** A type of medieval French poetry, often set to music by troubadours. **2** A 19th-cent. term, coined by CHOPIN, for a long, romantic instrumental piece.

ballet A dramatic entertainment in which dancers in costume perform to a musical accompaniment. Mime is often used in ballet to express emotions or to tell a story. Ballet has a long history that dates back to before the Middle Ages. In the 16th and 17th cents., ballets often included singing and consequently were closely linked to opera. By the end of the 18th cent., however, ballet had evolved more gymnastic qualities and, although it was still included as an integral part in many operas, it also kept a separate existence. In the 19th cent., ballet achieved new heights of popularity in France and spread to Italy and Russia where several schools of ballet were established that incorporated traditional dancing into their teaching. TCHAIKOVSKY's ballet scores (e.g. SWAN LAKE and *The* SLEEPING BEAUTY) had a massive influence on Russian ballet and greatly added to its international appeal. The Russian choreographer and entrepreneur, Sergei Diaghilev (1872–1929), encouraged young composers such as STRAVINSKY and RAVEL) to write ballet scores. At the start of the 20th cent. ballet became immensely popular in England. VAUGHAN WILLIAMS, BLISS and BRITTEN all composed notable pieces for ballet and the outstanding English choreographers Sir Frederick Ashton and Kenneth Macmillan helped to maintain the interest. In the USA, the choreographer George Balanchine had an equally powerful influence and many American composers have since writen ballet music. Meanwhile, PROKOFIEV's masterpieces (e.g. *Romeo and Juliet*) maintained Russia's great tradition in dancing. Today, ballet is witnessing a new revival with scores being produced by young composers and with energetic companies establishing new dancing techniques on both sides of the Atlantic.

Ballo in Maschera, Un *see* Masked Ball, A.

band A term used to describe virtually any group of instrumentalists except a concert orchestra, for example dance band, jazz band, pop band, military band.

banjo A guitar-like, stringed instrument of Black American origin. It comprises a shallow metal (sometimes wood) drum with parchment stretched over the top while the bottom is (usually) left open. Banjos can have between four and nine strings.

Bantock, Granville (1868–1946) An influential English composer and conductor who actively encouraged young composers (SIBELIUS dedicated his 3rd symphony to him). His works, which included symphonic poems, operas and choral pieces, followed the romantic tradition. Perhaps his best known work is his tone-poem *Fifine at the Fair*. He was knighted in 1930.

bar 1 A vertical line (bar line) drawn down one or more STAVES of music. **2** The space between two bar lines.

Barber, Samuel (1910–81) An American composer and singer who whose works include two operas (*Vanessa* and *Antony and Cleopatra*), ballets, symphonies, concertos, choral works and piano compositions. In 1931 he composed *Dover Beach*, a setting of Matthew Arnold's poem for string quartet and his own voice. His best known work is *Adagio for Strings* (1936).

Barber of Seville, The (*Il Barbiere di Siviglia*) The title of a comic opera by ROSSINI with a libretto by C. Sterbini (based on Beaumarchais' play of the same name). The story tells how Count Almaviva succeeds, with the help of Figaro (the barber of Seville), in wooing Rosina, the ward of the protective Dr Bartolo. MOZART's *The* MARRIAGE OF FIGARO is a sequel to the story. Rossini's opera, not to be confused with Paisiello's earlier version of the tale, was first performed in Rome, 1816.

barber-shop quartet A quartet of amateur male singers who perform close-harmony arrangements. The tradition originated in barber shops in New York in the late 19th century.

Barbiere di Siviglia, Il *see* Barber of Seville, The.

Barbirolli, John (Giovanni Battista) (1899–1970) An outstanding English conductor, of Italian origin. In 1943 he became conductor of Manchester's Hallé Orchestra, which he stayed with for the rest of his life and transformed into one of the world's leading orchestras. He was knighted in 1949.

barcarolle (Fr.) A boating song with a rhythm imitating that of songs sung by gondoliers.

bard A Celtic minstrel, part of whose job it was to compose songs for his master. Bards traditionally held annual meetings (*Eisteddfods*) in Wales and these have been revived in recent times as competition festivals.

Barenboim, Daniel (1942–) An Argentine-born Israeli pianist and conductor who is famed for his interpretation of late 19th and early 20th-cent. music.

baritone 1 A male voice, midway between bass and tenor with a range of approximately two octaves. **2** A brass instrument of the SAXHORN family.

baroque (Port.) Literally 'grotesque', but it has become a term used to describe the lush style of music typical of the 17th and early 18th cents.

Barraqué, Jean (1928–73) A French experimental composer who explored the possibilities of voice and percussion instruments, as in his piece entitled *Le Temps restitué*.

barrel organ A mechanical organ of the 18th and 19th cents. in which air was admitted into pipes by means of pins on a hand-rotated barrel. It was restricted to playing a limited number of tunes but was nonetheless frequently used in church services.

Bartered Bride, The A comic opera by SMETANA to a three-act libretto by K. Sabini. The story tells of a love intrigue set in a Bohemian village. The opera was first performed in Prague, in 1866.

Bartók, Béla (1881–1945) A Hungarian composer and pianist who was initially influenced by the works of LISZT and Richard STRAUSS but who later turned to the study of the traditional folk music of his homeland. He earned an enviable reputation in Europe as a virtuoso pianist but many of his compositions were not well received in Hungary until the staging of his ballet *The Wooden Prince* in Budapest in 1917. During the 1920s he resumed his career as a pianist and was given a salaried post at the Hungarian Academy of Sciences in 1934; his position at the academy was ostensibly offered to him so that he could continue to compile a collection of Hungarian folksongs. In 1940 he emigrated to the USA and taught at Columbia and Harvard universities.

Bartók's music has a highly individual quality, not always instantly accessible, that combines traditional folk elements with the contemporary. His intensely creative mind forced him into many problems with composition but his works remain powerful and contain a melodic and rhythmic quality that are unique to him. Although he died in poverty, he is now revered as one of the great forces of 20th cent. music.

Bartók's principal works include: *Duke Bluebeard's Castle* (opera); *The Miraculous Mandarin* (ballet); *Cantata profana* (a choral piece); and six influential string quartets. In addition he wrote many orchestral works, chamber pieces, piano sonatas, and numerous arrangements of folk songs.

baryton (Ger.) An 18th-cent. German stringed instrument, played with a bow.

Basie, William ('Count') (1904–84) A Black American jazz pianist, band leader and composer. He started his career as a variety show pianist but on 'discovering' jazz he formed his own band in 1935. His group made several recordings and became famous for its driving rhythms as well as its virtuoso soloists.

bass 1 The lowest adult male voice. **2** An abbreviation for DOUBLE BASS. **3** An addition to the instrument name to indicate the largest member of a family of instruments (except where CONTRABASS instruments are built).

bassa (It.) 'Low'.

bass-bar A strip of wood glued as reinforcement under the bridge inside the BELLY of instruments of the VIOLIN family.

bass clef *see* clef.

bass clarinet A single-reed instrument built an octave lower than the CLARINET, with a crook and upturned bell.

bass drum A large percussion instrument consisting of a cylindrical wooden hoop which is usually covered on both sides with vellum. It is common in military bands in which it is suspended vertically from the shoulders and beaten with two sticks.

basse danse (Fr.) Literally, 'low dance', i.e. a dance in which the feet are kept low to the ground.

basset horn An alto CLARINET.

bass flute An ALTO flute with a pitch a fourth lower than a 'concert' or normal flute.

basso continuo *see* figured bass.

bassoon A double-reed instrument dating back to the

16th cent. that consists of a wooden tube doubled back on itself. It has a compass from B flat below bass clef to E on the fourth line of the treble clef.

basso ostinato (It.) 'Obstinate bass', a ground bass, i.e. a bass FIGURE that is repeated many times throughout a composition (or part of a composition) while the upper parts vary.

baton The stick used by a CONDUCTOR to give his commands to performers.

batterie 1 (Fr.) (*also* battery) A 17th and 18th-cent. term for ARPEGGIO. **2** The percussion section of an orchestra.

battuta (It.) *see* beat.

Bax, Arnold Edward Trevor (1883–1953) An English composer and pianist who was greatly influenced by Irish folklore and by the poetry of Yeats. He adopted a richly romantic style in his compositions, the most notable of which are his symphonic poems (e.g. *The Garden of Fand*, *Overture to a Picaresque Comedy* and *Tintagel*). He also wrote 7 symphonies, concertos for violin and arranged many folk songs. He was knighted in 1937.

Bayreuth A town in Germany where WAGNER arranged for the building of a festival theatre which has subsequently become internationally famous for staging his operas.

beat 1 A unit of rhythmic measure in music, indicated to a choir or orchestra by the movement of a conductor's baton. The number of beats in a BAR depends on the TIME-SIGNATURE. **2** A form of 20th cent. popular music with a steady and powerful rhythm.

be-bop A jazz development of the 1940s in which complex rhythms and harmonic sequences were carried out against rapidly played melodic improvisation. It is particularly associated with the jazz saxophonist, Charlie PARKER.

Bebung (Ger.) Literally, 'trembling', i.e. a VIBRATO effect caused by shaking a finger holding down a key of a clavichord.

Bechstein, Friedrich Wilhelm Carl (1826–1900) A German piano manufacturer who, after working in Germany, France and England, established his own company in Berlin in 1856. Branches of his firm were subsequently formed in France, England and Russia. London's Wigmore Hall was originally named the Bechstein Hall.

Bedford, David (1937-) A prolific English composer who was, for a time, a member of the pop group The Whole World. His best known work is *Star's End* (1974), a composition for electric instruments as well as orchestra.

Beecham, Thomas (1879–1961) An English conductor of international repute. His early ambition was to compose but he took up conducting instead. He founded the London Philharmonic Orchestra in 1932 and the Royal Philharmonic Orchestra in 1946. He was responsible for introducing many new operas to a British audience, and was noted for his interpretations of BERLIOZ and DELIUS. He was knighted in 1914 and succeeded to his father's baronetcy in 1916.

Beethoven, Ludwig van (1770–1827) A German composer and pianist of Flemish descent. He left school at the age of 11 and was initially taught music by his talented father. In 1792 he was noticed by HAYDN, who invited him to Vienna, but the two of them did not get on well together and Beethoven took lessons elsewhere. He made his first public appearance in Vienna in 1795, playing his B flat major piano concert (Op. 19) and in 1800 he conducted his first symphony there. Apart from occasional excursions, Beethoven spent the rest of his life in Vienna composing a prodigious quantity of music. Yet he never found composing easy. In 1802 his increasing deafness may have led him to contemplate suicide; his struggle with his incurable ailment was expressed in the EROICA symphony (1804). By 1819 he was stone deaf and unmarried, although often in love; nevertheless it was during the last few years of his life that he composed some of his most profound works. His stature was recognized by his contemporaries, although they found his later music difficult.

Beethoven's influence on music is truly immense. He was a 'subjective composer' whose works express great emotional intensity. He revolutionized the emotional range of the symphony and the sonata form. Although much of his music reflects his tempestuous, restless nature, other pieces have a calmness that show a different side of his complex personality.

Beethoven's principal compositions include: 9 symphonies; FIDELIO (opera); *The Creatures of Prometheus* (ballet); *Christus am Olberg* (oratorio); 5 piano concertos; the violin concerto; 2 Masses; numerous pieces of chamber music; 32 piano sonatas; and several songs.

Beggar's Opera, The A ballad opera by JOHN GAY. It is essentially a play interspersed with songs to tunes of the day, and satirizes both contemporary politics and Italian operatic conventions. It was first performed in London in 1728.

Beiderbecke, Leon ('Bix') (1903–31) An American jazz cornet player, pianist and composer. He was one of the few white jazz players to influence black musicians and his cornet playing was famed for its beautiful tone.

bel A unit used in the measurement of the intensity of sound, named after its inventor, Alexander Graham Bell (1847–1922). *See* decibel.

bel canto (It.) Literally, 'beautiful singing'. A style of singing characterized by elaborate technique, associated with 18th-cent. Italian opera.

Bellini, Vincenzo (1801–35) An Italian composer famed for his operas which include *Il Pirata*, *La Sonnambula* and *I Puritani*.

bell (*orchestral*) Cylindrical metal tubes (tubular bells) of different lengths which are suspended from a frame and struck with a wooden mallet.

belly The upper part of the body or soundbox of a stringed instrument.

Belshazzar's Feast An oratorio by WALTON with words, taken largely from the Bible, arranged by Osbert Sitwell. It was first performed in Leeds in 1931. SIBELIUS wrote a piece on the same subject.

Belyayev, Mitrofan (1836–1904) A Russian music

publisher who was an enthusiastic sponsor of the 'new' composers. BORODIN, RIMSKY-KORSAKOV and many others used to congregate at his house regularly on Fridays and collectively wrote *Les Vendredis* (Fridays) in his honour.

ben, bene (It.) 'Well', as in *ben marcato* meaning 'well marked', 'well accented'.

Benedict, Julius (1804–85) An English composer and conductor who wrote many operas and oratorios but is best remembered for *The Lily of Killarney* (1862). He was knighted in 1871.

Benedicite (Lat.) A CANTICLE known as the *Song of the Three Holy Children*; it is used during Lent as an alternative to the TE DEUM in the Anglican service of Morning Prayer.

Benedictus (Lat.) **1** The second part of the SANCTUS of a Roman Catholic Mass. **2** The CANTICLE *Benedictus Dominus Israel* or Blessed be the Lord God of Israel.

Benjamin, Arthur (1893–1960) Australian composer and pianist who was renowned for his humorous but accomplished style. His principal operas include *The Devil Take Her* (1931) and *Prima Donna* (1931).

Bennett, Richard Rodney (1936–) An English composer and pianist who is best known for the popular tunes from his film scores, but he has written a great variety of work, including his operas *The Mines of Sulphur* and *A Penny for a Song*.

Bennett, William Sterndale (1816–75) English composer and pianist who was a friend of MENDELSSOHN and SCHUMANN and founded the Bach Society in 1849.

His works include a symphony, 4 piano concertos and songs. He was knighted in 1871.

Benvenuto Cellini An Opera by BERLIOZ to a libretto by L. de Wailly and A. Barbier. This was Berlioz's first opera and was based on the life of the famous Italian sculptor. When it was first produced in 1838, it received little acclaim but has since been recognized as a masterpiece.

berceuse (Fr.) A cradle song.

Berg, Alban (1885–1935) An Austrian composer who studied with SCHOENBERG and who was an exponent of atonal composition. He established his reputation with his first opera, *Wozzeck*, in 1921 and went on to write significant concertos and chamber music.

bergomask or **bergamasca 1** A popular 16th and 17th-cent. dance from Bergamo in Italy. **2** A 19th-cent. dance in quick 6/8 time.

Berio, Luciano (1925–) An Italian composer and conductor who has applied AVANT-GARDE techniques to his works. He gained a reputation with *Circles* in 1960, a piece with text by E.E. Cummings in which the female singer is given a certain amount of freedom with regard to which notes she sings.

Berkeley, Lennox Randal Francis (1903–89) An English composer who was influenced by STRAVINSKY and is best known for his symphonies and operas, for example *Nelson* and *A Dinner Engagement*.

Berlin, Irving (originally Israel Baline) (1888–1989) An American composer of Russian origin who was not technically knowledgeable but who nevertheless wrote some outstandingly successful songs. Among the best known are *Alexander's Ragtime Band*, *White Christmas* and *God Bless America*. He wrote most of the lyrics for his songs himself.

Berlioz, (Louis) Hector (1803–69) A French composer, conductor and critic. He was expected to follow in his father's footsteps and become a doctor but he soon gave up medicine and took lessons in composition instead. In 1827 he fell passionately in love with the Irish actress Harriet Smithson (whom he subsequently married but later left for Marie Recio), who was the inspiration for his first masterpiece, SYMPHONIE FAN-TASTIQUE (1830). Over the next ten years or so, he composed some of his most notable works but was invariably short of money. In 1858 he finished his most ambitious opera, *The Trojans*, but ironically he never heard it performed in its entirety before his death. He died an unhappy man, lonely and sick.

Berlioz's music is renowned for its extravagant style and startling rhythms; even during his lifetime he earned the reputation for being a Romantic composer *par excellence*. However, much of his grand and extrovert music is balanced by more subtle works. It was as an orchestrator that he was most innovative.

His principal compositions include: BENVENUTO CELLINI (opera); *The* TROJANS (opera); *Béatrice et Bénédict* (opera); SYMPHONIE FANTASTIQUE; *Harold in Italy* (viola and orchestra); *Romeo et Juliette* (dramatic symphony); and *Les Nuits d'été* (song cycle).

Berners, Lord (originally Gerald Hugh Tyrwhitt-Wilson) (1883–1950) An English composer who was also a diplomat, author and painter. He is mainly remembered for his ballets, e.g. *The Triumph of Neptune* and *A Wedding Bouquet*.

Bernstein, Leonard (1918–90) American conductor, composer and pianist. As a conductor, his specialities included the works of MAHLER, RAVEL and SIBELIUS; as a composer he achieved fame with such musicals as *West Side Story* and *On the Town*. He also wrote 3 symphonies, an opera and music for the film *On the Waterfront*.

Berwald, Franz Adolf (1796–1868) A distinguished Swedish composer and violinist whose work included 4 symphonies, concertos and several operas, e.g. *A Rustic Betrothal in Sweden*.

big band A large band, most commonly associated with the SWING era. Such bands were famed for the strong dance rhythms they produced.

Billings, William (1746–1800) An American who worked as a tanner and composed hymns, anthems and songs in his spare time. Although his knowledge of music was limited, he is considered to be the first 'all-American' composer of any worth.

Billy Budd 1 An opera by BRITTEN to a libretto by E.M. Forster and Eric Crozier. It is based on Herman Melville's story of a hapless mariner who is hanged for murder. It was first performed in London in 1951. **2** An opera by Ghedini to a libretto by Salvatore Quasimodo.

binary form A structure, common in Baroque music, consisting of two related sections which were repeated. SONATA FORM evolved from it.

Birtwistle, Harrison (1934–) An outstanding English

composer of operas and symphonies who has also occasionally dabbled with electronic music. He is noted for such works as *The Triumph of Time* (for orchestra), and *Punch and Judy* and *Gawain* (opera). He was knighted in 1991.

bis (Fr.) 'Twice'.

Bishop, Henry Rowley (1786–1855) An English composer and conductor who was the first British musician to be knighted (1842). He adapted a number of other composers' operas for the English stage, including MOZART'S MARRIAGE OF FIGARO. Although he wrote many works himself, much of it is forgotten, save his song *Home Sweet Home*.

bitonality The use of two keys simultaneously.

Bizet, Georges (originally Alexandre César Léopold Bizet) (1838–75) A French composer who is best known for his operas (for example, *The* PEARL FISHERS, IVAN THE TERRIBLE, CARMEN) but who also wrote a symphony and several songs. He did not achieve the recognition he deserved in his lifetime.

blanche (Fr.) Literally, 'white'; the French word for a MINIM.

Bliss, Arthur (1891–1975) An English composer who is noted for daringly adventurous works. Amongst his most famous pieces are *The Olympians* (opera), *Checkmate* and *Miracle of the Gorbals* (ballets), as well as *Rout* (a piece for soprano and 10 instruments).

Bloch, Ernest (1880–1959) An American composer who was born in Switzerland. His music is noted for being typically Jewish, for example *Hakdesh* (for baritone, chorus and orchestra), and his *Israel Symphony* and *American Symphony*.

block chords A harmonic procedure in which the notes of chords are moved simultaneously in 'blocks'.

Blomdahl, Karl-Birger (1916–68) A Swedish composer who wrote three symphonies and the opera, *Aniara* (1959), which is set on a space ship and contains electronic effects.

Blow, John (1649–1708) An English composer and organist who wrote numerous anthems and songs, and the masque, *Venus and Adonis*.

Bluebeard's Castle (Duke Bluebeard's Castle) An opera by BARTOK to a libretto by B. Balázs, which was first performed in Budapest, 1918.

Blue Danube, The A famous waltz written by Johann STRAUSS (the younger) in 1867.

Bluegrass A type of folk music originally from Kentucky, USA, (where Kentucky bluegrass grows); *see* country and western.

blues A 20th-cent. Black American song or lamentation following an essentially simple form of 12 bars to each verse. Blues music formed the basis for JAZZ; musicians favoured such instruments as the guitar and harmonica.

B Minor Mass A setting of the Latin Mass by BACH for soloists, chorus and orchestra, composed in 1733–8.

bocca chiusa (It.) Literally, 'closed mouth', i.e. humming.

Boccherini, Luigi (1743–1805) A prolific Italian composer and acclaimed cellist, who became neglected and died in poverty in Madrid. His work includes a total of 125 string quintets, 102 string quartets and the opera, *Clementina*.

Boehm system An improved system of keys and levers for the flute which is named after its German inventor, Theobald Boehm (1793–1881). The system is also applied to other instruments, e.g. the clarinet.

Bohème, La An opera by PUCCINI to a libretto by G. Giacosa and L. Illica. The story tells of the love affairs between Rodolfo and Mimi, and Marcello and Musetta, set in the Latin Quarter of Paris. It was first performed in Turin, 1896. Leoncavallo also wrote an opera of the this name.

Böhm, Karl (1894–1981) An Austrian conductor especially associated with the works of MOZART and Richard STRAUSS.

Boito, Arrigo (1842–1918) An Italian composer and librettist who wrote the libretti for VERDI'S FALSTAFF and OTELLO.

bolero (Sp.) A moderately fast Spanish dance in triple time. RAVEL'S *Bolero* (1928), a spiralling crescendo based on a repeated theme, was the music for a ballet choreographed by Nijinsky.

bones A pair of small sticks (originally bones) that are held in the hands and clicked together rhythmically.

bongos Pairs of small, upright Cuban drums that are often found in dance bands. They are played with the hands.

boogie-woogie A jazz and blues style of piano playing in which the left hand plays a persistent bass rhythm while the right hand plays a melody.

45

bop Short for BEBOP.

Boris Godunov An opera by MUSSORGSKY (who also wrote the libretto) which was first performed in its entirety in 1874. Recounting scenes from the life of the 16th-cent. Tsar Boris, it is considered one of the greatest of Russian operas.

Borodin, Alexander Porfirevich (1833–87) A Russian composer who was the illegitimate son of a Russian prince. As well as being a musician, he was a devoted and able scientist which explains why his output of music was comparatively small. He was a member of the FIVE and his most famous works include *In the Steppes of Central Asia* (tone-poem), and PRINCE IGOR (an opera completed after his death by RIMSKY-KORSAKOV and GLAZUNOV).

bouche fermée (Fr.) *see* bocca chiusa.

bouffe *see* opéra-bouffe.

Boughton, Rutland (1878–1960) An English composer of operas, the most famous of which were based on Arthurian legends, e.g. *The Immortal Hour* and *The Birth of Arthur*.

Boulanger, Juliette Nadia (1887–1979) A French composer and conductor but who is mainly remembered for being an outstanding teacher of composition.

Boulez, Pierre (1925–) A French composer, conductor and pianist who gave up a career as a mathematician in order to study music. He is reckoned to be one of the most important of AVANT-GARDE composers and his most noted works include *La Marteau sans maître* (for voice and chamber orchestra), and *Pli selon pli* (for soprano and orchestra).

Boult, Adrian Cedric (1889–1983) An English conductor who gained an international reputation after he conducted the first performance of HOLST's suite *The Planets* in 1918. He conducted many orchestras worldwide and had a particular penchant for the works of English composers. He was knighted in 1937.

bourrée (Fr.) A lively French dance dating from the 17th cent.

bouzouki A Greek stringed instrument with a long, fretted neck. Its six strings are plucked, often to provide an emotionally charged accompaniment to songs. The sound of the bouzouki reached a worldwide audience with the film music by the Greek composer Mikis Theodorakis.

bow A wooden stick which is strung with horse-hair and used to play instruments of the violin and viol family.

bowed harp A primitive violin, dating back to at least the 12th cent. It was held on the knee and played vertically.

bowing The technique of using a BOW to play an instrument. *See also* legno.

Boyce, William (1711–79) An English composer and organist whose works include 20 symphonies and numerous pieces of church and chamber music. He is most famous for writing the song *Heart of Oak*.

Brabançonne, La The Belgian national anthem, written in 1830.

brace The vertical line, usually with a bracket, which joins two STAVES of music to indicate that they are played together.

Brahms, Johannes (1833–97) A German composer and one of the most influential of the 19th cent. He had humble origins and was first taught by his father, a double-bass player. His ambitions to be a composer were encouraged by LISZT and SCHUMANN and his appointment as director of music to the Prince of Lippe-Detmold (1857) gave him time to concentrate on composing. It took him 20 years to write his first symphony but when it was performed in Karlsruhe in 1876, it was nicknamed 'Beethoven's 10th' and his reputation was assured.

Brahms' music was considered conservative by many of his contemporaries but few composers have managed to express deep emotions as eloquently. His symphonies and concertos are considered to be masterpieces.

Brahms' principal compositions include: 4 symphonies, 2 piano concertos, a violin concerto, a concerto for violin and cello, *A German Requiem* (chorus and orchestra), 3 piano sonatas and many outstanding pieces of chamber music.

Brain, Dennis (1921–57) An English horn player who became the outstanding exponent of this instrument in his day. BRITTEN wrote *Serenade* (for tenor, horn and strings) especially for him.

Brandenburg Concertos Six orchestral concertos by BACH which were written for Christian Ludwig, Margrave of Brandenburg, in 1721.

branle (Fr.) A French folk dance from the 15th cent. which had a swaying movement.

brass band A type of band, particularly associated

with the North of England, which consists of brass instruments and drums only.

brass instruments A family of wind instruments which are made of metal but not always brass. Instruments with reeds and those which used to be made from wood (such as the flute) are excluded. A characteristic of the family is that sound is produced by the vibration of the lips which are pressed into a funnel-shaped mouthpiece. A selection of notes can be produced by effectively lengthening the tubing, either with a slide (as in the trombone) or with valves (as in the trumpet).

bravura (It.) Literally, 'bravery', as in a 'bravura passage', a passage that demands a virtuoso display by the performer.

break 1 In jazz, a short, improvised, solo passage. **2** The point in a vocal or instrumental range where the REGISTER changes.

Bream, Julian (1933–) A virtuoso English guitar and lute player who has done much to revive interest in classical guitar music. Both WALTON and BRITTEN wrote pieces especially for him.

breit (Ger.) 'Broadly' or 'grandly'; a term used to describe the manner in which a piece should be played.

Brendel, Alfred (1931–) An Austrian pianist who lives in London and who has acquired an international reputation as a soloist.

breve Originally the short note of music (*c.*13th cent.), but as other notes have been introduced, it is now the longest note and is only occasionally used.

Brian, William Havergal (1876–1972) An English composer who was largely self-taught. He wrote 32 symphonies, which sometimes demanded outrageously large orchestras, and the opera, *The Tigers*.

bridge 1 A piece of wood that stands on the belly of stringed instruments and supports the strings. **2** A passage in a composition that links two important themes together.

Bridge, Frank (1879–1941) An English composer, viola player, conductor and teacher. He wrote numerous works of all kinds (e.g. *A Prayer*, for chorus and orchestra); BRITTEN was one of his pupils.

Brigg Fair The so-called 'English Rhapsody' for orchestra by DELIUS; it is based on Lincolshire folk-songs.

brindisi (It.) Literally, 'a toast'; a drinking song during which toasts are often given.

brio (It.) 'Vigour', so *con brio* means 'with vigour'.

brisé (Fr.) Literally, 'broken'; a term which indicates that a chord should be played in ARPEGGIO fashion or that music for stringed instruments should be played with short movements of the bow.

Britten, (Edward) Benjamin (1913–77) An English composer, conductor and pianist who started to write music when he was five. He is one of the few 20th-cent. composers who has succeeded in pleasing both 'radical' and 'conservative' audiences. Some of his greatest works were written in collaboration with the poet W.H. Auden and he wrote pieces specifically for his friend the tenor Peter PEARS, and the cellist ROSTROPOVICH. He had a special gift for setting words to music and his most impressive works are operas. He had a life-long love for the North Sea and the coastal town of Aldeburgh, where he lived and where he founded the ALDEBURGH FESTIVAL in 1948.

Britten's major works include the operas PETER GRIMES, THE RAPE OF LUCRETIA, ALBERT HERRING, BILLY BUDD and DEATH IN VENICE. He did, however, write numerous other pieces and is considered to be one of the most influential of all 20th-cent. composers.

broken octaves A term used to describe a passage of notes that are played alternately an octave apart; they frequently occur in piano music.

Brubeck, Dave (1920–) An American jazz pianist and composer. He had a sophisticated style and is especially known for adapting classical music for jazz.

Bruch, Max (1838–1920) A German composer of Jewish origin. His works include operas, 3 symphonies and 3 violin concertos. Perhaps the best known of all his work are his Second Violin Concerto and his setting of *Kol Nidrei* for cello and orchestra.

Bruckner, Anton (1824–96) An Austrian composer who is noted for his 10 symphonies as well as his choral and chamber music. He also wrote organ music and pieces for male-voice choirs. He was influenced by, and to some extent overshadowed by, WAGNER. Many of his symphonies are essentially religious. He wrote three Masses, including *Grosse Messe* (a Mass in F minor), and numerous other sacred vocal works.

brunette (Fr.) A folk love-song of the 17th and 18th cents.

buffa *see* opéra-bouffe.

bugle A simple BRASS INSTRUMENT with a conical tube and a cup-shaped mouthpiece which was widely used for giving military signals.

Bull, John (1563–1628) An English organist and composer whose best known works are keyboard and church music.

Bull, Ole Børneman (1810–80) A Norwegian violinist an composer who was largely self-taught. He excelled when performing his own works.

bullroarer *see* thunderstick.

Bülow, Hans Guido von (1830–94) A German pianist, conductor and composer who originally studied law. He is best remembered as a conductor who was greatly influenced by WAGNER (he conducted the first performances of *Tristan und Isolde* and *Die Meistersinger von Nürnberg*). As a pianist, he had an impressive repertoire.

Bumbry, Grace (1937–) A Black American soprano (formerly mezzo-soprano) who made her debut in 1960. She is especially noted for her interpretations of CARMEN, TOSCA and SALOME.

burla (burlesca) (It.) A short and jolly piece of music.

Busoni, Ferruccio Benvenuto (1866–1924) An Italian composer, pianist, theorist and teacher. He lived most of his life in Germany and is remembered mainly for his operas, e.g. *Die Brautwahl* and *Arlecchino*.

Buxtehude, Dietrich (1637–1707) A Danish composer and noted organist, much admired by BACH. He reinstituted the ABENDMUSIK concerts at Lübeck.

Byrd, William (1543–1623) An English composer who was for a time an organist at Lincoln Cathedral and a Gentleman of the Chapel Royal, and later organist there. His compositions include Masses and other church music.

Byzantine music Music of the Christian Church of the Eastern Roman Empire which was established in AD 330 and lasted until 1435. It influenced Western church music.

C

C 1 The key-note or tonic of the scale of C major. **2** An abbreviation for contralto, *con* (with), *col, colla* (with the).

C.A. Abbrev. for *coll' arco* meaning 'with the bow' (with reference to playing a stringed instrument).

cabaletta (It.) A term for a simple ARIA with and insistent rhythm, or an emphatically rhythmical ending to an aria or duet.

cabinet organ *see* American organ.

caccia (It.) Literally, a 'hunt', as in *corno da caccia*, hunting horn. It can also mean a 14th-cent. hunting poem set to music.

Caccini, Giulio (*c.*1550–1618) An Italian singer and composer who was a member of the Florentine group, the Camerata, which helped to establish opera. He wrote many songs and the early opera *L'Euridice*.

cachucha A Spanish solo dance in 3/4 time.

cacophony A discordant muddle of sound.

cadence A term used to describe the concluding phrase at the end of a section of music.

cadenza (It.) Literally, 'cadence', but it has come to have two specific meanings. **1** An elaborate ending to an operatic aria. **2** A flourish at the end of a passage of solo music in a concerto.

Cage, John (1912–) An American composer and pianist who is famed for his experimental works which do not conform to standard musical practice. He has incorporated elements of chance into his compositions as well as electronic and environmental sounds. His works include *Music of Changes* (for 'prepared' piano), and *4' 33*, which consists of 4 minutes 33 seconds of silence.

calando (It.) Literally, 'diminishing', i.e. in both volume and speed.

calcando (It.) 'Pressing forward', i.e. a term used to indicate an increase in speed.

Callas, Maria (originally Maria Kalogeropoulou) (1923–77) A soprano of Greek origins but who was born in the USA. She became the most celebrated singer of her day and was famed for her acting ability as well as her outstanding voice.

calypso A kind of song with syncopated rhythms from the West Indies, notably Trinidad; calypso lyrics are usually witty and topical, and are often a vehicle for political satire.

cambiata (It.) An abbreviation for *nota cambiata*, CHANGING NOTE.

camera (It.) Literally, a 'room', but in musical terms it refers to a type of music that can be performed in a place other than a church, music hall or opera house etc.; *see* chamber music.

campanelli (It.) *see* glockenspiel.

campanology The art of bell-ringing or the study of bells.

Campion (Campian), Thomas (1567–1620) An English poet and song writer who was also a physician and lawyer. He published several books of lute songs and many MASQUES for performance at court.

can-can A Parisian music-hall dance of the late 19th cent. in quick 2/4 time. Famous examples of the dance are found in OFFENBACH's operettas.

cancel (US) *see* natural.

cancrizans A type of music that makes sense if it is played backwards.

Cannabich, Christian (1731–98) A German violinist, composer and conductor. His conducting was particularly admired by MOZART.

canon A COUNTERPOINT composition in which one part is imitated and overlapped by one or more other parts, e.g. a soprano lead with a tenor follow up. In a 'strict' canon, the imitation is exact in every way.

cantabile (It.) Literally, 'song-like'; it is a term applied to instrumental pieces indicating that they should be played in a singing style.

cantata Originally a piece of music of the BAROQUE period that is sung (as opposed to a SONATA, a piece which is played). It has come to be a term used to describe a vocal or choral piece, with an instrumental accompaniment. German cantatas were generally religious works. In many ways, the form is similar to

OPERA and ORATORIO, but it tends not to be so elaborate.

canticle A hymn that has words from the bible, other than a psalm.

cantor (Lat.) A 'singer'; nowadays the term refers to the chief singer in a choir or the lead singer in a synagogue.

cantus firmus (Lat.) 'Fixed song', i.e. a melody in polyphonic music, often taken from PLAINSONG, with long notes against which COUNTERPOINT tunes are sung.

canzone, canzona, canzon Literally, 'song'; a vocal work, or and instrumental piece that is modelled on music for the voice.

canzonet 1 A short kind of CANZONE. **2** A type of MADRIGAL or a simple solo song.

capotasto (It.) The 'head of the fingerboard', i.e. the raised part or 'nut' at the top of the fingerboard of a stringed instrument that defines the lengths of the strings. A moveable capotasto, comprising a wood or metal bar that can be clamped to the fingerboard, is occasionally used on fretted instruments to shorten all the strings at the same time, thus raising the pitch.

cappella, a *see* a cappella.

capriccio (It.) 'Caprice'; a short, lively piece.

carillon 1 A set of bells which can be played by electrical or mechanical means to produce a tune. **2** An organ stop which produces a bell-like sound.

Carissimi, Giacomo (1605–74) An Italian composer, particularly of church music. He is noted for his oratorios, for example *Jonas Baltazar*.

Carmen An opera by BIZET to a libretto by H. Meilhac and L. Halévy. It tells the tragic story of the sergeant of the guard, Don José, who falls in love with a gypsy girl, Carmen. It was first performed in Paris in 1875.

Carmina Burana (Songs from Beuren) An oratorio or cantata by Carl ORFF first performed in Frankfurt, 1937. The mainly Latin text is based on medieval poems about women, drink and love.

Carnegie Hall A famous concert hall in New York endowed by the philanthropist and millionaire, Andrew Carnegie (1835–1919), who was born in Scotland but made his fortune in the USA.

Carnival of the Animals (*Le carnaval des animaux*) A popular satirical suite by SAINT-SAENS, composed in 1886. Each of the 14 movements depicts a different animal.

carol Originally, any medieval English song with a refrain, but now it means a song associated with Christmas.

Carpenter, John Alden (1876–1951) A successful American businessman who was also a noted composer. His works include *Krazy Kat* (jazz pantomime) and *Skyscrapers* (ballet).

Carreras, José (1946-) A Spanish tenor, one of the most respected and admired of the late 20th cent.

Carter, Elliot (1908-) A major American composer of ballets, chamber music and symphonies. He held many teaching posts at prestigious American colleges and his works include *Variations for Orchestra* and *Symphony of 3 Orchestras.*

Caruso, Enrico (1873–1921) A legendary Italian tenor who made more than 600 appearances at the New York Metropolitan Opera House. He was the first tenor to make recordings, which earned him a handsome fortune.

Casals, Pablo (1876–1973) A Catalan cellist, conductor and composer whose worldwide performances did much to raise the status of the cello as a solo instrument. He made his home in Puerto Rico in 1956. His compositions include the oratorio *El pessebre* (The Manger).

Casella, Alfredo (1883–1947) An Italian composer, conductor and pianist who was also an author. He was passionate about modern Italian music and he helped to establish the Venice *Biennale* festivals. His works include *Il deserto tentato* (opera) and *Il convento veneziano* (ballet).

cassation An 18th-cent. term for instrumental music devised for open-air performance, similar to the serenade.

Casse-Noisette *see* Nutcracker, The.

castanets A Spanish percussion instrument comprising two shell-like pieces of wood which are clicked together by the fingers. In orchestras, they are occasionally shaken on the end of sticks.

castrato (It.) An adult male singer with a soprano or contralto voice produced by castration before puberty. Castrati were popular singers in the 17th and 18th. The practice was abandoned during the 19th cent.

catch A ROUND for three or more voices. The words are often humorous and frequently contain puns, e.g.

Ah, how Sophia which, when sung, sounds like 'Our house afire'.

Cavalieri, Emilio de' (*c*.1550–1602) An amateur Italian composer of the Medici Court in Florence. He wrote four music-dramas which heralded the way for the oratorio form. His best-known work is the morality play *La rappresentazione de anima e di corpo* (The Representation of Soul and Body).

Cavalli, Pietro Francesco (originally Pier Caletti-Bruni) (1602–76) An Italian composer who wrote more than 40 operas as well as church music. He was one of the first composers to inject humour and exaggerated drama into his operas, e.g. *L'Ormindo* and *La Calisto*.

cavatina (It.) A short and often slow song or instrumental piece.

CB Abbrev. for *contrabasso* (double bass).

cebell A 17th-cent. English dance similar to the GAVOTTE.

Cecilia, St The patron saint of music who was martyred in the 2nd or 3rd cent. Her feast day is 22 November.

ceilidh A gathering at which songs, folk music and dances are performed; ceilidhs are particularly associated with Scotland and Ireland.

celesta A small keyboard instrument in which hammers are made to strike metal bars suspended over wooden resonators; the sound produced has an ethereal, bell-like quality.

cello *see* violoncello.

cembalo (It.) **1** A DULCIMER. **2** An abbreviation of *clavicembalo* which is the Italian for HARPSICHORD.

Cesti, Antonio (1623–69) An Italian opera composer who was originally a friar but was released from his vows in 1658. He was musical director at the Medici Court in Florence until 1652. He then served the Hapsburgs in Austria. His works helped to develop the operatic form, e.g. *Orontea*.

C.F. Abbrev. for CANTUS FIRMUS.

Chabrier, Alexis Emmanuel (1841–94) A French composer who worked as a civil servant for 18 years and who was largely self-taught. He was a devotee of WAGNER, whose influence can be heard in some of his operas, especially *Gwendoline*. His most famous piece is his lively orchestral rhapsody, *España*.

chaconne (Fr.) A slow dance in triple time that is thought to have originated in Mexico.

Chaikovsky, Piotr Ilyich *see* Tchaikovsky.

Chaliapin, Fedor Ivanovich (1873–1933) A Russian bass who had formidable stage presence as well as a magnificent voice. He is best remembered for his role in *Boris Gudunov*.

chalumeau (Fr.) **1** A generic term for a type of reed-pipe. **2** A term now used for the lower register of the CLARINET.

chamber music Originally, chamber music was a term used to describe any type of music that was suitable for playing in a room of a house as opposed to a church or concert hall. However, it has come to mean music for a small number of intruments (e.g. flute and piano) or group of performers (e.g. string quartet, sextet etc.), with one instrument to each part.

chamber orchestra A small orchestra, sometimes solely of stringed instruments, for performing CHAMBER MUSIC.

Chaminade, Cécile (1857–1944) A French pianist and composer who is best known for her songs and piano works, although she did write a number of more ambitious pieces, for example *Konzertstück* (for chorus and orchestra).

champêtre (Fr.) 'Rural' or 'rustic'.

change-ringing An English method of ringing a peal of church bells; the bells are rung in an established order, which then passes through a series of changes.

changing note A dissonant PASSING NOTE which is a third away from the preceding note, before being resolved.

chanson (Fr.) A song for either a solo voice or a choir. In some contexts it can also mean an instrumental piece of song-like quality.

chant A general term for a type of music which is sung as part of a ritual or ceremony. It is a term which is used particularly for unaccompanied singing in religious services.

chanter The pipe of a BAGPIPE, on which a melody is played.

chanterelle (Fr.) Literally, the 'singing one', i.e the highest string on a bowed, stringed instrument (for example, the E string on a violin).

Chapel Royal The body of musicians and clergymen who serve a British monarch in his or her court. It also refers to the building where services are held.

character piece A term used by composers for a short

instrumental piece, such as may attempt to describe a specific mood.

charleston A ballroom dance, similar to the foxtrot, which was evolved by the Blacks of the Southern USA.

Charpentier, Gustave (1860–1956) A French composer whose works include instrumental pieces and songs. His most memorable piece, however, is *Louise*, an opera concerning the low-life of Paris.

Charpentier, Marc-Antoine (1634–1704) A French composer of stage and church music but whose most impressive works were the operas, *Les Amours d'Acis et de Galatée* and *Médée*.

Chausson, Ernest (1855–99) A French composer of romantic operas and orchestral pieces, including *Le Roi Arthur* (opera).

Chávez, Carlos (1899–1945) A noted Mexican composer and conductor whose work was much influenced by Indian folk music and folklore.

Cherubini, (Maria) Luigi (Carlo Zenobia Salvatore) (1760–1842) An Italian composer who settled in Paris in 1788. He wrote operas (e.g. *Médée* and *Les Deux Journées*) and other works, and was much admired by BEETHOVEN.

chest voice The lower register of voice, so called because notes seem to emanate from the chest.

chevalet (Fr.) The BRIDGE of a stringed instrument.

chiaro, chiara (It.) 'Clear', 'distinct'.

chitarrone (It.) A large LUTE.

choir 1 The place, defined by special seats or 'choir stalls' in a large church or cathedral where singers are positioned. **2** A body of singers, such as a male-voice choir, church choir. **3** (US) A section of the orchestra, for example 'brass choir'.

choirbook A large medieval volume that (usually) included both words and music and was designed to be read by various members of a choir while it was stationed on a centrally placed lectern.

choir organ The section of an ORGAN that is played from the lowest MANUAL and is soft enough to accompany a church choir.

Chopin, Frédéric François (originally Fryderyk Franciszek Chopin) (1810–49) A Polish-born composer and pianist who was the son of a French father and Polish mother. He was a prodigy, taking his first music lessons at six, composing at seven and giving recitals at eight. He settled in Paris in 1831 and, although he had already gained a worthy reputation as a pianist, he earned a living as a teacher to aristocratic families and this allowed him time to concentrate on composing. He became friendly with the leading musicians of his era (such as LISZT, MENDELSSOHN, BERLIOZ) and fell in love with the novelist George Sand (Amandine Aurore Dupin), who devotedly nursed him when he began to suffer from tuberculosis, the disease from which he was to die. Whilst he was living with Sand (they never married), he composed his most impressive works. When their relationship broke up in 1848, he toured Britain to earn money but died the following year.

As well as being an exuberant, virtuoso pianist, Chopin was an outstanding composer, especially of keyboard music. He advanced the concept of the NOCTURNE, as expressed by FIELD, and developed subtle and unconventional harmonics in his compositions for piano. His reputation as a Romantic, in every sense of the word, did, for a time, hinder him in being accepted as an innovative composer (although nobody has ever doubted his talent as a pianist).

Chopin's principal works include: pieces for piano and orchestra (e.g. *Variations on Là ci darem la mano*); piano solos (e.g. 4 *Ballades*), 27 *Études*; and many chamber music works and songs.

choral 1 An adjective used to describe music that involves a CHORUS, for example choral symphony.

chorale A hymn-tune of the Lutheran Church, but dating back to the 15th cent.

chorale cantata A CANTATA that was written to be performed in a (Lutheran) church.

Chorale Fantasia 1 A work by BEETHOVEN (Op. 80) for piano, chorus and orchestra. **2** A setting by HOLST for soprano, chorus, organ, brass, strings and percussion of words by Robert Bridges.

choral symphony 1 A symphony in which a chorus is used at some point (or, indeed, a symphony written entirely for voices). **2** The popular name of BEETHOVEN's symphony no. 9 in D minor.

chord A combination of notes played simultaneously, usually not less than three.

chordophone Any instrument in which stretched strings are vibrated to produce sound, for example a violin.

chorus 1 A body of singers. *See* choir. **2** Music written for a body of singers (usually to follow an introductory piece). **3** A refrain that follows a solo verse.

Christmas Oratorio The name given to a series of six church cantatas by BACH (1734).

'Christmas' Symphony Another nickname given to HAYDN'S 'LAMENTATION' SYMPHONY.

chromatic (from Gk. *chromatikos*, 'coloured') A term used to describe notes which do not belong to a prevailing scale, e.g. in C major all sharps and flats are chromatic notes. The 'chromatic scale' is a scale of 12 ascending or descending semitones; and a 'chromatic chord' is a chord that contains chromatic notes.

Ciaccona (It.) *see* chaconne.

Cilèa, Francesco (1866–1950) An Italian composer, best known for his successful operas, including *Adriana Lecouvreur*.

Cimarosa, Domenico (1749–1801) An Italian composer of operas (e.g. *The Secret Marriage*) also working in St Petersburg and Vienna, and one of the most important operatic composers of his era. He also wrote Masses and oratorios.

cimbal, cimbalom *see* dulcimer.

circular breathing The technique of sustaining a note when playing a wind instrument by breathing in through the nose while sounding the note.

citole A medieval instrument and ancestor of the CITTERN.

cittern A pear-shaped stringed instrument of the GUITAR family popular from the 16th cent. to the 18th cent. It was similar to the LUTE except that it had a flat back and wire strings, and was easier to play.

Clair de lune A piano piece by DEBUSSY, which forms the third movement of the *Suite bergamasque,* composed 1890–95.

clappers Virtually any kind of percussion instrument comprising two similar pieces that can be struck together, for example bones, spoons, sticks.

clarinet A single-reed woodwind instrument dating back to the 17th cent. It has a cylindrical tube and nowadays comes in two common sizes: B flat and A. It is an instrument common to both classical music and jazz.

Clarke, Jeremiah (*c.*1673–1707) An English composer who was, for a time, organist at St Paul's Cathedral in London. His compositions include many anthems and pieces for harpsichord, but he is best remembered for 'The Prince of Denmark's March', otherwise known as the TRUMPET VOLUNTARY (formerly attributed to PURCELL).

clàrsach A small harp of the Scottish Highlands and Ireland.

classical 1 A term used to describe a certain form of music which adheres to basic conventions and forms that are more concerned with carefully controlled expression rather than unrestrained emotion. **2** A term used to describe 'serious' music as opposed to popular music.

clavecin (Fr.) *see* harpsichord.

claves Short sticks that are held in the hand and clicked together to emphasize a beat or rhythm. They originated in Cuba.

clavicembalo (It.) *see* harpsichord.

clavichord A keyboard instrument dating from the 15th cent. in which the strings are struck by a brass 'tangent' and can be made to sound a note of variable pitch until the key is released. However, the sound is soft and keyboard is limited; the instrument fell out of favour with the introduction of the piano.

clavier 1 A practice KEYBOARD which makes no sound save clicks. **2** Any keyboard instrument that has strings (esp. Ger., US), e.g. harpsichord, piano.

clef A symbol positioned on a line of a STAVE which indicates the pitch of the line and consequently all the notes on the stave. Three clefs are commonly used: alto (tenor), treble and bass.

Clementi, Muzio (1752–1832) An Italian composer and pianist whose works exploit the potential of the piano (as opposed to the harpsichord). He knew MOZART, BEETHOVEN and HAYDN and taught John FIELD in London. He wrote many symphonies and some 60 piano sonatas.

'Clock' Symphony The nickname of HAYDN's Symphony no. 101 in D major, so called because of the 'tick-tock' rhythm of the second movement.

close harmony Harmony in which the notes of the chords are close together. In singing, this means that each voice remains fairly close to the melody.

Coates, Eric (1886–1957) An English composer and violist whose orchestral works (e.g. *Countryside* and *The Three Bears*) are light but well crafted.

Cockaigne A concert overture by ELGAR subtitled 'In London Town' and dedicated to 'my friends the members of British orchestras'.

coda (It.) Literally, a 'tail', meaning a passage at the end of a piece of music which rounds it off.

codetta (It.) A 'little tail', i.e. a shorter version of a CODA.

col, coll', colla, colle (It.) Literally, 'with the', so *col basso* means 'with bass'; *colle voce*, with voice.

Coleridge-Taylor, Samuel (1875–1912) An English composer whose mother was English and father was from Sierra Leone. He wrote famous settings for Longfellow's poems, e.g. *Hiawatha's Wedding Feast* and *The Death of Minnehaha*, and also composed orchestral, stage and chamber music.

col legno (It.) *see* legno.

coloratura (It.) The florid ornamentation of a melodic line, especially in opera.

colour The tone-quality of instruments and voices.

combo An abbreviation of 'combination', especially a collection of musicians that make up a jazz band.

combination tone A faint (third) note that is heard when two notes are sounded simultaneously; also called a 'resultant tone'.

comic opera An opera which has an amusing plot, or (sometimes) an opera which includes some spoken dialogue.

common chord A major or minor chord, usually consisting of a keynote and its third and fifth.

comodo (It.) 'Convenient', as in *tempo comodo*, meaning at a 'convenient speed'.

compass The musical range of a voice or instrument.

composition 1 A work of music. **2** The putting together of sounds in a creative manner. **3** The art of writing music.

compound interval An INTERVAL which is greater than an octave.

compound time Musical time in which each beat in a bar is divisible by three, for example 6/8, 9/8 and 12/8 time.

computer-generated music Music that is created by feeding a formula or program into a computer which then translates the program into sounds.

Comus A MASQUE by Milton with music by Henry LAWES. It was first performed in 1634.

concert A public performance of secular music other than an opera or ballet.

Concertgebouw (Dutch) Literally, a 'concert building', but usually taken to mean Amsterdam's main concert hall (completed 1883).

concert grand A large grand piano that is used in concert halls.

concertina A type of ACCORDION, hexagonal in shape, with small studs at each end which are used as keys.

concert-master (US) The first violinist, or leader, of an orchestra.

concerto (It.) **1** Originally, a work for one or several voices with instrumental accompaniment. **2** A work for several contrasted instruments. **3** An orchestral work in several movements, containing passages for groups of solo instruments (*concerto grosso*). **4** A piece for a solo instrument and an accompanying orchestra.

concert overture An orchestral piece of one movement, similar to an opera overture, but written for performance in a concert hall. It originated in the 19th cent.

concert pitch The internationally agreed PITCH, according to which A above middle C (in the middle of treble clef) is fixed at 440 hertz (cycles per second).

Concertstück (Ger.) A short concerto.

Concierto de Aranjuez A concerto for guitar and orchestra by RODRIGO which was first performed in 1940.

concitato (It.) 'Agitated'.

concord A combination of sounds (such as a chord) that are satisfactory and sound agreeable. The opposite to DISSONANCE.

concrete music *see* musique concrète.

conducting The art of directing and controlling an orchestra or choir (or operatic performance) by means of gestures. As well as indicating the speed of a piece, a conductor, who often uses a BATON to exaggerate his or her arm movements, is also responsible for interpreting the music.

conga 1 A tall, narrow drum which is played with the hands. **2** An entertaining dance in which the participants form a long, moving line one behind the other.

conjunct A succession of notes of different pitch.

conservatory A school that specializes in musical training. The term originates from the kind of charitable institutions for orphans called *conservatorio* in

16th and 17th-cent Italy, where music was taught to a high standard.

consort An old spelling of the word 'concert', meaning an ensemble of instruments, e.g. a consort of viols.

Contes d'Hoffmann, Les *see* Tales of Hoffmann.

continuo (It.) An abbreviation of *basso continuo*. *See* figured bass.

contrabass 1 (adjective) An instrument that is an octave lower than the normal bass of the family, e.g. contrabass tuba. **2** (noun) A double bass.

contralto The lowest female voice, which usually has a range of about two octaves.

contrapuntal Relating to COUNTERPOINT.

contrary motion *see* inversion.

contratenor The 14th and 15th-cent. word for a voice with approximately the same range as a TENOR.

contredanse (Fr.) A French corruption of 'country dance', i.e. a lively dance.

Coperario, John (*c.*1575–1626) An English composer and noted player of the lute and viola da gamba. His name was originally John Cooper but he changed it because Italian music was fashionable.

Copland, Aaron (1900–90) An American composer, conductor and pianist who was also an influential teacher. He championed the cause of modern music and wrote several books on the subject. His best known works include the ballets *Billy the Kid*, *Appalachian Spring* and *Rodeo*.

Coppélia A ballet with music by DELIBES which was first performed in 1870.

cor (Fr.) *see* French horn.

cor anglais (Fr.) Literally, 'English horn', but it is neither English nor a horn. It is in fact an alto OBOE pitched a fifth below the standard oboe.

coranto (It.) *see* courante.

corda (It.) A 'string', as in 'piano string'; the term *una corda* literally means 'one string', an indication to use the 'soft' pedal on the piano.

Corelli, Arcangelo (1653–1713) An Italian violinist and composer who spent much of his early life in France and Germany as a virtuoso performer. His most important pieces include sonatas (e.g. *12 Sonate a tre*) and 12 *Sonate da camera a tre*.

Cornelius, Peter (1824–74) A German composer and writer who was a friend of WAGNER and LISZT. His works include the operas *The Barber of Baghdad* and *The Cid*.

cornet 1 A BRASS INSTRUMENT with three valves that has a quality of tone lying between a HORN and a TRUMPET; it has great flexibility and is often used in military and jazz bands. **2** An organ stop used for playing flourishes.

cornett (Fr.) An obsolete wind instrument dating from the Middle Ages. It comprised a tube of wood, pierced with holes which were stopped by fingers, and a cup-shaped mouthpiece.

Coronation Concerto The name given to MOZART's piano concerto in D major which was played at the coronation of Leopold II in 1790.

Coronation Mass MOZART's Mass in C major, so called because it was associated with the annual crowning of a statue of the Virgin near Salzburg.

Coronation of Poppaea, The *see* Incoronazione de Poppea, L'.

corranach A lament sung at Scottish funerals.

Così fan tutte ('Women are all the same') An opera by MOZART to a libretto by L. da Ponte which has the subtitle, '*La scuola degli amante*' (The School for Lovers). It was first performed in Vienna in 1790 and relates the story of two sisters and their fickle love for two soldiers.

cotillion A popular ballroom dance of the early 19th cent.

cottage piano A small upright piano.

counterpoint The combination of two or more independent melodic lines that fit together to create a coherent sound texture. The classical conventions of harmony are based on counterpoint.

counter-subject A melody, found in FUGUE, that is contrapuntal to the main theme (subject), i.e. after singing the subject, a voice carries on to sing the counter-subject while the answer is sung.

counter-tenor The highest natural male voice (not to be confused with FALSETTO).

country and western A generic term for a form of 20th-cent. American folk music, originating from the south-east of the USA, with Nashville, Tennessee, as its traditional home. It is usually played by small bands using fiddles, guitars, banjos and drums etc. The songs are typically of a sentimental, sometimes tragic, nature. Lively 'bluegrass' music is a form of country and western.

Couperin, François ('le Grand') (1668–1733) The most

important member of a French family of musicians. He was an organist and wrote music for the harpsichord. His book *L'Art de toucher le clavecin* gave instructions on how to play his harpsichord pieces and it had an influence on BACH.

couplet 1 The same as DUPLET. **2** A two-note SLUR. **3** A song in which the same music is repeated for every stanza.

courante (Fr.) Short for *danse courante* or 'running dance', i.e. a lively Baroque dance in triple time.

Covent Garden Theatre An opera house in London, now known as The Royal Opera House. It is the home of the Royal Ballet and the Royal Opera companies.

Coward, Noël (1899–1974) An English playwright, songwriter, singer and actor, noted in particular for his witty songs, such as 'Mad Dogs and Englishmen'. He wrote songs and scores for a number of revues and musicals (e.g. *Bitter Sweet*) as well as stage plays.

cow bell As used as a percussion instrument in an orchestra, an ordinary square cow bell with the clapper taken out. It is played with a drumstick.

Cowell, Henry Dixon (1897–1965) An American composer, pianist, teacher and writer who was largely self-taught but nevertheless rose to become a revered experimenter. He developed a technique of playing what he called 'tone clusters' on the piano, which involved hitting the keyboard with a fist or elbow. He wrote 20 symphonies and the opera *O'Higgins of Chile*.

Cramer, Johann Baptist (1771–1858) A German-born

composer and pianist who came to live in London where he gained a high reputation. He is most noted for his piano pieces and his book of *Studies*, which he wrote to pass on his skills and which is still used by young pianists today.

Creation, The An oratorio by HAYDN to a text by Baron van Swieten (a translation of an English libretto, including passages from Milton's *Paradise Lost*).

'Creation' Mass The nickname for a mass in B flat major by HAYDN.

credo (Lat.) 'I believe', the first word in the Roman Catholic Creed.

crescendo (It.) 'Increasing', i.e. getting gradually louder.

Creston, Paul (originally Joseph Guttoveggio) (1906–) An American, self-taught composer of Italian origin. His works include 5 symphonies, choral pieces and concertos, some of which were written for unusual instruments (such as harp, accordion).

Cristofori, Bartolomeo (1655–1731) An Italian instrument maker who first devised the hammer mechanism for the piano.

croche (Fr.) A quaver.

Croft, William (1678–1727) An English composer who was for a time organist at Westminster Abbey. He is best known for his odes and anthems, especially the hymn-tune 'St Anne' to which is sung 'O God our Help in Ages Past'.

crook 1 A detachable section of tubing that was inserted into a brass or woodwind instrument between the mouthpiece and the body of the instrument to give it a different key (by increasing the length of the air-column). Performers often had as many as 12 crooks but the introduction of valved instruments in the 1850s virtually dispensed with their necessity. **2** A curved metal tube between the mouthpiece and the body of large wind instruments, such as the bassoon and bass clarinet.

crooning A soft, sentimental style of singing, often to dance music. Bing Crosby was a noted 'crooner'.

Cross, Joan (1900–) An English soprano who was one of the greatest of the 20th cent. She was particularly associated with the works of BRITTEN.

Crosse, Gordon (1937–) An English composer whose works include pieces for children (e.g. *Ahmet the Woodseller*) and 3 operas (e.g. *Purgatory*).

cross rhythms Rhythms that appear to have conflicting patterns and are performed at the same time as one another.

crotchet (US, 'quarter note') A note with a quarter of the time value of a whole note (semibreve).

crumhorn *see* Krumhorn.

csárdás *see* czárdás.

cuckoo A short pipe with a single finger hole; it gives two notes that imitate the sound of the bird.

Cui, César Antonovich (1835–1918) A Russian composer, critic and member of 'The FIVE'. He wrote 11 operas (e.g. *The Captive of the Caucasus*) but is best remembered for his witty writings.

curtain music *see* act tune.

curtall A small bassoon of the 16th and 17th cents.

cycle a series or sequence of pieces of music, written

by a given composer, which have a common theme or idea.

cymbals Percussion instruments comprising two metal plates which are held in the hands and clashed together. They are mounted on stands for jazz and popular music drum kits, where they are operated by pedals or struck with sticks.

cymbalon *see* dulcimer.

czárdás A Hungarian dance with two parts (a slow section and a fast section) that alternate.

Czerny, Karl (1791–1857) An Austrian-born composer and piano teacher who was taught by BEETHOVEN and in turn taught LISZT. He published many influential books on piano playing.

D

D 1 The second note of the scale of C major. **2** Abbrev. for DOMINANT, and for doctor (as in D. Mus., Doctor of Music).

da capo (It.) 'From the head'; it is an instruction to repeat the beginning of the piece. Abbrev.: D.C.

Dallapiccola, Luigi (1904–75) An Italian composer whose work includes anti-fascist songs (e.g. *Canti di prigionia* or 'Songs of Captivity') and several operas (e.g. *Il Prigioniero*, 'The Prisoner').

dal segno (It.) 'From the sign', i.e. go back to the point in the music marked by the relevant symbol and repeat the music which follows it. Abbrev.: D.S. (See Appendix).

damp, to To stop the vibrations of an instrument by touching it, or part of it, for example the strings of a harp, the skin of a drum.

Dämpfer (Ger.) *see* mute.

Damrosch, Walter (1862–1950) An American composer and conductor of German descent who was particularly noted for conducting works by WAGNER. His best known operas include *Cyrano de Bergerac* and *The Scarlet Letter*. His brother (Frank Heino) and father (Leopold) were also notable composers and musicians.

Daphnis et Chloé A ballet by RAVEL which was commissioned by the impressario Diaghilev. It was first performed in 1912 and includes pieces for chorus as well as orchestra.

Dargomizhsky, Alexander Sergeievich (1813–69) A Russian composer who was largely self-taught. His works include the operas *The Russalka* and *The Stone Guest* as well as songs and orchestral fantasias.

Davies, Peter Maxwell (1934–) An English composer and one of the 'MANCHESTER SCHOOL'. Many of his compositions are influenced by medieval techniques. Since 1971 he has lived in the Orkney Islands, which have provided inspiration. As well as writing operas (e.g. *Taverner*) and orchestral pieces, he has also composed film music (e.g. for Ken Russell's *The Devils*).

Davis, Colin (1927–) An English conductor who is especially associated with the works of MOZART, STRAVINSKY, BERLIOZ and TIPPETT. He was knighted in 1978.

Davis, Miles (1926–91) A Black American jazz trumpeter who was a devotee of Charlie PARKER. He was one of the most influential of all contemporary jazz players and was especially well known for his 'cool' style. He made numerous recordings which include *Sketches of Spain* and *Miles Ahead*.

Death and the Maiden (*Der Tod und das Mädchen*) A song by SCHUBERT to words by M. Claudius, composed in 1817; also a string quartet in D minor by Schubert, which incorporates this song.

Death and Transfiguration (*Tod und Verklärung*) A symphonic poem by Richard STRAUSS. It was first performed in 1889.

Death in Venice An opera by BRITTEN to a libretto, based on the novel by Thomas Mann, by Myfanwy Piper.

D.C. *see* da capo.

Debussy, Claude Achille (1862–1918) A French composer who was one of the most influential of his era. He lived in Russia and Italy before settling in his native France and was friendly with the Impressionist painters, whose ideals he admired and whose style he attempted to imitate in music. The poet Mallarmé was also a friend and he 'illustrated' his poem in *Prélude à l'après-midi d'un faune*; the orchestral piece is considered to be one of his greatest. His opera *Pelléas et Mélisande* took him 10 years to write and was partly inspired by his reaction to the music of WAGNER. His work is powerfully suggestive, but is nevertheless meticulously constructed.

Debussy's principal works include: NOCTURNES, *La*

MER, *Printemps* and PRELUDE A L'APRES MIDI D'UN FAUNE (orchestral pieces); *Suite bergamasque*, *Pour le piano* and *Etudes* (for piano); *L'Enfant prodigue* (choral work); and PELLEAS ET MELISANDE (opera). He also wrote various pieces of chamber music and many songs.

début (Fr.) 'Beginning', i.e. a first appearance.

decibel One tenth of a BEL, a unit for measuring sound. A decibel represents the smallest change in loudness that can be detected by the average human ear.

deciso (It.) Literally, 'decided', i.e. with decision or 'play firmly'.

decrescendo (It.) 'Decreasing', i.e. getting gradually softer.

de Falla *see* Falla, Manuel de

degree A step of a SCALE; the position of each note on a scale is identified by its degree.

Delibes, Clément Philibert Léo (1836–91) A French composer of opera and organ pieces who was also a teacher. His best known works include the ballet, COPPELIA and the opera LAKME.

delicato (It.) 'Delicate'.

delicatamente (It.) 'Delicately'.

Delius, Frederick (1862–1934) An English composer of German parents who had settled in Bradford. His father refused to admit to his son's musical talents and pushed him into a career as a businessman. He lived in Florida as an orange grower for a time, but returned to Europe and became friendly with many artists and composers, including RAVEL and the painter Gauguin.

He visited Norway and became a close friend of GRIEG, who greatly influenced his compositions. In Britain, his music was slow to be recognized but was championed by Sir Thomas BEECHAM. Delius was happily influenced by the music he heard wherever he travelled and hints of SPIRITUALS and Norwegian folk songs are evident in some of his works. He is considered a romantic composer and his works tend to be robust frequently demand large orchestras.

His principal works include: *Over the hills and far away*, *Appalachia*, BRIGG FAIR and ON HEARING THE FIRST CUCKOO IN SPRING (for orchestra); *A* VILLAGE ROMEO AND JULIET and *Fennimore and Gerda* (opera); and several choral works and pieces of chamber music.

Dello Joio, Norman (1913–) An American composer, pianist and organist. He has written operas (e.g. *The Ruby* and *The Trial at Rouen*) as well as organ, chorus and piano music.

Del Mar, Norman (1913–) An English conductor particularly associated with 20th-cent. music. He is a guest conductor with many international orchestras.

descant A soprano part, sometimes improvised, sung above a hymn tune while the tune itself is sung by the rest of the congregation or choir.

Deutschland über alles (Germany beyond Everything) The German national anthem written just before the revolution of 1848 and sung to a tune by HAYDN.

deux temps (Fr.) In 2/2 time. *Valse à deux temps* is a waltz which has only two dance steps to every three beats of the bar.

development The expansion or changing in some way of parts of a theme of music that have already been heard, for example, by varying the rhythm or elaborating the phrase to give it new impetus.

Diabelli, Anton (1781–1858) An Austrian composer and founder of a firm of music publishers. He was a friend of BEETHOVEN and HAYDN and wrote many simple piano pieces himself. He is, however, best known for inviting a number of composers to write variations on a waltz tune of his own. Beethoven wrote 33 which have subsequently become known as the *Diabelli Variations*.

Diamond, David Leo (1915–) An American composer whose works include eight symphonies as well as concertos for piano, violin and cello. *Rounds*, for string orchestra, is probably his best known piece.

diapason 1 The term given to a family of organ stops which are largely responsible for the tone of the instrument. **2** (Fr.) A tuning fork; *diapason normal* means the same as CONCERT PITCH.

diatonic Belonging to a SCALE. The diatonic notes of a major scale consist of five tones (T) and two semitones (S), arranged TTSTTTS. *Compare* chromatic.

Dibdin, Charles (1745–1814) A self-taught English composer who wrote successful short operas (e.g. *The Padlock*) and numerous songs. He also wrote a book, *The Musical Tour of Mr Dibdin*.

Dido and Aeneas An opera by PURCELL, first performed in 1689. The story (taken from Virgil) concerns the events leading up to Dido's suicide after being deserted by Aeneas.

dièse (Fr.) Sharp.

Dies Irae ('Day of Wrath') A part of the REQUIEM Mass, with a PLAINSONG melody which has often been used by Romantic composers.

digital 1 One of the keys on the keyboard of a piano or organ. **2** In sound recording, a method of converting audio or analogue signals into a series of pulses according to their voltage, for the purposes of storage or manipulation.

diminished interval A perfect or major INTERVAL reduced by one semitone by flattening the upper note or sharpening the lower one.

diminished seventh chord A chord which covers a minor SEVENTH diminished by one semitone, i.e. C–B flat diminished to C–A. (This is in fact equivalent to a major sixth, but the term diminished seventh is often used.) It is frequently employed as a means of transition into another key.

diminished triad A minor TRIAD in which the fifth is flattened (diminished) (e.g. in the key of C major, C–E–G flat).

diminuendo (It.) 'Diminishing', i.e. getting gradually quieter.

diminution The shortening of note time-values, so that a melody is played more quickly, usually at double speed.

D'Indy *see* Indy, Vincent D'.

direct A sign placed at the end of a line or page of old music that indicates the pitch of the following note or notes.

discord A chord or combination of notes which create

an an unpleasant or jarring sound that needs to be resolved.

dissonance The creation of an unpleasant sound or DISCORD.

Dissonance Quartet A string quartet in C major by MOZART, composed in 1785, so named because of the dissonance of the opening section.

divertimento (It.) An 18th-cent. term for a piece of music that was intended to be a light entertainment, i.e. a diversion.

divertissement (Fr.) **1** A short ballet incorporated into an opera or play. **2** A short piece that includes well-known tunes taken from another source. **3** A DIVERTIMENTO.

divisé (Fr.) *see* divisi.

divisi (It.) 'Divided'; a term used to indicate that, where a part is written in double notes, performers should not attempt to play all the notes but should divide themselves into groups to play them. It is particularly used in music for strings.

divisions 1 A 17th-cent. type of VARIATION in which the long notes of a melody were split up into shorter ones. **2** An obsolete term for long vocal runs used by composers such as BACH and HANDEL.

'Dixieland' A simple form of traditional JAZZ which originated in New Orleans at the start of the 20th cent.

do (It.) *see* doh.

dodecaphonic Relating to dodecaphony, the TWELVE-NOTE SYSTEM of composition.

'Dog' Waltz *see* Minute Waltz.

doh The spoken name for the first note of a major scale in TONIC SOL-FA.

Dohnányi, Ernö (Ernst von) (1877–1960) A Hungarian composer and pianist who travelled the world giving recitals and eventually settled in the USA. His compositions tended to follow the German, rather than Hungarian, tradition and he is best known for his *Variations on a Nursery Theme* (for piano and orchestra). He also wrote 3 operas (e.g. *The Tenor*) and 3 symphonies amongst other pieces.

dolce (It.) 'Sweet' or 'gentle'.

dolcissimo (It.) 'Very sweet'.

dolente (It.) 'Sorrowful'.

doloroso (It.) 'Sorrowfully'.

dominant 1 The fifth note above the TONIC of a major or minor scale. **2** The name given to the RECITING NOTE of GREGORIAN CHANTS.

Domingo, Placido (1941–) A Spanish tenor of international repute who is particularly well known for performing in Italian operas, although he has a repertoire of more than 40 roles.

Don Carlos An opera by VERDI to a French libretto by F. J. Méry and C. du Locle. The story tells of Don Carlos, the heir to the Spanish throne, who falls in love with Elisabeth de Valois, who is destined to marry his father. It was first performed in 1867.

Don Giovanni (full title: *Il dissoluto punito, ossia Don Giovanni*, The Rake punished, or Don Juan) A comic opera by MOZART to a libretto by L. da Ponte. The story concerns the amorous adventures of the legendary Don Juan. It was first performed in 1787.

Donizetti, Gaetano (1797–1848) A prolific Italian composer who wrote no fewer than 75 operas, some serious, others comic. Many of his compositions are considered superficial, but some are perennial favourites, in particular DON PASQUALE, LUCCIA DI LAMMERMOOR, LUCREZIA BORGIA and *La Favorita*.

Don Pasquale A comic opera by DONIZETTI, who also wrote the libretto with Ruffini. The story tells of an old bachelor, Don Pasquale, who is conned into a false marriage contract.

Don Quixote 1 A tone poem by Richard STRAUSS, based on the novel by Cervantes, first performed in 1898. **2** An opera by MASSENET, first performed in 1910. **3** A suite by TELEMANN.

doppio (It.) 'Double', as in *doppio movimento*, meaning 'twice as fast'.

Dorian mode A term applied to the ascending scale which is played on the white keys of a piano beginning at D.

dot A mark used in musical notation. When it is placed after a note, it makes the note half as long again; when it is placed above a note it indicates STACCATO.

dotted note *see* dot.

double 1 A word used to describe certain instruments that are built an octave lower than normal, e.g. a double bassoon (also called a 'contrabassoon') is built an octave lower than a standard bassoon. **2** A term used to describe a type of VARIATION found in 17th-cent. French instrumental music in which melody notes are embellished with ornamentation.

double bass The largest and lowest pitched of the

bowed string instruments. It used to have three strings but now it has four (sometimes five).

double counterpoint Counterpoint in which the two parts can change places, i.e. the higher can become the lower and vice versa.

double fugue 1 A fugue with two subjects. In one type of double fugue, both subjects are introduced at the start; in another type, the second subject appears after the first and the two are eventually combined.

Dowland, John (1563–1626) An English composer and lute player who was famous as a performer during his lifetime and who is now considered to be a great and innovative composer of songs. He published four volumes of airs and a celebrated collection of 21 instrumental pieces called *Lachrimae*. His son, Robert Dowland, followed in his father's footsteps and also became a noted lutenist and composer.

down-beat The downward movement of a conductor's baton or hand which usually indicates the first beat of a bar.

D'Oyly Carte, Richard (1844–1901) An English impresario who brought together GILBERT and SULLIVAN and subsequently founded the D'Oyly Carte Opera Company to perform their operas, for which he built the Savoy Theatre in London.

Dreigroschenoper, Die *see* Threepenny Opera.

drone A pipe that sounds a continuous note of fixed pitch as a permanent bass. The BAGPIPES, for example, have several drone pipes. Also, a similar effect produced by stringed instruments fitted with 'drone strings'.

drum A percussion instrument of which there are numerous types, such as TIMPANI, SIDE DRUM etc. Most drums consist of a hollow metal or wood cylinder over which is stretched a skin. Sound is produced by beating the skin with a stick or with the hands.

drum kit A set of drums and cymbals that are arranged in such a way that they can all be played by one person sitting on a stool. Some of the instruments (such as the bass drum) are played with a foot pedal, but most are struck with sticks or brushes. Drum kits are used by jazz and pop drummers and can vary enormously in size.

D.S. An abbreviation of DAL SEGNO.

due corde (It.) Literally, 'two strings'; a term used in violin music indicating that a passage that could theoretically be played on one string should nevertheless be played on two to produce the desired effect.

duet A combination of two performers or a composition for such a pair, for example, piano duet.

Dufay, Guillaume (c.1400–74) A Flemish composer who was the most important of his time. Although he wrote some secular songs, he is best known for his church music and masses (for example *L'Homme armé*) based on a secular theme.

Dukas, Paul (1865–1935) A French composer and critic who was at first influenced by the works of WAGNER but became increasingly drawn by the Impressionist movement. His output was comparatively small but includes some of the most important works of the early 20th cent., such as *The* SORCERER'S APPRENTICE and *Ariadne and Bluebeard* (opera), and *La Peri* (ballet).

dulcimer An ancient instrument which was introduced to Europe from the East in the Middle Ages. It consists of a shallow box over which strings are stretched. The instrument is placed on the knees and the strings are struck with small hammers. In the USA, an instrument similar to the ZITHER is sometimes called a dulcimer.

dulcitone A keyboard instrument containing tuning forks which are struck with hammers as in a piano.

Dumbarton Oaks Concerto A concerto in E flat major for 15 instruments by STRAVINSKY. It is so called because it was first performed, in 1938, at Dumbarton Oaks, the estate in Washington D.C. belonging to R.W. Bliss, who commissioned it.

dumka A Slavonic folk ballad or lament, which may have a fast middle section.

Dunstable, John (*c.*1390–1453) An English musician, astrologer and mathematician of whose early life very little is known. However, he is considered one of the most important composers of the 15th cent. and was probably one of the first to write instrumental accompaniments to church music.

duplet A group of two notes of equal value which are played in the time normally taken by three.

duple time A form of musical time in which the number of beats in a bar is a multiple of two, for example 2/4 (2 crotchets) and 6/8 (6 quavers in two groups of three).

Du Pré, Jacqueline (1945–1987) An celebrated English

cellist who was renowned for her interpretation of ELGAR's cello concerto. In 1967 she married the conductor Daniel BARENBOIM, but her life was cut tragically short by multiple sclerosis.

dur (Ger.) 'Major', as in major key.

Dussek, Jan Ladislav (originally Dusík) (1760–1812) A Czech pianist and composer who earned a reputation as a virtuoso performer in his own lifetime. He was a prolific composer and his works include 28 piano sonatas and 15 piano concertos.

Dvořák, Antonín (1841–1904) A Czech composer of modest origins who learned to play the violin at an early age. He went on to become a viola player with the Prague National Theatre, with which he stayed for 11 years. His talent for composing was encouraged by BRAHMS, who helped to get some of his pieces published. He travelled to England, where he was fêted, and to the USA, where he stayed for three years. In the USA he was influenced by Black music (as seen in the AMERICAN QUARTET) and this, coupled with homesickness, inspired him to write his most famous, and last, symphony, entitled FROM THE NEW WORLD. When he eventually returned to Czechoslovakia, he concentrated on writing symphonic poems and operas. All Dvořák's work is carefully constructed, yet fresh and exciting. BRAHMS, SMETANA and WAGNER influenced his work, but so too did his love of folk music.

His principal works include: *The Devil and Kate* and *Armida* (operas); *Te Deum* (choral piece); 9 symphonies; and many chamber music compositions, piano pieces and songs.

dynamic accents ACCENTS which correspond to the regular rhythm of a piece of music, as indicated by the TIME SIGNATURE.

Dyson, George (1883–1964) An English composer and teacher who for a time studied in Italy and Germany. His works include one symphony and several cantatas, such as *The Canterbury Pilgrims*. He was knighted in 1941.

E

E The third note (MEDIANT) of the scale of C major.

écossaise An abbreviation of *danse écossaise*, i.e. 'Scottish dance', although in fact the term has little to do with Scottish dancing and merely refers to a quick dance in 2/4 time.

Egk, Werner (1901–83) A German composer and conductor who was influenced by STRAVINSKY. His important works include the operas, PEER GYNT, *Irish Legend* and *The Government Inspector*. He also wrote ballet and choral music.

eighth-note (US) A quaver.

Eighteen Twelve (1812) A concert overture by TCHAIKOVSKY, written in 1882, the 70th anniversary, to commemorate Napoleon's retreat from Moscow. It includes *La* MARSEILLAISE and optional parts for canon, church bells and a military band.

Einem, Gottfried von (1918–) An Austrian composer who was born in Switzerland. He is most noted for his operas *Danton's Death* and *The Old Lady's Visit*, and the ballet *Princess Turandot*. He has also written orchestral and choral pieces.

electronic instruments A generic term for instruments that convert electrical energy into sound, such as the synthesizer.

Elektra An opera by Richard STRAUSS to a libretto (based on Sophocles' *Electra*) by Hugo von Hofmannsthal. The story concerns the revenge of Elektra on her mother, Clytemnestra, for the death of her father, Agamemnon. It was first performed in 1909.

Elgar, Edward William (1857–1934) An English composer who had no formal musical training but learned from his father, who ran a music shop and was a part-time piano tuner. For a time he earned a living teaching the violin and it was not until his famous piece for orchestra, ENIGMA VARIATIONS, was first performed in London in 1899 that his reputation as a composer was established. The next 15 years of his life were the most fruitful and he wrote many impressive works, among them the oratorios *The Dream of Gerontius* and *The Kingdom*; two symphonies and the cello concerto. The work for which he is most famous, No. 1 of a set of the POMP AND CIRCUMSTANCE marches, was first performed in 1901. He was knighted in 1904 and became a baronet in 1931.

Although Elgar was an overtly romantic composer, he was an undoubted master of orchestration. His Roman Catholic faith and his love of England were lasting influences throughout his life. Unlike many of his contemporaries, Elgar realized the potential of the gramophone and he made several recordings of his own work.

His principal works include: *The Apostles*, *The Dream of Gerontius* (oratorios); *Coronation Ode*, *The Spirit of England* (choral works); FALSTAFF (a tone poem); the cello concerto; *Enigma Variations*. In addition, he wrote many pieces for orchestra, chorus and organ.

Elisir d'amore, L' An opera by DONIZETTI to a libretto by F. Romani. The story tells of a youth who buys a love potion (elixir) from a quack doctor; this turns out to be nothing more than wine, but love results none the less.

Ellington, Edward Kennedy 'Duke' (1899–1974) A Black American jazz composer, pianist and band leader whose experiments with jazz (such as his jazz impressions of classical pieces) opened up new horizons for the genre. He was called 'Duke' because of his aristocratic air. His most memorable compositions include *Mood Indigo*, *Concerto for Cootie* and *Creole Rhapsody*.

embouchure 1 The mouthpiece of a BRASS or WIND INSTRUMENT. **2** The correct tensioning of the lips and facial muscles when playing woodwind and brass instruments to create good tone.

encore (Fr.) Literally, 'again'; the call from an English audience (the French equivalent is in fact *bis*) for more music. If the performance does continue, the additional music is also known as an 'encore'.

end pin *see* tail pin.

enharmonic intervals Intervals that are so small that they do not exist on keyboard instruments; an example is the interval from A sharp to B flat.

Enigma Variations (Variations on an Original Theme) A famous work for orchestra by ELGAR, first performed in 1899. The enigma may be an unheard theme (possibly the Scottish ballad 'Auld lang syne'), and 14 of the variations are dedicated to friends, whose personalities he attempted to portray in the music; the 15th is devoted to himself.

ensemble (Fr.) Literally, 'together'; a term meaning a group of players or singers, a movement in opera for several singers, or the precision with which such a group performs together.

Entführung aus dem Serail, Die (The Abduction from the Harem) A comic opera with spoken dialogue by MOZART to a libretto by Gottlieb Stephanie after a play by Bretzner. It tells of the rescue of Constanze by her lover Belmonte from the court of Pasha Selim. It was first performed in 1782.

entr'acte (Fr.) The music played between the acts of a play or opera.

episode 1 In FUGUE, a passage that connects entries of the subject. **2** In RONDO, a contrasting section that separates entries of the principal theme.

equal temperament A convenient, but technically incorrect, way of tuning a keyboard in which all semitones are considered equal, e.g. F sharp and G flat are taken to be identical notes when theoretically they are not. Such a system makes complex MODULATIONS practicable.

Erlkönig (The Erl-King) A setting of Goethe's ballad by SCHUBERT, who wrote it when he was 18.

Eroica (It.) The popular, abbreviated title of BEET-HOVEN's symphony no. 3 in E flat major, composed 1803–4. It was originally entitled *Sinfonia grande Napoleon Bonaparte*, but Beethoven was so annoyed that Napoleon proclaimed himself emperor (in 1804) that he changed the name to *Sinfonia eroica, composa per festeggiare il souvenire d'un grand' uomo* (Heroic Symphony, composed to celebrate the memory of a great man). It was first performed in 1804.

escapement The mechanism in a piano which releases the hammer, allowing a string to vibrate freely after it has been struck.

espressivo (It.) 'Expressively'.

esquisse (Fr.) A 'sketch', a title sometimes given to short instrumental pieces.

Estampes (Engravings) A set of three piano pieces by DEBUSSY, which were first performed in 1904.

estampie (Fr.) A form of dance accompanied by song, dating from the 12th cent., which may constitute the oldest type of instrumental composition in Western music.

Esther An oratorio by HANDEL with words by Pope and Arbuthnot, based on Racine. It was originally composed as the MASQUE *Haman and Mordecai*, but the Bishop of London refused to allow a religious story to be performed on stage so Handel expanded it into an oratorio, which was first performed in 1732.

estinto (Lat.) Literally, 'extinct', i.e. as soft as possible.

étude A 'study' or piece of music evolved from a single phrase or idea.

Eugene Onegin An opera by TCHAIKOVSKY, who also wrote the libretto (from Pushkin) in conjunction with K. Shilovsky. The story concerns the love of Tatiana for Onegin, a proud man, who refuses to return her affections until much later, by which time it is too late, and as a result he kills himself. It was first performed in 1879 by students.

euphonium A large brass instrument, a tenor TUBA, which is mainly used in brass and military bands.

eurhythmics A system of teaching musical rhythm by graceful physical movements. It was invented by Emile JAQUES-DALCROZE in 1905.

Evans, Geraint (1922–) A Welsh baritone and opera producer of international repute. He is particularly famous for his roles in MOZART operas. He was knighted in 1969.

evensong *see* Nunc Dimittis.

exposition 1 In the SONATA FORM, the first section of a piece in which the main themes are introduced before they are developed. **2** In FUGUE, the initial statement of the subject by each of the parts.

expressionism A term borrowed from the visual arts which implies the expression of inner emotions.

extemporization *see* improvisation.

F

F 1 The fourth note (or SUBDOMINANT) of the scale of C major. **2** In abbreviations, *f* means *forte* (loud); *ff*, *fortissimo* (very loud) and *fp*, *forte piano* (loud and then soft).

fa In the TONIC SOL-FA, the fourth degree in any major scale.

faburden Literally, 'false bass' or 'drone', the lowest of three voices in the English 15th-cent. improvised harmonization of PLAINSONG melody (15th cent.)

Façade An 'entertainment' by WALTON for six instruments and a narrator of a series of poems by Edith Sitwell. It was first performed in 1923.

fado (Port.) A type of melancholy song with a guitar accompaniment.

Fairy Queen, The An operatic MASQUE with music by PURCELL. The words, which include spoken dialogue, are based on Shakespeare's *Midsummer Night's Dream*. It was first performed in 1692.

Falla, Manuel de (1876–1946) A Spanish composer and pianist who was first taught the piano by his mother. He won a prize from the Madrid Academy of Fine Arts for his opera *La vida breve* (Life is Short) in 1905, but it was not performed. For a time he lived in Paris where he met, amongst others, RAVEL and DEBUSSY, who both influenced his compositions. He returned to Spain until the beginning of the Spanish Civil War when he left for Argentina, where he died. His work is full of Spanish vitality but he was rarely satisfied with his own work and his output was small.

His principal compositions include the ballets, *El amor brujo* (LOVE THE MAGICIAN), *El sombrero de tres picos* (The Three-cornered Hat); a work for piano and orchestra, *Noches en los jardines de España* (NIGHTS IN THE GARDENS OF SPAIN); and the piano piece *Fantasia bética*.

false relation In harmony, the occurrence of a note bearing an accidental which is immediately followed, in another part, by the same note which does not bear an accidental, or vice versa.

falsetto (It.) An adult male voice, used in the register above its normal range. It has often been used, to comic effect, in operas.

Falstaff 1 A comic opera by VERDI to a libretto by A. Boito (after Shakespeare's *Merry Wives of Windsor* and *Henry IV, Parts 1 and 2*). This was Verdi's last opera and was first performed in 1893. **2** A symphonic study in C minor by ELGAR.

Fanciulla del West, La *see* Girl of the Golden West, The.

fancy *see* fantasia.

fandango A lively Spanish dance, thought to be South American in origin, in triple time. It is usually accompanied by guitar and castanets.

fanfare A flourish of trumpets, or other instruments (e.g. organ) that imitate the sound of trumpets.

fantasia (It.) A piece in which the composer follows his imagination in free association rather than composing within a particular conventional form; when such a piece is played, it can sound as if it is being improvised.

Fantasie (Ger.), **fantaisie** (Fr.) *see* fantasia.

Farewell Symphony HAYDN's symphony no. 45 in F sharp minor. Haydn intended the piece to be a hint to his patron, Prince Esterházy, that his orchestra needed a holiday. In the last movement, the performers stop playing and leave one by one until just two violinists are left.

Fauré, Gabriel Urbain (1845–1924) A French composer, organist and teacher who was a pupil of SAINT-SAENS. He later taught composition (to RAVEL, among others). The last 20 years of his life were marred by deafness. He particularly excelled at writing songs and, although some of his pieces were influenced by WAGNER, they were all unmistakeably French.

His principal works include: *Promethée* and *Pénélope* (operas); PELLEAS ET MELISSANDE (incidental music); *Ballade* (for piano and orchestra); a Requiem Mass; and the songs *La Chanson d'Eve* and *Le Jardin clos*.

Faust An opera by GOUNOD to a libretto by J. Barbier and M. Carré (after Goethe's *Faust*). It was first performed in 1859 and remains one of the most popular of all operas.

Faust Overture, A An orchestral overture by WAGNER, first performed in 1844.

Faust Symphony, A A symphony for orchestra and chorus by LISZT. It was first performed in 1857.

fauxbourdon (Fr.) A 15th-cent. continental technique of improvising a bass part for a PLAINSONG melody.

Feldman, Morton (1926–) An American composer who was greatly influenced by CAGE and the paintings of the abstract expressionists (such as Jackson Pollock), whose work he has attempted to emulate in music. He has experimented with alternative forms of music and music notation and his most noted pieces include *Projections* (chamber music) and *Vertical Thoughts* (keyboard pieces).

feminine cadence An ending in which the final chord occurs on a weak beat of the bar and not the more usual strong beat.

Ferguson, Howard (1908–) A Northern Irish composer and teacher whose works include the ballet *Chaunteclear* as well as chamber and piano music.

fermata (It.) *see* pause.

Ferrabosco, Alfonso (1543–88) An Italian composer who came to live in England when he was young. He wrote several madrigals, motets and pieces for lute. He left England in 1578 but his son, Alfonso (*c*.1575–1628), remained and was employed as a violinist by James I. He composed music for MASQUES, and some fine instrumental music.

Ferrier, Kathleen (1912–53) An English contralto who was probably the most famous of her generation. The part of Lucretia in BRITTEN's opera RAPE OF LUCRETIA was written for her, but she was best known for her BRAHMS and WAGNER recitals. She was made a C.B.E. in 1953 but died of cancer shortly afterwards.

ff *see* F (2).

fiddle 1 A generic term for a range of primitive stringed instruments played with a bow, as used in parts of Asia, Africa and Eastern Europe. **2** A colloquial term for a violin, especially in folk music.

Fidelio (full title: *Fidelio, oder Die eheliche Liebe*, Fidelio, or Married Love) BEETHOVEN's only opera, originally to libretto by J. Sonnleithner. The story tells of the rescue of Florestan, a prisoner of Pizarro, by his wife Leonora, who is disguised as a jailer named Fidelio. Beethoven wrote four LEONORA overtures for the opera. It was first performed, in the first of its three versions, in 1805.

Field, John (1782–1837) An Irish pianist and composer who was an apprentice to CLEMENTI. He travelled all over Europe demonstrating pianos and earned the reputation of being a virtuoso performer. He eventually settled in Russia, where he died. He invented the NOCTURNE form, which CHOPIN later developed, and wrote 7 piano concertos and 4 sonatas.

fife A small flute still used in 'drum and fife' bands.

fifth An INTERVAL of five notes (the first and last notes are counted) or seven semitones, for example, from C to G.

figure A short musical phrase that is repeated in the course of a composition.

figured bass The bass part of a composition which has numerical figures written below the notes to indicate how the harmony above should be played. It is, in effect, a type of musical shorthand in which the bass line and melody are written down while the numbers indicate which chords should be played. The system was used during the 17th and early 18th cents.

finale (It.) **1** The last movement of a work. **2** The concluding section of an opera act.

Fingal's Cave (Alternative title: The Hebrides) An overture in B minor by MENDELSSOHN, said to have been inspired by a visit to the Isle of Staffa. It was first performed in 1832.

fingering A type of notation that indicates which fingers should be used to play a piece of music.

Finlandia An orchestral tone-poem by SIBELIUS, nationalistic in character, containing melodies which resemble Finnish folk tunes. It was first performed in 1900. *See also* nationalism.

fino (It.) 'As far as', so *fino al segno* means 'as far as the sign'.

Finzi, Gerald (1901–56) An English composer who is best known for his musical settings of poems by Thomas Hardy, and for *Dies natalis*, for voice and strings.

fioritura (It.) 'Flowering', i.e. an embellishment.

fipple flute *see* flageolet; recorder.

Firebird, The A ballet with music by STRAVINSKY and choreography by Fokine. It was first performed in 1910.

Fireworks Music The popular title of HANDEL's *Music for the Royal Fireworks*, a suite of eight movements. It was originally composed for a wind band as accompaniment to the fireworks display in London celebrating the Peace of Aix-la-Chapelle in 1749. Handel subsequently added string parts.

Fischer-Dieskau, Dietrich (1925–) A German baritone and conductor who is especially admired for his huge repertoire, including the *Lieder* of SCHUBERT and WOLF.

Fitzwilliam Virginal Book A highly important manuscript collection of keyboard music of the late 16th and early 17th cents.

Five, The The name given to a group of nationalistic 19th-cent. Russian composers who were known in Russia as *moguchaya kuchka* (The Mighty Handful). The five were RIMSKY-KORSAKOV, BALAKIREV, BORODIN, CUI and MUSSORGSKY.

flageolet A small, end-blown flute with six holes, four in front and two at the back, popular in the 17th cent.

Flagstad, Kirsten (1895–1962) A Norwegian soprano who was especially famous for singing WAGNER roles.

flamenco A generic term for a type of Spanish song from Andalusia, usually sad and often accompanied by guitar and dancing. Flamenco guitar playing relies heavily on the strumming of powerful, dynamic rhythms.

flat 1 A note which is lowered by one semitone as indicated by the flat sign (see Appendix). **2** A note (or notes) produce at too low a pitch and hence 'out of tune'.

Fledermaus, Die (The Bat) An operetta by Johann STRAUSS the Younger to a libretto by C. Haffner and R. Genée. The title refers to a fancy-dress costume which has a crucial effect on the plot. It was first performed in 1874.

Fliegende Holländer, Der *see* Flying Dutchman, The.

Flight of the Bumble-Bee, The The orchestral interlude in RIMSKY-KORSAKOV's opera *The Legend of the Czar*

Saltan, which describes how a prince becomes a bee. It has been arranged for many different instruments.

Flotow, Friedrich von (1812–83) A German composer who is best known for his operas such as *Alessandro Stradella* and *Martha*.

flue pipes All organ pipes which have narrow openings, or flues, into which air passes; the other pipes are REED PIPES.

Flügelhorn (Ger.) A soprano brass instrument invented by Adolphe Sax, similar to a bugle in shape, but with three pistons.

flute 1 The tranverse or German flute is a member of the WOODWIND family of instruments, although these days it is normally made of silver or other metal. One end of the instrument is stopped and sound is produced by blowing across the mouthpiece formed around an aperture cut into the side of the instrument at the stopped end. The pitch is controlled by means of a lever system. **2** The English flute is a beaked, end-blown, wind instrument with finger holes, now more usually called the RECORDER.

Flying Dutchman, The (*Der Fliegende Holländer*) An opera by WAGNER, who also wrote the libretto. It tells the story of the Flying Dutchman, who is condemned by the Devil to wander the seas forever but is saved by the love of Senta. It was first performed in 1843.

folía (Sp.) 'The folly', a wild and noisy Portuguese dance.

folk dance Any dance, performed by ordinary people, in a pre-industrial society, that has evolved over the years and gained a traditional form. Folk dances differ widely in character and some have symbolic significance, such as war dances, fertility dances etc.

folk song Properly, any song which has been preserved by oral tradition. Many composers and pop musicians have written new compositions that imitate old folk songs.

forlana (It.) An Italian dance from northern Italy that is especially associated with Venetian gondoliers.

form The structure of a composition. The basic elements of musical composition which define a given piece's form are repetition, variation and contrast. Examples of recognized forms include FUGUE, RONDO, SONATA FORM etc.

forte (It.) 'Loud'. Abbrev.: *f*.

fortepiano (It.) An early word for PIANOFORTE. Not to be confused with *forte piano* (loud then soft).

fortissimo (It.) 'Very loud'. Abbrev.: *ff*.

Forty-Eight, The The popular name of BACH's *48 Preludes and Fugues*, also called *The Well-Tempered Clavier*.

forza (It.) 'Force', so *con forza* means 'with force'.

forzato (It.) 'Forced'.

Foss, Lukas (originally Fuchs) (1922–) A composer of German parentage who settled in the USA in 1937. He has written several operas (e.g. *The Jumping Frog of Calaveras County*), a symphony and the oratorio, *A Parable of Death*.

Foster, Stephen Collins (1826–64) A self-taught American composer of popular songs, such as *My old Kentucky Home*, *Camptown Races*, *Jeannie with the Light Brown Hair* and *Oh! Susanna*.

Four Last Songs (*Vier letzte Lieder*) Four short, but exquisitely executed settings of poems for soprano and orchestra by Richard STRAUSS. They were his last compositions and were first performed in 1950.

Four Seasons, The (*Le quattro stagioni*) A set of four perennially popular violin concertos by VIVALDI.

fourth An INTERVAL of four notes (including the first and last) or five semitones, e.g. C to F.

foxtrot A dance, originating in the USA, in duple time. It first became popular in 1912.

fp Abbreviation for *forte piano* (It.) meaning 'loud then soft'.

Françaix, Jean (1912–) A French composer of operas, ballets and orchestral works, for example *Les Demoiselles de la nuit* (ballet), and *La Maine de Gloire.*

Franck, César Auguste (1822–90) A Belgian composer and organist whose work is marked by its chromatic and romantic style. His principal compositions include: *Ruth, La Tour de Babel, Rebecca* (oratorios); *Hulda, Ghiselle* (operas); and *Variations symphoniques* (for piano and orchestra).

Frankl, Peter (1935–) A Hungarian-born pianist who has been a British citizen since 1967. He is a member of a chamber music trio and is a renowned concert hall soloist.

Franz, Robert (1815–92) A German composer admired by SCHUMANN and LISZT, who wrote more than 250 songs. He became deaf in 1868 and was forced to give up his music.

free-reed A type of reed found in such instruments as the accordion and harmonica. It consists of a small metal tongue which vibrates freely in a metal slot when air is blown over it. The pitch of the reed is determined by its thickness and length.

French horn *see* horn.

French sixth *see* augmented sixth.

Frescobaldi, Girolamo (1583–1643) An Italian composer who was one of the outstanding organists of his era. He wrote many keyboard pieces, toccatas, arias and madrigals.

fret (Fr.) One of a series of thin pieces of metal fitted into the wooden finger-board of a stringed instrument to make the stopping of strings easier and more accurate. Each fret represents the position of a specific note. Frets are found on guitars, mandolins and banjos.

'Frog' Quartet The nickname of HAYDN's string quartet in D major (1787); it is so called because the theme in the last movement sounds like croaking.

From the New World The title of DVORAK's symphony no. 9 in E minor, composed in 1893. It was written while Dvořák was in the USA and is his impression of the country. It shows influences of Black American music and the music of the native Indians.

front man The person who stands at the front of the stage during a performance of JAZZ and who is therefore the focus of the audience's attention. He or she is often, but not always, the leader or singer of the band.

frottola (It.) Literally, 'little mixture'; a type of Italian polyphonic song which was popular in the 15th cent.

fugue A contrapuntal composition for two or more parts (commonly called 'voices') which enter successively in imitation of each other. The first entry is called the 'SUBJECT' and the second entry (a fifth higher or lower than the subject) is called the 'ANSWER'. When all the voices have entered, the EXPOSITION is complete and is usually followed by an EPISODE which connects to the next series of subject entries. A COUNTER-SUBJECT is a melodic accompaniment to the subject and answer and is often in DOUBLE COUNTERPOINT. A fugue may be written for voices, instruments or both. The form dates back to the 17th cent.

full close *see* cadence.

full organ A term used in organ music to indicate that all the loud stops are to be used together.

funk A form of heavily syncopated, rhythmic Black dance music, originating in the USA. The adjective, often used in JAZZ terminology, is *funky*.

fuoco (It.) 'Fire', so *con fuoco* means 'with fire'.

furioso (It.) 'Furious'.

Für Elise (For Elise) A BAGATELLE in A minor for piano by BEETHOVEN, written *c*.1810. The word 'Elise' on the manuscript may have been an erroneous transcription of Therese; Beethoven was in love with Therese von Brunswick, among whose papers the score was found.

Fux, Johann Joseph (1660–1741) An Austrian composer and theorist who specialized in church music. He wrote over 400 works including 10 oratorios, 18 operas and 50 masses.

fz Abbrev. for FORZATO.

G

G The fifth note (or DOMINANT) of the scale of C major.

Gabrieli, Andrea (*c*.1515–86) An Italian organist and composer of madrigals, motets, masses and instrumental pieces.

Gabrieli, Giovanni (*c*.1557–1612) The nephew of Andrea GABRIELI, and also a noted composer, organist and teacher. He was one of the greatest Venetian composers of motets.

Gade, Niels Wilhelm (1817–90) A Danish composer who travelled to Italy and Germany, where he was encouraged by MENDELSSOHN. His output was influenced by Mendelssohn and SCHUMANN, and his principal works include 8 symphonies, 6 overtures and several cantatas, e.g. *The Crusaders*.

galant (Fr.) 'Polite'; a term applied to certain graceful styles of court music, especially of the 18th cent.

galanterie An 18th-cent. German term for a keyboard piece in the GALANT style.

galliard (Fr.) A lively court dance, usually in triple time, which dates back to the 16th cent.

galop A lively dance in duple time that originated in Germany and was popular in the 19th cent.

Galway, James (1939–) A Northern Irish flautist and composer who has done much to popularize the flute with his many recordings and television appearances. Before he embarked on a solo career, he was principal flautist with several of the world's leading orchestras, notably the Berlin Philharmonic Orchestra.

gamelan A type of traditional orchestra found principally in Indonesia and South-East Asia. Although such an orchestra includes strings and woodwind instruments, it is the array of gongs, drums and chimes, which produce the unique and highly complex rhythms of gamelan music. DEBUSSY was especially influenced by gamelan.

gamut 1 The note G on the bottom line of the bass clef. **2** An alternative (now obsolete) word for the key of G. **3** The whole range of musical sounds, from the lowest to the highest, hence the common phrase 'to run the gamut'.

gavotte An old French dance, in 4/4 time, which usually starts on the third beat of the bar. It was favoured by LULLY in his ballets and operas and has been revived in the 20th cent. by such composers as PROKOFIEV and SCHOENBERG.

Gay, John (1685–1732) An English poet and playwright who is best known for writing the words of *The* BEGGAR'S OPERA.

Gazza Ladra, La *see* Thieving Magpie, The.

gedämpft (Ger.) 'Muted'.

Geige (Ger.) 'Fiddle' or 'violin'.

Geistertrio (Ger.) (The Ghost Trio) The nickname of BEETHOVEN's piano trio in D major. It is so called because of the sinister character of the slow movement, which Beethoven intended to use in an opera version of *Macbeth*.

Geminiani, Francesco (*c.*1679–1762) An Italian violinist who lived in Paris, London and Dublin. He had a highly successful solo career and wrote a ballet (*La* *foresta incantata*) and several impressive sonatas, trios and concertos. His book *The Art of Playing on the Violin*, was the first of its kind.

gemshorn (chamois horn) **1** An early type of recorder made from the horn of an animal. It fell out of favour in the 16th cent. **2** An organ stop with a light tone.

Generalpause (Ger.) A rest of one or more bars for all the members of an orchestra. Abbrev.: G.P.

German, Edward (originally Edward German Jones) (1862–1936) A Welsh composer who is best known for the incidental music he wrote for Shakespeare's plays, for example *Henry VIII*. He also composed the operettas *Merrie England* and *Tom Jones*. He was knighted in 1928.

German sixth *see* augmented sixth.

Gershwin, George (1898–1937) An American composer and pianist who wrote songs for many musical shows, often in conjunction with his lyricist brother, Ira, such as *Lady, be Good*, *Funny Face* and *Girl Crazy*. His most famous concert piece is *Rhapsody in Blue* for piano and jazz orchestra, and he also wrote the opera *Porgy and Bess*.

Gesualdo, Carlo (*c*.1560–1613) An Italian composer and lutenist who was also Prince of Venosa. He wrote outstanding madrigals and motets which were far in advance of their time. He gained a certain notoriety for ordering the murder of his wife and her lover. STRAVINSKY was just one 20th-cent. composer who was captivated by his compositions.

'Ghost' Trio *see* Geistertrio.

Gibbons, Orlando (1583–1625) An important English

111

composer and organist who wrote motets, madrigals and stately anthems (for example, *This is the Record of John*). His son, Christopher, was also an organist and composer of note.

Gibbs, Cecil Armstrong (1889–1960) An English composer who is best known for his songs. He also composed an opera as well as a choral symphony, *Odysseus*.

giga (It.) *see* gigue.

gigue (Fr.) A lively dance or jig.

Gilbert, William Schwenk (1836– 1911) A British writer whose successful collaboration, as librettist, with the composer Arthur SULLIVAN produced a string of highly successful and ever-popular comic operas.

Gillespie, 'Dizzy' (1917–) An American jazz trumpeter and band leader, with a distinctive trumpet, the bell of which stuck out at an angle. He was a virtuoso performer of BEBOP. He earned his nickname 'Dizzy' because his playing reached such virtuoso heights.

Ginastera, Alberto (1916–) An Argentinian composer whose earlier works had a traditional and nationalistic flavour. In later works he has explored modern techniques and styles. He is particularly well known for his operas, *Don Rodrigo*, *Bomarzo* and *Beatrix Cenci*, but he has also written ballets, concertos and several pieces for voice and orchestra.

giocoso (It.) 'Merry'.

gioioso (It.) 'Joyful'.

Giordano, Umberto (1867–1948) An Italian composer of operas, for example, *Mala vita*, *Andrea Chénier* and *Fedora*.

Girl of the Golden West, The (*La Fanciulla del West*) An opera by PUCCINI to a libretto by G. Civinini and C. Zangarini. Set in the Wild West, the story tells of Minnie, the owner of a bar, who falls in love with Dick Johnson, a bandit.

giusto (It.) 'Exact', as in *tempo giusto*, which can mean either 'strict time' or 'appropriate speed'.

Glass, Philip (1937–) An American composer, a pupil of Nadia BOULANGER and Ravi SHANKAR, whose work shows the influence of oriental music and SERIALISM. His music tends to use minimal themes, repeated over and over again, but the overall effect is often richly textured, with great poise. His work includes pieces for voice and a broad variety of instruments, as well as the opera *Einstein on the Beach*.

glass harmonica At its simplest, a set of goblets which are played by rubbing a moistened finger around the rims. This idea was taken further by the scientist and statesman Benjamin Franklin (1706–90), who invented a glass harmonica in which a gradated series of glass bowls is fixed to a rotating spindle and played with the fingers. Both BEETHOVEN and MOZART wrote music for the instrument, which produces a high-pitched humming sound.

Glazunov, Alexander Konstantinovich (1865–1936) A Russian composer who was a pupil of RIMSKY-KORSAKOV. His first symphony, written when he was 17, was hailed as a masterpiece but he never entirely fulfilled his promise. In all, he wrote 8 symphonies and 7 quartets, and his other works include the ballet *Raymonda*.

glee A simple, unaccompanied composition for male voices in several sections.

Glière, Reinhold Moritzovich (1875–1956) A Russian composer of Belgian descent. His most important works include the opera *Shah Senem* and the ballet *Red Poppy*.

Glinka, Mikhail Ivanovich (1804–57) A Russian composer, influenced by folk–music. His best known works are his operas *A Life for the Tsar (Ivan Sussanin)* and *Russlan and Ludmilla*. He composed numerous other works including orchestral pieces and chamber music.

glissando (It.) 'Sliding'; a rapid sliding movement up or down a scale.

Glockenspiel (Ger.) Literally, 'a play of bells', an instrument, produced in a variety of sizes, comprising steel bars of different lengths which are arranged like a keyboard; each bar sounds a different note. Played with hammers, it produces sounds that have a bell-like quality. It is used in orchestras and military bands (in which it is held vertically).

Gloria (Lat.) The first word of *Gloria in excelsis Deo* (Glory to God in the highest), the hymn used in both Roman Catholic Masses and in Anglican services. Many composers have set the gloria to music. It is also the first word of the doxology *Gloria Patri* (Glory be to the Father), which is sung after a psalm.

Gluck, Christoph Willibald (von) (1714–87) A German composer who, after studying and working in Prague, Rome, London and Paris, eventually settled in Vienna. He is best known for his operas, especially

Orfeo ed Euridice, which revolutionized the Italian style of opera by simplifying it and relating the music to the drama. In all, he wrote some 100 operas (many are now lost) and he had a profound influence on the works of MOZART and BEETHOVEN. In addition to his massive output of operas, he also wrote ballets and assorted pieces of miscellaneous music.

Glyndebourne A small, but prestigious, opera house established by John Christie (1882–1962) on his estate near Lewes, in the heart of the English countryside. An annual opera festival has been held there since 1934.

Gobbi, Tito (1915–84) An Italian baritone who was one of the greatest singing actors of the 20th century. He had a reputation as a professional that was second to none and he was particularly impressive in PUCCINI's *Tosca* and VERDI's *Falstaff*.

God Save the Queen/King The British national anthem and possibly one of the best known tunes in the world. However, the authorship of both the tune and the words remains obscure.

Gondoliers, The An operetta by SULLIVAN with a libretto by GILBERT. The tale concerns the Duke of Plaza Toro and two gondoliers who find themselves jointly reigning as kings. It was first performed at the Savoy Theatre, London, in 1889.

gong A percussion instrument that originated in the Far East. Gongs are made in many sizes and shapes, but an orchestral gong consists of nothing more that a large sheet of metal with a pronounced rim. Sound is produced by striking it with a hammer.

Goodman, Benny (1909–86) An American jazz clarinetist who formed the original SWING band in 1934. Although jazz was his first love, he was also a notable classical player and gave virtuoso performances of MOZART concertos. Pieces by BARTOK and COPLAND were commissioned by him.

Goossens, Eugene (1893–1962) An English conductor and composer who worked all over the world, championing the cause of modern music. His works include the operas *Judith* and *Don Juan de Mañara*, as well as two symphonies and various pieces of incidental and chamber music. His brother, Léon, and father, also Eugene, were influential musicians.

gospel song A type of popular religious song originated by Black American slaves who sang hymns to pulsating blues rhythms. Such songs, which are still sung fervently today in religious services, were one of the originating forces of jazz.

Götterdämmerung *see* Ring des Nibelungen, Der.

Gottschalk, Louis Moreau (1829–69) An American composer and pianist who earned fame as a virtuoso performer whilst travelling the globe. He also composed memorable pieces such as *The Aeolian Harp* and *The Dying poet* for piano.

Gould Glenn (1932–82) A Canadian pianist with an international reputation and very broad repertoire, noted in particular for his interpretation on the piano of works by BACH.

Gould, Morton (1913–) An American composer, conductor and pianist, who is known for having composed a concerto for tap dancer and orchestra. He also wrote three symphonies, a ballet (*Fall River Legend*) and several musicals.

Gounod, Charles François (1818–93) A French composer whose original ambition was to become a priest. He lived in England for a period and is best known for his opera *Faust*, although he wrote many other pieces, including cantatas, oratorios and symphonies.

G.P. An abbreviation of GENERALPAUSE.

grace note An ornamental, extra note, usually written in small type, used to embellish a melody.

Gradus ad Parnassum (Steps to Parnassus) **1** A work on counterpoint by FUX. **2** A collection of piano studies by CLEMENTI.

Grainger, Percy Aldridge (originally George Percy) (1882–1961) An Australian-born composer and pianist who settled in the USA in 1914. He was influenced by GRIEG into collecting folk songs and is best known for composing the songs *Country Gardens* and *Handel in the Strand*.

Granados, Enrique (1867–1916) A Spanish composer, pianist and conductor. Much of his work, which includes 7 operas and 2 symphonic poems, has a distinctly Spanish flavour.

grandioso (It.) 'In an imposing manner'.

grand opera A term originally used to distinguish serious opera, sung throughout, from opera that contained some spoken dialogue. The term is now also used to describe a lavish production.

grand orchestre (Fr.) A full orchestra.

grand orgue (Fr.) A great organ (as opposed to a swell organ etc.) *See* organ.

Grappelli, Stephane (1908–) A French jazz violinist, a member of the quintet the Hot Club de France (1934–9), noted for his highly individual, sliding style.

Graun, Karl Heinrich (1704–59) A German composer and singer. He wrote some 30 operas (for example, *Montezuma*) as well as cantatas, church music and piano concertos. His brother, Johann Gottlieb, was also a noted composer and violinist.

grave (It.) 'Slow' or 'solemn'.

grazia (It.) 'Grace'.

grazioso (It.) 'Gracefully'.

Great C Major Symphony The name given to SCHUBERT's symphony no. 9; so called to distinguish it from his shorter 6th symphony, also in C major.

great stave A stave created by pushing the stave with the treble clef and the stave with the bass clef closer together so that both clefs can be located on one exaggerated stave.

Gregorian chant A term that refers to the large collection of ancient solo and chorus PLAINSONG melodies preserved by the Roman Catholic Church. They are named after Pope Gregory I (*c*.540–604) but date from about 800. Until recently they were sung at specific ceremonies, such as baptism, Mass etc.

Grieg, Edvard Hagerup (1843–1907) A Norwegian composer who started writing music at the age of nine. He travelled all over Europe, visiting England and Italy, where he met LISZT. Grieg remains perennially popular with 20th-cent. audiences for his lyricism and atmospheric writing and his PEER GYNT (for orchestra) has frustrated cognoscenti, who have peristently panned it, by being a regular favourite. Much of Grieg's music gains its strength from its use of national idiom and, without doubt, he remains the most prominent of all Norwegian composers. His works include violin sonatas, piano pieces, choral works, compositions for orchestra (including the *Holberg Suite*) and many songs.

Griffes, Charles Tomlinson (1884–1920) An American composer who was influenced by the Impressionist movement. His works include the symphonic poem *The Pleasure Dome of Kubla Khan* and the dance drama *The Kairn of Koridwen*.

Grosse Fuge A fugue in B flat major for string quartet by BEETHOVEN. It was published as a separate work (Op. 133).

ground bass A bass line that is constantly repeated throughout a composition, as a foundation for variation in the upper parts.

Grove, George (1820–1900) An English scholar, editor and writer on music. He edited *The Dictionary of Music and Musicians*, the authorative music dictionary which, many editions later, still bears his name. He was also the first director of the Royal College of Music. He was knighted for his achievements in 1883.

Groves, Charles (1915–) An English conductor of outstanding merit, and a noted champion of British music. He has conducted many of the world's leading orchestras and was knighted in 1973.

Grumiaux, Arthur (1921–86) A Belgian violinist of

international repute whose playing was especially admired by fellow violinists for its classical purity.

grupetto (It.) Literally, a 'little group'; a general term used to describe various ORNAMENTS of one or more decorative notes.

Guarneri A famous family of violin-makers who were based in Cremona. The first member was Andrea who was a pupil of AMATI (with STRADIVARI). The greatest was Giuseppe (1687–1744).

guitar A plucked string instrument which may have been introduced to Spain from North Africa. Unlike the lute, it has a flat back and usually carries 6 strings suspended over a fretted finger-board (12-string guitars were favoured by certain BLUES musicians, such as LEDBETTER). The acoustic ('soundbox') guitar has been played by classical, flamenco and folk musicians for generations, but the electric guitar is a comparatively new development. The body may be hollow (or 'semi-acoustic') or solid, with 'pick-ups' (electrically motivated resonators that respond to the vibration of the strings) mounted under the BRIDGE. The vibrations received by the pick-ups have to be electrically amplified or else they are virtually featureless. Electric guitars have a huge COMPASS which has been exploited by jazz, pop and rock musicians.

Gurney, Ivor Bertie (1890–1937) An English composer and poet who suffered terribly during World War I. He was eventually confined to a mental hospital but he composed some memorable works, including the song-cycle *Ludlow and Teme*.

gusto (It.) 'Taste', so *con gusto* means 'with taste'.

H

H (Ger.) B natural.

habanera (Sp.) A dance of Cuban origin with a powerful, syncopated rhythm; it is, however, most usually associated with Spain.

'Haffner' Symphony The symphony in D by MOZART, so called because it was written for the Haffner family.

Haitink, Bernard (1929–) A Dutch conductor with an international reputation and formidable repertoire, including in particular MAHLER.

Halévy, Jacques François (1799–1862) A French composer of operas and ballets, the most notable being *La Juive* (opera). He was also a teacher and instructed both GOUNOD and BIZET.

half note (US) A MINIM.

half step (US) A SEMITONE.

Hallé, Charles (1819–95) A German-born conductor and pianist who settled in Manchester in 1848 and founded the internationally famous Hallé Orchestra in 1857. He was knighted in 1888.

Hallelujah Chorus The name of several pieces of music, the most famous being that written by HANDEL which brings Part II of the MESSIAH to a close.

halling A lively Norwegian dance, in 2/4 time, during which men leap high into the air.

Hammerstein, Oscar (II) (1895–1960) An American lyricist, responsible for numerous highly successful Broadway musicals, written in collaboration first with Jerome KERN, then with Richards RODGERS.

121

Hammond organ The brand name of an electric organ first produced by the Hammond Organ Company, Chicago, in 1935. The sound it produces is electronically manufactured and attempts to reproduce the sound of the pipe organ. It cannot be said to succeed in this, but its unique temperament has been exploited by jazz, pop and music-hall musicians the world over.

handbells Bells, of various pitch, that are held in the hands of a group of performers and rung in sequence to create a tune.

Handel, George Frideric (originally Georg Friederich Händel) (1685–1759) A German-born composer who settled in England and took English nationality. His father was a barber-surgeon who sent his son to study law at Halle University, but the young Handel rebelled and became a violinist at the Hamburg Opera House, where his first operas, *Almira* and *Nero*, were produced. He lived in Italy for three years but settled in London in 1712. He readily found favour with the English court of Queen Anne and, subsequently, George I. His talent was allowed to flourish in England and he wrote some 20 operas. However, he eventually abandoned the writing of 'Italian' operas for commercial reasons, and instead composed oratorios. This process led to MESSIAH, possibly his greatest, and certainly his most well known, piece of music. During the last years of his life he was troubled with blindness.

Handel succeeded is amalgamating Italian and German styles and traditions with his own notable originality. In his oratorios, in particular, he has given the world some of the most stupendous and magnificent music ever written. His principal works include: the operas *Almira*, *Rodrigo*, *Agrippa*, *Rinaldo*, *Allessandro*, *Orlando*, *Arianna*, *Atlanta*, *Imeneo*; the passion *St John Passion*; the oratorios *Esther*, *Israel in Egypt*, MESSIAH, *Samson*, *Hercules*, *The Triumph of Time and Truth*; the secular choral works ACIS AND GALATEA, *Ode for St Cecilia's Day*; the orchestral pieces WATER MUSIC, FIREWORKS MUSIC; and many other pieces for harpsichord and chamber orchestras, in addition to songs and cantatas.

Hansel and Gretel An opera by HUMPERDINCK to a libretto by the composer's sister, Adelheid Wette. The story is taken from the tale by the Brothers Grimm. It was first performed in 1893.

hardanger fiddle A Norwegian violin used in folk music. It is somewhat smaller than an ordinary violin, and has four SYMPATHETIC STRINGS.

harmonica A small, FREE-REED instrument commonly called the 'mouth organ'. Although it is a small and apparently inconsequential instrument (often considered a toy),many BLUES and folk musicians have illustrated its potential by exploiting its emotive power.

harmonics The sounds that can be produced on stringed instruments by lightly touching a string at one of its harmonic nodes, i.e. at a half-length of a string, quarter-length and so on.

harmonium A small, portable REED-ORGAN which developed in the 19th cent. Air is pumped to the reeds (which are controlled by stops and keys) by pedals worked continuously by the feet.

harmony 1 The simultaneous sounding of two or more notes, i.e chords. A harmonious sound is an agreeable or pleasant sound (CONCORD); but harmonization may also produce sounds, which to some ears at least, are unpleasant (DISCORD). **2** The structure and relationship of chords.

harp An instrument, of ancient origin, consisting of strings stretched across an open frame. It is played by plucking the strings, each of which is tuned to a separate note.

harpsichord A keyboard instrument, developed in the 14th and 15th cents., in which the strings are plucked (not struck) by quills or tongues (plectra). The tongues are connected to the keys by a simple lever mechanism. The harpsichord went out of favour during the late 18th cent. due to the introduction of the piano. However, the instrument has seen a revival in the 20th cent., and new compositions exploiting its 'twangy' sound have been written for it.

Harris, Roy (1898–1979) A prolific American composer who succeeded in amalgamating some of the qualities of American folk songs with modern composition methods. His works include 16 symphonies and works for chorus and orchestra.

Hauptwerk (Ger.) A great organ, as distinct from a swell organ etc. *See* organ.

hautbois (Fr.) Literally, 'high' or 'loud wood'. *See* oboe. From the Elizabethan period to the 18th cent., the English equivalent was 'hautboy'.

Hawaiian guitar A style of guitar playing in which a steel bar is moved up and down the strings (as opposed to the more usual stopping of strings with the fingers) to produce a distinctive slurred sound. The guitar is usually played horizontally. Electrically amplified instruments are now frequently used.

Haydn, Franz Joseph (1732–1809) An Austrian composer who, like many great musicians, started his career as a choirboy in Vienna. In 1761 he was employed by the aristocratic Esterházy family as an assistant KAPEELLMEISTER, and then Kapellmeister from 1766. He stayed with the Esterházys for 30 years and, although he was committed to carrying out certain administrative duties, he was allowed time to compose. He gradually earned a reputation as an outstanding and original composer and he received many commissions including one from the Concert de la Loge Olympique in Paris for six symphonies. By this time he was friendly with MOZART and the two composers had the highest regard for each other. When Prince Nikolaus Esterházy died in 1790, Haydn was no longer required to live at Esterháza (although his salary was maintained) and he took the opportunity to visit England where he received more commissions, most notably from the impresario J.P. Salomon for an opera, six symphonies and assorted other pieces of music. After a year, he returned to Vienna and bought a house (where he taught BEETHOVEN). He returned to London again in 1794 where he was fêted, and he wrote a further six symphonies for Salomon. In 1795 he rejoined the Esterházy household but his official duties were light and he concentrated on composing. Over the next six years, he completed six magnificent Masses and the great choral works *The* CREATION and *The Seasons*. The last years of his life were uneventful and he wrote little, preferring to live quietly in Vienna.

Haydn is often called the father of the SYMPHONY because, although he did not invent it, he extended its range and expressive power, and each of his 104 symphonies is startlingly original. Later, his music was overshadowed by the works of Beethoven and Mozart and it was the mid-20th cent. before it was generally recognized how innovative and influential his compositions were. He produced a colossal amount of work and was never afraid to experiment with new ideas and techniques.

Haydn's principal works include: 18 operas (for example *Il Mondo della Luna*, ARMIDA); 104 symphonies; 8 oratorios and cantatas; 84 string quartets; 52 piano sonatas; 12 Masses; and 47 songs.

Haydn, Johann Michael (1737–1806) An Austrian composer and the brother of Franz Joseph HAYDN. His works include 24 Masses, 2 Requiem Masses and many miscellaneous compositions for orchestra.

head voice The upper register of a voice, so called because the sound seems to vibrate in the head of the singer. *Compare* chest voice.

Hebrides Overture, The *see* Fingal's Cave.

Heckelphone A double-reed instrument which is effectively a baritone OBOE. It was used by Richard STRAUSS in his opera *Salome*.

Heifetz, Jascha (1901–87) A Russian-born violinist who became an American citizen in 1925. Noted for his technical mastery, he had several works composed for him, e.g. by WALTON.

Heldentenor (Ger.) Literally, a 'heroic tenor', i.e. a tenor with a strong voice suitable for Wagnerian heroıs roles.

Heller, Stephen (1813–88) A Hungarian virtuoso pianist and composer who travelled Europe giving recitals. He composed some 150 pieces for the piano, mainly using innovatory techniques.

Helmholtz, Hermann Ludwig Ferdinand von (1821–94) A German physiologist and physicist who published highly important and influential books on sound theory. His work *On the Sensations of Tone*, which was first published in 1862, is the foundation of the modern theory of acoustics.

hemisemidemiquaver The 64th note, i.e. a note with a value of a quarter of a semiquaver or a 1/64th of a semibreve.

hemiola A rhythm in which two bars in triple time are played as though they were three bars in duple time.

Hen, The The nickname given to HAYDN's symphony no. 83 in G minor. It is so called because in the first movement the oboes make a clucking sound.

Henry VIII (1491–1547) The king of England from 1509–47. He is said to have been an accomplished musician and he wrote a number of compositions, including songs and instrumental pieces.

Henze, Hans Werner (1926–) A German composer

127

who has never been tied down to a particular style and his compositions are extraordinarily diverse. He was at first influenced by STRAVINSKY and SCHOENBERG and he made a name for himself with the opera *Boulevard Solitude* in 1952. His political thinking moved dramatically to the far Left in the 1960s and his music drama *The Raft of The Medusa* is dedicated to the revolutionary, Che Guevara. His works include operas, ballets, symphonies, concertos and choral pieces such as *Voices*, which has a text partly written by Ho Chi Minh.

Herbert, Victor (1859–1924) An Irish-born composer, conductor and cellist who settled in the USA. He is best known for his operettas (for example *Babes in Toyland*) but he also wrote a cello concerto, a symphonic poem and various pieces of orchestral music.

Here Comes the Bride *see* Lohengrin.

Hérold, Louis Joseph Ferdinand (1791–1833) A French composer of ballets and operas, e.g. *Zampa* and *Le Pré aux clercs*.

Heseltine, Philip *see* Warlock, Robert.

heterophony (Gr.) Literally, 'difference of sounds', i.e. two or more performers playing different versions of the same melody simultaneously.

hexachord A scale of six notes which was used in medieval times.

Hindemith, Paul (1895–1963) A German composer, teacher, conductor and virtuoso viola player. He was considered degenerate by the Nazis and stayed in the USA for the duration of the Second World War. He was ultimately revered as one of the most important and versatile musicians of his era. He was a great believer in making music that could be readily understood and he composed pieces for children and amateurs, as well as sophisticated concertos and operas. His principal works include: operas (for example, *Cardillac*, *News of the Day*); orchestral pieces (for example, *Symphonic Metamorphoses*); and many pieces for chamber orchestra. He also wrote several influential books on musical theory, such as *The Craft of Musical Composition*.

H.M.S. Pinafore An operetta by GILBERT and SULLIVAN. The story, set on board a British warship, tells of the romance between Sir Joseph Porter, First Lord of the Admiralty, and Josephine, the Captain's daughter. It was first performed in 1878.

hocket (Fr.) The breaking up a melody very short phrases or single notes with rests in between them.

Hoddinott, Alun (1929–) A Welsh composer and teacher who is best known for his romantic, yet serious, operas (for example, *The Magician*, *The Beach of Falesá*), symphonies, and the oratorio *Job*.

Holbrooke, Joseph (1878–1958) An English composer, pianist and conductor. His works include the trilogy of Celtic operas *The Cauldron of Annwen,* and the symphonic poem *The Raven*. He was also a controversial writer on music.

Holiday, Billie (1915–59) An American jazz singer who had a remarkably sensuous and evocative voice. Drug addiction brought her life to a tragic end.

Holst, Gustav Theodore (1874–1934) An English composer and teacher of Swedish descent. He had a range of diverse interests, from English folk music to Sanskrit literature, which at various times influenced his compositions. His most famous orchestral piece is *The* PLANETS, but he also wrote operas (for example, *Avitri*, *At The Boar's Head*), choral pieces (for example, *Hymns from the Rig-Veda*, *The Hymn of Jesus*) and many songs.

homophony A term applied to music in which the parts move 'in step' and do not have independent rhythms. *Compare* polyphony.

Honegger, Arthur (1892–1955) A Swiss composer who spent most of his life in France. He was a member of the group of composers called *Les* SIX and achieved fame with his orchestral piece *Pacific 231*, which is a representation of a locomotive engine. His other works include the oratorio *Le Roi David*, the operas *Antigone* and *The Eaglet*, and 5 symphonies.

hook The black line attached to the stem of all notes of less value than a crotchet.

hootenanny An American term for a small festival of folk music.

horn A BRASS INSTRUMENT consisting of a conical tube coiled into a spiral and ending in a bell. The lips are pushed into a funnel-shaped mouthpiece. The modern orchestral horn is called the French horn (because that is where it was developed) and is fitted with three (sometimes four, sometimes seven) valves which open and close various lengths of tubing so that the pitch of the notes can be changed. There are two common 'horns', which are in fact woodwind instruments, the BASSET HORN (alto clarinet) and the English horn or COR ANGLAIS (alto oboe).

hornpipe 1 A single-reed wind instrument played in Celtic countries. **2** A 16th-cent. dance in triple time, originally accompanied by the hornpipe and later erroneously associated with sailors.

Horowitz, Vladimir (1904–87) A Russian-born pianist who settled in the USA in 1928. He achieved virtuoso status and was especially noted for his interpretation of music by CHOPIN and SCARLATTI.

Hovhaness, Alan (1911–) An American composer who has often relied upon oriental subjects and instruments for inspiration. His most famous piece *And God Created Whales* is for a taped whale solo and orchestra, but he has also written some 20 symphonies and several operas.

Howells, Herbert (1892–1983) An English composer who was much influenced by ELGAR and VAUGHAN WILLIAMS. His works include choral pieces (for example *Hymnus Paradisi*), organ and piano compositions, and chamber music.

Hummel, Johann Nepomuk (1778–1837) An Austrian composer and pianist who studied under MOZART. He wrote 9 operas and 7 piano concertos in addition to choral pieces.

humoresque (Fr.), **Humoreske** (Ger.) A word used by, for example, SCHUMANN as the title for a short, lively piece of music.

Humperdinck, Engelbert (1854–1921) A German composer of operas, incidental music and songs who was for a time an assistant to WAGNER. His best known opera is HANSEL AND GRETEL.

Hunter, Rita (1933–) An English soprano with an international reputation. Her best known role is that of Brünhilde in WAGNER's RING cycle.

hurdy-gurdy A medieval stringed instrument, shaped like a viol. A wooden wheel, coated in resin, is cranked at one end to make all the strings resonate. The strings are stopped by rods operated by keys. The hurdy-gurdy was often used to provide dance music.

hymn In the Christian Church, a poem sung to music in praise of God.

Hypoaeolian, Hypodorian *see* mode.

I

Ibert, Jacques François Antoine (1890–1962) A French composer who was famed for his light and witty music. His best known compositions include the symphonic poem *The Ballad of Reading Jail* (after Wilde), his opera *Le Roi d'Yvetot*, and his orchestral piece *Escales*.

idée fixe (Fr.) 'Fixed idea', i.e. a recurring theme.

idiophone Any instrument in which sound is produced by the vibration of the instrument itself, for example, cymbals, bells, castanets etc.

Idomeneo, Rè di Creta (Idomeneo, King of Crete) An opera by MOZART to a libretto by G.B. Veresco, in which Idomeneo promises Neptune that if he is saved from a storm, he will sacrifice the first person he sees on returning home. The victim turns out to be his son. Neptune, however, is appeased and Idomeneo's son takes over the throne. It was first performed in 1781.

imitation A device in COUNTERPOINT whereby a phrase is sung successively by different voices.

'Imperial' Symphony The nickname for HAYDN's symphony no. 53 in D. It is so called because of the grand introduction to the first movement.

impetuoso (It.) 'Impetuously'.

impressionism A style of painting of the late 19th cent. in which forms were conveyed by dappled effects rather than by rigid outlines. By analogy, the word is also used to identify certain types of atmospheric music, such as the music of DEBUSSY and RAVEL.

impromptu A type of piano music that sounds as if it has been improvised, i.e. written in a free and easy style.

improvisation The art of playing or 'inventing' music that has not already been composed, i.e. spontaneous composition. Some forms of music (especially JAZZ) often rely heavily on the ability of performers to improvise certain sections. It has the same meaning as extemporization.

in alt *see* alt.

incalzando (It.) 'Pressing forward', i.e. working up speed and force.

incidental music Music written to accompany the action in a play, but the term is also commonly applied to overtures and interludes.

inciso (It.) 'Incisive', hence an instruction that a strong rhythm is required.

Incoronazione di Poppaea, L' (The Coronation of Poppaea) An opera by MONTEVERDI to a libretto by G.F. Busenello. Set in ancient Rome, it tells of the ambitions of Poppaea to become empress. It was first performed in 1642.

indeciso (It.) 'Undecided', i.e. the pace of a piece of music can be varied according to the performer's feelings.

indeterminacy A term used by John CAGE to describe music that does not follow a rigid notation but leaves certain events to chance or allows performers to make their own decisions when performing it.

Indy, Paul Marie Theodore Vincent d' (1851–1931) A French composer who also wrote music text books and important biographies of BEETHOVEN and FRANCK. His compositions include the operas *Fervaal*, *L' Etranger* and *La Légende de St Christophe*, symphonies, and pieces of chamber music.

inflected note A note with an ACCIDENTAL placed before it, i.e. it is sharpened or flattened.

In nomine (Lat.) (In the name [of the Lord]) A type of CANTUS FIRMUS used by English composers of the 16th cent. It was first used by TAVERNER in his setting of *In nomine Domini* for one of his Masses.

inner parts The parts of a piece of music excluding the highest and lowest; for example, in a work for soprano, alto, tenor and bass, the alto and tenor roles are inner parts.

instrumentation *see* orchestration.

instrument In music, a device on which or with which music can be played. There are five traditional categories of instrument: WOODWIND, BRASS, PERCUSSION, KEYBOARD and STRING. However, ELECTRONIC and MECHANICAL INSTRUMENTS also exist.

interlude A title sometimes used for a short part of a complete composition; for example, a piece of music performed between the acts of an opera.

intermezzo (It.) **1** A short piece of piano music. **2** A short comic opera performed between the acts of a serious opera, especially in the 16th and 17th cents.

Internationale The international Communist anthem. The words are by E. Pottier and the music is by P. Degeyter.

interpretation The way in which a performer plays a piece of composed music. No composer can possibly indicate exactly how a piece should be played and, to some degree, it is up to the performer to play it as he or she thinks fit.

interval The gap or 'sound distance', expressed numerically, between any two notes, i.e. the difference in PITCH between two notes. For example, the interval between C and G is called a FIFTH because G is the fifth note from C. *Perfect intervals* are intervals that remain the same in major and minor keys (i.e. fourths, fifths, octaves.)

intonation A term used to describe the judgement of pitch by a performer.

intone To sing on one note. A priest may intone during a Roman Catholic or Anglican service.

introduction A section, often slow, found at the start of certain pieces of music, notably symphonies and suites.

Introit An ANTIPHON, usually sung in conjunction with a psalm verse, in the Roman Catholic and Anglican liturgies.

invention A title used by BACH for his two-part keyboard pieces in contrapuntal form.

inversion A term which literally means turning upside down. It can refer to a chord, interval, theme, melody or counterpoint. For example, an inverted INTERVAL is an interval in which one note changes by an octave to the other side, as it were, of the other note.

Iolanthe (subtitled, The Peer and the Peri) A comic opera by GILBERT and SULLIVAN. The story concerns the love of Strephon, the son of the fairy Iolanthe and the Lord Chancellor, for a maiden named Phyllis. It was first performed in 1882.

Ionian mode A MODE which, on the piano, uses the white notes from C to C.

Iphigénie en Aulide (Iphigenia in Aulis) An opera by GLUCK to a libretto by F.L.L. du Roullet based on Racine and Euripides. It relates the story of the sacrifice of Iphigenia, the daughter of Agamemnon and Clytemnestra. It was first performed in 1774.

Iphigénie en Tauride (Iphigenia in Tauris) An opera by GLUCK to a libretto by N.F. Guillard based on Euripides. It is the sequel to IPHIGENIE EN AULIDE and tells of how Iphigenia is rescued by her brother, Orestes. It was first performed in 1779.

Ireland, John (1897–1962) An English composer who was greatly influenced by French music and is best known for his orchestral works, e.g. *The Forgotten Rite*, *Mai-Dun* and *Satyricon*.

isorhythm A term used to describe a short, rhythm pattern that is repeatedly applied to an existing melody which already has an distinct rhythm.

Italian sixth *see* augmented sixth.

Ivan the Terrible 1 An opera by BIZET to a libretto by Leroy and Trianon, composed in 1865. **2** The name given by Diaghilev to RIMSKY-KORSAKOV's opera *The Maid of Pskov*.

Ives, Charles Edward (1874–1954) An American composer who is regarded as a pioneer of 20th-cent. music although his works were largely ignored during his lifetime. He explored the possibilities of mixing apparently discordant sounds to create a satisfactory result; he wanted everyday sounds (such as radio transmissions) to be incorporated into compositions to make the music more readily understood. He is best known for his orchestral pieces, for example *General Booth enters into Heaven*, *The Unanswered Question* and *Central Park in the Dark*.

J

jam session A 20th-cent. slang expression for an occasion when a group of musicians join forces to improvise music. It is usually only appropriate to jazz, blues and rock music.

Janáček, Leoš (1854–1928) A Czech composer, conductor and organist who was also an influential teacher. He was particularly drawn to the rhythms and constructions of folk songs and is best known for the operas that he wrote in old age, such as *The Excursions of Mr Brouček*, *The Cunning Little Vixen* and *From the House of the Dead*. However, he also wrote numerous other pieces, which include the symphonic poem *Tarus Bulba* and his famous *Sinfonietta*.

Janissary music The music of Turkish military bands which influenced European composers during the 18th cent. It is particularly associated with cymbals, drums and tambourines.

Jaques-Dalcroze, Emile (1865–1950) A Swiss composer and teacher who developed the concept of musical teaching through EURHYTHMICS. He also composed some 5 operas and 2 noted violin concertos.

Järnefelt, Armas (1869–1958) A Finnish composer and conductor who elected to become a Swedish national in 1910. He is best known for his orchestral, choral and piano works, such as *Berceuse*.

jazz A term used to describe a style of music that evolved in the Southern States of the USA at the turn of the century. It owes a great deal to the rhythms and idioms of BLUES and SPIRITUALS, but many of the favoured instruments (e.g. saxophone, trumpet and trombone) were European in origin. Jazz traditionally relies upon a strong rhythm 'section', comprising bass and drums, which provides a springboard for other instruments. Jazz developed from being a form of music played in the back streets of New Orleans to a sophisticated art form performed by small dedicated groups as well as 'big bands' or 'jazz orchestras'.

Self-expression, and therefore improvisation, has always been a crucial aspect of jazz and this has allowed many individuals (such as Louis ARMSTRONG and Benny GOODMAN) to blossom and further its cause. *See also* bebop.

Jerusalem A famous choral song by Sir Hubert PARRY to words by William Blake, composed in 1918.

Jeune France (Young France) The name adopted by a group of French composers, including JOLIVET and MESSIAEN, who identified their common aims in 1936.

Jew's harp A simple instrument consisting of a small, heart-shaped, metal frame to which a thin strip of hardened steel is attached. The open-ended neck of the frame is held against the teeth and the strip is twanged to produce sound, which is modified by using the cavity of the mouth as a soundbox.

jig A generic term for a lively dance.

jingles 1 An instrument consisting of a number of small bells or rattling objects on a strap, which are shaken to produce sound. **2** In the singular, a short, catchy piece of music with equally catchy lyrics, often used to enliven the commentary of radio stations broadcasting popular music.

jingling johnny An instrument, of Turkish origin, comprising a long stick to the head of which was attached a series of small bells, much used in the past in military bands.

Joachim, Joseph (1831–1907) A Hungarian violinist celebrated for his performances of BACH, BEETHOVEN, MENDELSSOHN and, notably, BRAHMS. He was also the composer of several works for violin and orchestra.

John Brown's Body A marching tune that was popular during the American Civil War, probably composed in about 1850. The doggerel words about the abolitionist John Brown were replaced in 1861 by the song 'Mine eyes have seen the glory of the coming of the Lord', which became known as 'The Battle Hymn of the Republic'.

Jolivet, André (1905–74) A French composer and a founder member of the JEUNE FRANCE group. He was influenced by oriental music and he is best known for his opera *Dolores*, oratorio *La Verité*, and ballets.

jongleur A medieval minstrel.

Joplin, Scott (1868–1917) A Black American RAGTIME composer and pianist. Although he wrote two ragtime operas, he is best known for his RAGS, such as *Maple Leaf Rag* and *The Entertainer*.

Joshua An oratorio by HANDEL to a libretto by T. Morell. It was first performed in 1748.

Josquin des Prés (Deprez) (*c*.1440–1521) An innovatory Flemish composer, the most celebrated of his day. He worked in both France and Italy and composed some 30 Masses and 50 motets.

jota A Spanish dance from Aragon in 3/4 time usually accompanied by castanets; the dancers occasionally sing.

juke box An automatic, coin operated, machine that plays records.

Jupiter Symphony The name given to MOZART's symphony no. 41 in C. It is so called because of the stately opening to the first movement.

K

K When followed by a number, a reference to either a catalogue of MOZART's works (compiled by Ludwig von KOCHEL), or a catalogue of SCARLATTI's works (compiled by Ralph Kirkpatrick).

Kabalevsky, Dmitri Borisovich (1904–87) A Russian composer of ballets, symphonies, piano pieces and operas (for example, *Invincible* and *The Sister*).

Kapellmeister (Ger.) Literally, 'master of the chapel', i.e. director of music to a noble court or bishop.

Karajan, Herbert von (1908–1989) An Austrian conductor who worked with most of the world's leading orchestras, and particularly the Berlin Philharmonic Orchestra. He was well known for conducting works by BEETHOVEN, BRAHMS, WAGNER, SCHUMANN and VERDI.

Karelia An overture and orchestral suite by SIBELIUS, composed in 1893 and named after the province of Finland in which he lived.

kazoo A simple instrument consisting of a short tube with a small hole in the side which is covered with a thin membrane. When a player hums down the tube, the membrane makes a buzzing sound. It is usually considered a children's instrument although it is frequently used by folk and jazz musicians.

Kern, Jerome (1885–1945) An American composer of musical comedies. His shows include *Sally*, *Very Good Eddie* and *Show Boat*. Some of his songs (e.g. *Ol' Man River* and *Smoke gets in your Eyes* are considered 'classics'.

kettledrum *see* timpani.

key 1 On a piano, harpsichord, organ etc., one of the finger-operated levers by which the instrument is played. **2** On woodwind instruments, one of the metal, finger-operated levers that opens or closes one or more of the soundholes. **3** A note that is considered to be the most important in a piece of music and to which all the other notes relate. Most pieces of Western music are 'written in a key', i.e. all the chords in the piece are built around a particular note, say F minor. The concept of a key is alien to certain types of music, such as Indian and Chinese.

key note *see* tonic.

key signature The sign (or signs) placed at the beginning of a composition to define its KEY. A key signature indicates all the notes that are to be sharpened or flattened in the piece; should a piece move temporarily into another key, the relevant notes can be identified with ACCIDENTALS.

Khachaturian, Aram Ilich (1903–78) A Russian Armenian composer who was influenced by the folk music of Armenia. He wrote music that was generally acceptable to the Soviet authorities of the time, although his second symphony was not well received. His works include symphonies, piano concertos, pieces for chorus and orchestra, and the ballet *Spartacus*.

Kindertotenlieder (Songs on the death of children) A cycle of five songs for voice and orchestra by MAHLER with words by F. Rückert.

Kirbye, George (*c*.1565–1634) An inventive English composer of motets and madrigals.

kit A miniature violin which was particularly popular with dancing masters of the 17th and 18th cents. who could carry one in the pocket and thereby provide music for lessons.

Klangfarbenmelodie (Ger.) Literally, 'melody of tone colours'. A term used by SCHOENBERG to describe a form of composition in which the pitch does not change; 'colour' is achieved by adding or taking away instruments.

klavier *see* clavier.

Klebe, Giselher (1925–) A German composer who has experimented with various musical forms and who has used electronic instruments. He has written several operas (such as *Die Räuber*) as well as orchestral and chamber music.

Kleine Nachtmusik, Eine (A Little Night Music) A popular serenade by MOZART for a small orchestra or string quartet, composed in 1787.

Klemperer, Otto (1885–1973) A German conductor and composer who was forced to leave Germany during the Second World War, when he went to live in the USA. After the war, he returned to Europe and dedicated himself to conducting. He was especially famous for conducting the works of BRAHMS and BEETHOVEN. His compositions include two symphonies and a Mass.

Köchel, Ludwig Alois Friedrich, Ritter von (1800–77) An Austrian scientist who was a great admirer of MOZART and catalogued the great composer's works, giving each one a 'K[öchel] number'.

Kodály, Zoltán (1882–1967) A Hungarian composer

143

and teacher who was greatly influenced by Hungarian folk songs. He wrote operas (for example, *The Spinning Room*), choral works (for example, *Psalmus Hungaricus*), chamber music, and various pieces for orchestra.

Koechlin, Charles (1867–1950) A prolific French composer, most of whose music is rarely heard today. His works include ballets, chamber music and several symphonic poems which were inspired by Kipling's *Jungle Book*. He was also an author of textbooks and a treatise on DEBUSSY.

Korngold, Eric Wolfgang (1897–1957) A prolific Austrian-born composer who was a child prodigy. He went to live in the USA in 1938 (becoming an American citizen in 1943) and settled in Hollywood where he wrote film music (for example, *The Adventures of Robin Hood*, *The Sea Hawks*). His other works include operas, chamber music and various pieces for orchestra.

koto A Japanese zither which has 13 silk strings stretched over a long box. The strings pass over moveable bridges and are played with plectra worn on the fingers. The instrument is placed on the ground and produces a distinctive, somewhat harsh, sound.

Kreisler, Fritz (1875–1962) A celebrated Austrian violinist, for whom ELGAR wrote his violin concerto. He settled in the USA, and wrote a variety of pieces, including some which he initially attributed to 17th and 18th-cent. composers.

Křenek, Ernst (1900–) An American composer, conductor and pianist of Czech origin. He emigrated to the USA in 1938 and was influenced by jazz before writing TWELVE-NOTE MUSIC. He has experimented with various styles of music and has composed for electronic instruments. His works include operas (for example, *Tarquin*, *Dark Waters*), choral pieces, ballets (for example, *Mammon*, *Eight Column Line*), and compositions for orchestra and piano.

Kreuzer Sonata The nickname given to BEETHOVEN's sonata for violin and piano in A, Op. 47 (1802–3), which he dedicated to the French violinist Rudolphe Kreutzer.

Krumhorn (Krummhorn) (Ger.) (crumhorn) A double-reed instrument, common in the 16th and early 17th cents. The tube was curved at the lower end and the reed was enclosed in a cap into which the player blew. It was made in several sizes: treble, tenor and bass.

Kyrie Eleison (Gk.) 'Lord have Mercy', the formal invocation at the start of the Mass and communion service.

L

la (lah) 1 The note A. **2** In the TONIC SOL-FA, the sixth note (or SUBMEDIANT) of the major scale.

lacrimoso (It.) 'Tearful'.

lai (Fr.) A 13th and 14th-cent. French song usually consisting of 12 irregular stanzas sung to different musical phrases.

Lakmé An opera by DELIBES to a libretto written by

E. Gondinet and P. Gille. The story is set in India where Lakmé, the daughter of a priest, falls in love with a British Army officer. It was first performed in 1883.

Lalo, Victor Antoine Edouard (1823–92) A French composer of Spanish descent who is best known for his *Symphonie espagnole* for violin and orchestra. His other works include operas (for example, *Le Roi d'Ys*), a ballet (*Namouna*), concertos, and songs.

lambeg drum A large, double-headed bass drum from Northern Ireland.

Lambert, Constant (1905–51) An English composer, conductor and critic who was commissioned by Diaghilev to write the music for the ballet *Romeo and Juliet*. His other works include a piano sonata, choral pieces and several songs.

lament A Scottish or Irish folk tune played at a death or some disaster, usually on the bagpipes.

'Lamentation' Symphony The nickname for HAYDN's symphony no. 26 in D minor. It is so called because some themes resemble the PLAINSONG melodies sung in Roman Catholic services during Holy Week.

lamentoso (It.) 'Mournfully'.

Lancers, The A type of QUADRILLE in which 8 or 16 couples take part.

Landini (Landino, Francesco) (*c*.1335–97) An Italian composer, organist and lute player who was blind from childhood. Among the most important musicians of his time, he composed numerous songs.

Ländler A country dance in slow waltz time from Austria and Bavaria.

Land of my Fathers (Hen Wlad fy Nhadau) A song adopted by the Welsh as their 'national' anthem. The words were written by Evan James and the tune by James James in 1860.

langsam (Ger.) 'Slow'.

languido (It.) 'Languidly'.

Lanner, Joseph (1801–43) An Austrian composer and conductor who was a contemporary of Johann STRAUSS 'the Elder', with whom he formed a quintet. He composed some 100 waltzes and many other dances.

l'aprés-midi d'un faune *see* aprés-midi d'un faune, Prélude à l'.

largamente (It.) Literally, 'broadly', meaning slowly and in a dignified manner.

larghetto (It.) 'Slow' or 'broad', but not as slow as LARGO.

largo (It.) Literally, 'broad', meaning slow and in a dignified manner .

'Lark' Quartet The nickname of HAYDN's string quartet Op. 6, No. 5, in D. It is so called because of the high-soaring violin notes at the beginning of the first movement.

Larsson, Lars-Erik (1908–86) A Swedish composer, conductor and critic who was influenced by BERG. His works include 3 symphonies, 3 concert overtures, a saxophone concerto and film music.

Lassus, Roland di (Orlando di Lasso) (1532–94) A Flemish composer who experimented with a wide range of musical forms and was one of the most prolific and versatile composers of his era. His compositions include Masses, motets, madrigals and many other choral pieces.

Last Post, The A bugle call of the British Army to signal the end of the day at 10 p.m. It is also played at military funerals.

Lawes, Henry (1596–1662) An English composer whose works were admired by the aristocracy; he composed the coronation anthem *Zadok the Priest* for Charles II. He wrote the music for Milton's masque *Comus*, and many songs and madrigals.

Lawes, William (1602–45) An English composer and the brother of Henry LAWES. He composed psalms, anthems and songs. He was killed in the Civil War.

lay clerk An adult male member of an Anglican cathedral choir.

leader 1 In Britain, the title of the principal first violin of an orchestra or the first violin of a string quartet or similar ensemble. **2** The leader of a section of an orchestra. **3** In the USA, an alternative term for conductor.

leading motif *see* Leitmotiv.

leading note The seventh note of the scale; it is so called because it 'leads to' the TONIC, a semitone above.

Leclair, Jean-Marie (1697–1764) A French composer and violinist. He wrote the opera *Scylla et Glaucus*, ballets and many pieces for violin. He was murdered outside his home, perhaps by his nephew. His younger brother, who rather confusingly had exactly the same name, was also a composer and violinist.

Ledbetter, Huddy ('Leadbelly') (1885–1949) A Black

American blues singer, composer, 12-string guitarist and piano player. He led a violent life and was imprisoned several times. He reputedly earned his nickname from the number of lead bullets that remained in his body. His most famous songs include *Goodnight Irene* and *Fannin Street*.

ledger lines *see* leger lines.

legato (It.) 'Smooth'.

leger lines, ledger lines Short lines added above or below a STAVE to indicate the pitch of notes that are too high or low to be written on the stave itself.

leggiero (It.) 'Light'.

legno (It.) 'Wood'; *col legno* is a direction to a violinist to turn the bow over and to tap the strings 'with the wood'.

Lehár, Franz (originally Ferencz) A Hungarian-born composer. After conducting military bands for a while, he settled in Vienna where he composed operettas, the most famous being *The* MERRY WIDOW, *The Count of Luxembourg* and *The Land of Smiles*.

Leigh, Walter (1905–42) An English composer who is best known for his operettas, for example, *The Jolly Roger*. He was killed in action during the Second World War.

leise (Ger.) 'Soft' or 'gentle'.

Leitmotiv (Ger.) Literally, a 'leading theme', i.e. a recurring theme of music, commonly used in opera, that is associated with a character or idea, thus enabling the composer to tell a story in terms of music.

'Leningrad' Symphony The subtitle of SHOSTAKOVICH's symphony no. 7, which was composed during the siege of Leningrad during the Second World War.

Lennon, John (1940–80) A British rock musician who was a founder member of the group The Beatles (1961–70). In partnership with Paul McCARTNEY, he was one of the most influential songwriters of the 20th cent., a career that was brought to a tragic close by his murder in New York.

lentamente (It.) 'Slowly'.

lento (It.) 'Slow'.

Leoncavallo, Ruggiero (1858–1919) An Italian composer who started his musical career as a café pianist. He is best known for his opera *I Pagliacci*, although he composed several others. He also wrote a ballet and the symphonic poem *Serafita*.

Leoninus (Léonin) (12th cent.) A French composer and organist of whom little is known. He is thought to have been one of the first musicians to use time-values.

Leonora overtures The title of three overtures written by BEETHOVEN for his opera FIDELIO, in which Leonore is the heroine. A fourth, definitive overture, *Fidelio*, was composed in 1814. Today, the 'Three Leonoras' are invariably played as concert overtures.

L.H. An abbreviation for 'left hand', commonly found in piano music.

Liadov, Anatol Konstantinovich (1855–1914) A Russian composer, teacher and conductor who was a pupil of RIMSKY-KORSAKOV. His most famous works are the symphonic poems *Baba Yaga*, *The Enchanted Lake* and *Kikimora*.

liberamente (It.) 'Freely', i.e. as the performer wishes.

libretto (It.) Literally, 'little book'. It is a term used for the text of an opera or oratorio.

licenza (It.) 'Licence' or 'freedom'; *con alcuna licenza* means 'with some freedom'.

Lied, Lieder (Ger.) 'Song, songs'.

Lied von der Erde, Das *see* Song of the Earth.

ligature 1 A 12th-cent. form of notation for a group of notes. **2** A slur indicating that a group of notes must be sung to one syllable. **3** The tie used to link two notes over a bar line. **4** The metal band used to fix the reed to the mouthpiece of a clarinet etc.

Ligeti, György (1923–) A Hungarian composer who has settled in Austria. He is renowned for composing sophisticated yet easy-to-listen-to pieces such as *Atmospheres* and *Lontano* for orchestra. He has also composed an opera, *Le Grand Macabre*, and pieces for flute and oboe.

Lilburn, Douglas (1915–) New Zealand's most famous composer, who studied in England for a period. He has experimented with electronic instruments but is best known for his more conservative works, which include three symphonies and his *Aotearoa Overture*.

Lilliburlero A 17th-cent. dance tune, of uncertain origin, which made fun of Irish Roman Catholics. It has subsequently been adopted as an Orangemen song with new words ('Protestant Boys').

Linley, Thomas (1733–95) An English composer and teacher who wrote incidental music for plays, including Sheridan's *The Duenna* and *School for Scandal*.

He also wrote madrigals, songs and cantatas. His son, also Thomas, was a violinist and friend of MOZART; and his daughter, Elizabeth Ann, was a noted soprano who married Sheridan.

'Linz' Symphony The nickname of MOZART's symphony no. 36 in C. It is so called because it was first performed in Linz in 1783.

lira da braccio, lira da gamba Italian stringed instruments of the 15th and 16th cents. The *lira da braccio* had seven strings and was played like a violin; the *lira da gamba* was a bass instrument, played between the knees, and had anything up to 16 strings.

lira organizzata A type of HURDY-GURDY that included a miniature organ.

l'istesso tempo (It.) 'The same tempo'.

Liszt, Ferencz (Franz) (1811–86) A Hungarian composer and pianist who was a great showman as well as a formidable musician. He went to Vienna as a child prodigy in 1823 and impressed BEETHOVEN amongst others. He travelled to France and England and his reputation as a virtuoso performer became legendary. In 1835 he eloped to Switzerland with Countess d'Agoult (who adopted the pseudonym of Daniel Stern when she became a novelist) and their daughter, Cosima, who eventually married WAGNER. In 1847 he settled in Germany with his new mistress, Princess Carolyne Sayn-Wittgenstein. During this period his composing flourished and, amongst other works, he wrote his famous *Hungarian Rhapsodies* for piano. He also became deeply religious and lived in Rome for a time where he composed two oratorios.

Liszt was undoubtedly one of the greatest (and most flamboyant) virtuoso pianists of all time. He was also an accomplished composer and he greatly furthered the development of piano music. He also wrote symphonies and symphonic poems (a term which he invented) and several choral works. His principal compositions include: the FAUST and *Dante* symphonies; 12 *Études d'Exécution Transcendante* and 20 *Hungarian Rhapsodies* for piano; several choral pieces; and 12 symphonic poems.

'Little Russian' Symphony The nickname for TCHAIKOVSKY's symphony no. 2 in C minor. It is so called because it uses Ukrainian (Little Russian) folk tunes.

'Little' Symphony The nickname for SCHUBERT's symphony no. 6 in C. It is so called to distinguish it from his Great C Major Symphony.

liturgy A term for any official, and written down, form of religious service.

Locke, Matthew (*c*.1630–77) An English composer who was employed by Charles II. His works include incidental music for Shadwell's *The Tempest*, several anthems and many pieces for the recorder.

loco (It.) Literally, 'place'. It is used in music to indicate that a passage is to be played at normal pitch, after a previous, contrary instruction, i.e. the music reverts to its original 'place' on the stave.

Loeffler, Charles Martin (1861–1935) An Alsatian-born composer and violinist who settled in the USA. He was influenced by DEBUSSY and is best known for the orchestral pieces *La Morte de Tintagiles*, *A Pagan Poem* and *The Canticle of the Sun* (with voice).

Loewe, Frederick (1904–88) An Austrian-born composer who settled in the USA in 1924 and became an American citizen. In collaboration with the lyricist Alan Jay Lerner, he created many famous musicals including *Paint Your Wagon*, *My Fair Lady* (from Shaw's *Pygmalion* and *Camelot*. He also wrote, with Lerner, the songs for the film *Gigi*.

Loewe, Johann Karl Gottfried (1796–1869) A German composer, conductor, pianist and singer who was the son of a noted musician of the same name. He wrote some 500 songs, 5 operas, 18 oratorios and many other pieces.

Lohengrin An opera by WAGNER, who also wrote the libretto. It relates how the knight Lohengrin, the son of Parsifal, tries to protect Elsa against the warlord, Friedrich. It contains the famous 'Here Comes the Bride' wedding march and was first performed in 1850.

London Symphony 1 The nickname given to HAYDN's last symphony, no. 104 in D, which was first performed in London in 1795. **2** VAUGHAN WILLIAMS's second symphony (1914), which includes sounds associated with London, such as street cries and the chimes of Big Ben.

lontano (It.) 'Distant'.

Lortzing, Albert (1801–51) A German composer, singer and conductor who is best known for his comic operas which he wrote to his own libretti, e.g. *Zar und Zimmermann*.

loure A type of bagpipe played in northern France, especially Normandy.

Love of Three Oranges, The An opera by PROKOFIEV, who also wrote the libretto. It is a play within a play and concerns a prince who loves three oranges and finds his desired princess in the third. It was first performed in 1921.

Love, the Magician *see* Amor Brujo, El.

Lucia di Lammermoor A tragic opera by DONIZETTI to a libretto by S. Cammarano (based on Walter Scott's *The Bride of Lammermoor*). It relates the story of Lucia, who falls in love with Edgar with disastrous consequences. It was first performed in 1835.

Lucio Silla An opera by MOZART to a libretto by G. de Gamera. It was first performed in 1835. Other operas of the same name were composed by Anfossi and J.C. BACH.

Lucrezia Borgia An opera by DONIZETTI to a libretto by F. Romani. It tells of how Lucrezia causes the death of her own son and ultimately commits suicide.

Lully, Jean-Baptiste (originally Giambattista Lulli) A French composer of Italian origin who worked in the court of Louis XIV. He composed many comedy-ballets (for example, *Le marriage forcé*, *Le Sicilien*), in which he acted and danced himself. He became immensely rich as a favourite of the king, but worked tirelessly at writing operas (some 20 in all) and helped to establish a distinctive French opera style. He died from an abscess after striking his foot with his conductor's baton. In addition to operas, his principal compositions include church music and two orchestral suites.

Lulu An unfinished opera by BERG, who also wrote the

libretto (after plays by Wederkind). The story concerns Lulu, a *femme fatale*, who causes the death of her lovers, but is ultimately killed by Jack the Ripper.

lunga pausa (It.) A 'long pause'.

Lupu, Radu (1945–) A Romanian pianist, currently living in Britain, who has worldwide reputation as a virtuoso performer.

lur A primitive Scandinavian bronze instrument, similar to a bugle. Lurs came in pairs and resembled the horns of a ram.

lusingando (It.) Literally, 'flattering', i.e. in a cajoling manner.

lute A plucked stringed instrument with a body resembling that of a half-pear. It is thought to have a history dating back some 3,000 years and was particularly popular during the 16th and 17th cents.; it has since been revived by 20th-cent. instrument makers. It has a fretted finger-board with a characteristic 'peg-box' (a string harness) bent back at an angle to the finger-board. A lute can have anything up to 18 strings. It was traditionally used as an instrument for accompanying dances, but many solo works have also been written for it.

Lutoslawski, Witold (1913–) A Polish composer who is renowned for his AVANT-GARDE pieces, e.g. *Funeral Music for Strings*.

Lydian mode 1 A scale used in ancient Greek music, the equivalent of the white notes on a piano from C to C. **2** From the Middle Ages onwards, the equivalent of a scale on the white notes on a piano from F to F.

lyre An instrument familiar to the ancient Greeks, Assyrians and Hebrews. It comprised a small, hollow box from which extended two horns that supported a cross bar and anything up to 12 strings, which could be plucked or strummed. It is traditionally taken to represent a token of love (Orpheus played the lyre).

lyric A short poem, or sequence of words, for a song. The term has a particular application to 20th-cent. musicals and pop songs. A 'lyricist' is the person who writes the words to a popular tune.

M

m (me) In TONIC SOL-FA, the third note (or MEDIANT) of the major scale.

Macbeth 1 An opera by VERDI to a libretto by F.M. Piave. It tells the familiar Shakespeare tale and was first performed in 1847. **2** A symphonic poem, on the same subject, by Richard STRAUSS (1890). **3** An opera by BLOCH to a libretto by E. Fleg (1910). **4** An opera by Lawrence Collingwood (1934).

McCabe, John (1939–) An English composer and pianist who has specialized in performing 20th-cent. pieces and works by HAYDN. His compositions include operas (for example, *The Play of Mother Courage*), ballets (for example, *Mary, Queen of Scots*), 3 symphonies, and many miscellaneous pieces for orchestra and/or chorus.

McCartney, Paul (1942–) A British rock musician who

was a founder member of the group The Beatles (1961–70). He is one of the most successful songwriters of the 20th cent., and many of the songs which he wrote in partnership with John LENNON are now considered 'classics'.

MacCunn, Hamish (1868–1916) A Scottish composer and conductor whose best known work is the concert overture *Land of the Mountain and the Flood*.

MacDowell, Edward Alexander (1861–1908) An American composer who studied in Europe, where he met LISZT. He is remembered for his piano pieces and symphonic poems.

Machaut, Guillaume de (*c*.1304–77) A French composer, poet and diplomat. He composed many motets and madrigals, several using his own poems. One of his most important works is his Mass, *Messe de Notre Dame*, for four voices.

Madam Butterfly An opera by PUCCINI to a libretto by G. Giacosa. It tells the tragic story of the Japanese girl, Cio-Cio-San (Madame Butterfly), who marries a Lieutenant Pinkerton of the US Navy. It was first performed in 1904 and is one of the most popular of all operas.

Maderna, Bruno (1920–73) An Italian composer and conductor. He composed piano, flute and oboe pieces and also favoured electronic instruments as in his *Musica su due dimensioni* (for flute, percussion instruments and electronic tape). As a conductor, he was a renowned interpreter of contemporary music.

madrigal A musical setting of a secular poem, usually for unaccompanied voices. The first madrigals date back to the 14th cent.; in the 17th cent. they were superseded by cantatas.

Maelzel, Johann Nepomuk (1772–1828) A German-born inventor who settled in Vienna where he constructed various mechanical instruments. He is best known for patenting the first clockwork METRONOME.

maestoso (It.) 'Majestic' or 'dignified'.

maggiore (It.) 'Major mode'.

Magic Flute, The (*Die Zauberflöte*) An opera (with dialogue) by MOZART to a libretto by E. Schikaneder. It tells the story of how Prince Tamino rescues Pamina, the daughter of the Queen of the Night, from the priest, Sarastro. The Queen gives him a magic flute for his protection. A parallel tale concerns Papageno, a bird catcher, who searches for his Papagena. It was first performed in 1791.

Magnificat (Lat.) The canticle of the Virgin Mary sung at Roman Catholic Vespers and Anglican Evensong. It is usually chanted, but many composers, such as BACH, have set it to their own music.

Mahler, Gustav (1860–1911) An influential Austrian composer and conductor who started to learn the piano when he was six and was giving public recitals four years later. He studied in Vienna and was impressed by the work of BRUCKNER. He conducted at many of Europe's leading opera houses before becoming the director of the Vienna State Opera in 1897. For much of his life, he spent the summer months composing and the winter ones conducting. In 1907 he went to the USA where he became conductor of the New York Metropolitan Opera, but returned to

Vienna in 1911 because of his flagging health. He died of pneumonia, aged 49.

Mahler was famous in his lifetime as a conductor but many of his compositions were not well received. However, his works have subsequently been hailed as masterpieces and are perceived to form a musical link between the 19th and 20th cents. Towards the end of his short life, he became obsessed with the fear of death, which he expressed eloquently in his music. He is particularly famed for the way in which he used voices, especially with his vocal symphonies.

Mahler's principal works include: 10 symphonies (the 10th was unfinished); the song cycles *Lieder eines fahrenden Gesellen* (Songs of the Wayfarer) and KINDERTOTENLIEDER; the song symphony *Das Lied von der Erde* (*The* SONG OF THE EARTH); and numerous individual songs.

main (Fr.) Literally, 'hand', so *main droite* means 'right hand' (particularly in piano music).

malagueña A Spanish dance 3/4 or 3/8 time, named after the town of Malaga. The tune is often sung as it is danced.

malinconia (It.) 'Melancholy'.

Malipiero, Gian Francesco (1882–1973) An Italian composer who is best known for his operas (for example, *Julius Caesar*, *Antony and Cleopatra*, oratorios, piano pieces, and songs.

mancando (It.) 'Fading away'.

Manchester School The name applied to a group of British composers who studied music at the Royal Manchester College during the 1950s. They include

Harrison BIRTWISTLE and Peter Maxwell DAVIES, among others.

mandolin, mandoline A stringed instrument, similar to the lute, but smaller and usually played with a plectrum. It has four pairs of strings and has occasionally been used as an orchestral instrument.

mano (It.) 'Hand'.

Manon Lescaut An opera by PUCCINI to a libretto by M. Praga, D. Oliva and L. Illica based on the novel by Prévost. The story tells of Manon, who is torn between her love for de Grieux and her lust for wealth. It was first performed in 1893. It is also the subject of several other operas and a ballet.

manual A keyboard on an organ or harpsichord; organs may have four manuals, named Solo, Swell, Great, and Choir.

maracas A pair of Latin-American percussion instruments made from gourds filled with seeds, pebbles or shells. Sound is produced by shaking the gourds.

Marbeck, John *see* Merbecke, John.

Marcello, Benedetto (1686–1739) An Italian composer, librettist and writer on music who was also a lawyer. He is known for his cantatas, psalm settings, oratorios and concertos. His brother, Alessandro, was also a composer of worth.

march A piece of music with a strict rhythm to which soldiers can march.

marcia (It.) 'March', so *alla marcia* means 'in a marching style'.

Marenzio, Luca (1553–99) An Italian composer who worked in Poland as well as in Rome. He is most famous for his madrigals, the style of which was influential.

mariachi (Sp.) A Mexican folk group of variable size; it normally includes violins and guitars.

Maria Theresa or **Maria Theresia** The nickname for HAYDN's symphony no. 48 in C. It is so called because it was written when Empress Maria Theresa visited Haydn's patron, Prince Esterházy (1773).

marimba A Latin American instrument which may have originated in Africa. It is similar to a large XYLOPHONE and can be played by up to four people at the same time.

Marriage of Figaro, The (*Le Nozze di Figaro*) An opera by MOZART to a libretto by L. da Ponte. It is the sequel to ROSSINI's opera *The* BARBER OF SEVILLE and tells how Figaro foils Count Almaviva's plans to make off with Susanna (who is betrothed to Figaro). It was first performed in 1786.

Marriner, Neville (1924–) An English conductor and pianist who founded the famous Academy of St Martin-in-the-Fields in 1956.

Marseillaise, La The French national anthem which was composed by Rouget de Lisle in 1792 and is so called because it was sung by men from Marseille as they entered Paris in the same year.

martelé (Fr.) *see* martellato.

martellato (It.) Literally, 'hammered'; a term used mainly in music for strings to indicate that notes should be played with short, sharp strokes of the bow. The term is also occasionally used in guitar and piano music.

Martin, Frank (1890–1974) A Swiss composer, pianist and harpsichordist who settled in Holland. In his later years, he composed TWELVE-NOTE MUSIC. He is best known for his operas *The Tempest* and *Monsieur Pourceaugnac*, ballets, orchestral pieces (for example, *Petite Symphonie Concertante*), incidental pieces and choral works.

Martinu, Bohuslav (1890–1959) A Czech composer who at various times lived in France, the USA and Switzerland. He wrote 13 operas (for example, *Comedy on the Bridge*, *The Greek Passion*) 6 symphonies, choral works, ballets, sonatas and many pieces of chamber music.

marziale (It.) 'Warlike'.

Mascagni, Pietro (1863–1945) An Italian composer whose outstanding early work, the opera *Cavalleria Rusticana*, was so successful that it overshadowed virtually everything else he wrote. His other operas include *L'Amico Fritz*, *Iris* and *Il Piccolo Marat*. He was a confirmed fascist, as his opera *Nerone* shows.

Masked Ball, A (*Un Ballo in Maschera*) An opera by VERDI to a libretto by A. Somma. The story originally concerned the assassination of Gustav III of Sweden at a masked ball in Stockholm but, for political reasons, the action was transferred to Boston, Massachusetts. It was first performed in 1859.

Mason, Daniel Gregory (1873–1953) An American composer and writer on music. His works include three symphonies (for example, *A Lincoln Symphony*). He was the grandson of Lowell Mason, an American organist and influential teacher.

masque A spectacular court entertainment that was especially popular during the 17th cent. It combined poetry and dancing with vocal and instrumental music to tell a simple story that invariably flattered its aristocratic audience.

Mass In musical terms, the setting to music of the Latin Ordinary of Mass (those parts of the Mass that do not vary). The five parts are the KYRIE ELEISON, GLORIA, CREDO, SANCTUS with BENEDICTUS, and AGNUS DEI.

Massenet, Jules Emile Frédéric (1842–1912) A French composer and teacher who was much influenced by WAGNER, but whose music is considered rather more sweet and melodious. He wrote 27 operas (for example, *Le Roi de Lahore*, *Manon*, *Don Quichotte*), ballets, oratorios and some 200 songs.

Master of the Queen's Musick An honorary position (in Britain) awarded to a prominent musician of the time; it is his (or her) duty to compose anthems etc. for royal occasions.

mastersingers (Ger., *Meistersinger*) Musicians or minstrels who operated in German cities from the 14th cent. until the 19th cent. They were usually craftsmen or tradesmen who composed poems and music and they formed themselves into powerful guilds.

Mastersingers of Nuremberg, The *see* Meistersinger von Nürnberg, Die.

Mathias, William (1934–) A Welsh composer and pianist, a pupil of Lennox BERKELEY, who has written a broad variety of work, including a symphony, concertos, choral music and chamber music.

Matins The name given to the first of the 'Canonical Hours' of the Roman Catholic Church. The term also refers to Morning Prayer in the Anglican Church.

Má Vlast (My Country) A cycle of six symphonic poems by SMETANA, who was inspired by the Czechoslovakian countryside and history (1874–9).

Mazeppa 1 An opera by TCHAIKOVSKY to a libretto by V.P. Burenin. Mazeppa was a Cossack ruler who revolted against Peter the Great. It was first performed in 1884. **2** A symphonic poem by LISZT on the same subject.

mazurka A Polish folk dance of the 17th cent. for up to 12 people. The music can vary in speed and is often played on bagpipes. CHOPIN, amongst other composers, was influenced by the music and wrote some 55 'mazurkas' for piano.

me In the TONIC SOL-FA, the third note (or MEDIANT) of the major scale.

measure (US) A BAR (of music).

mechanical instruments Instruments that can play complex music through the programming of their mechanism (for example, by punched paper or pins on a spindle) when supplied with power (through foot pedals, clockwork, steam power, electricity etc.)

mediant The third note in a major or minor scale above the TONIC (lowest note), e.g. E in the scale of C major).

Mehta, Zubin (1936–) An Indian conductor, violinist and pianist. He is best known as a conductor and has worked with most of the world's leading orchestras, notably the New York Philharmonic Orchestra.

Meistersinger (Ger.) *see* mastersingers.

Meistersinger von Nürnberg, Die (The Mastersingers of Nuremberg) An opera by WAGNER, who also wrote the libretto. The story concerns Walther and his love for Eva, the daughter of Pogner, who promises his daughter's hand to the winner of the Mastersinger's contest. Walther eventually wins the challenge. It was first performed in 1868.

Melba, Nellie (originally Helen Porter Armstrong, née Mitchell) (1859–1931) An Australian soprano who became extremely famous in Europe and the USA for her operatic roles. She chose her stage name, Melba, in tribute to the city of Melbourne. She was honoured in several ways: she was made a D.B.E. in 1918, and the ice-cream dessert, peach Melba, and Melba toast were both named after her.

melodic minor scale *see* scale.

melodic sequence *see* sequence.

melodica (It.) A free-reed instrument which was developed from the harmonica. It is box-shaped and has a small keyboard; the player blows down a tube and plays notes by pressing the keys.

melodrama Originally, a part of a play or opera in which words are spoken to a musical accompaniment. From this, the word has come to mean an exaggeratedly dramatic or sensational play.

melody A succession of notes, of varying pitch, that create a distinct and identifiable musical form. Melody, HARMONY and RHYTHM are the three essential ingredients of music. The criteria of what constitutes a melody change over time.

membranophone The generic term for all instruments in which sound is produced by the vibration of a skin or membrane, e.g. DRUM, KAZOO.

Mendelssohn, Felix (Jakob Ludwig Felix Mendelssohn-Bartholdy) (1809–47) A German composer, organist, pianist and conductor who was first taught music by his mother. He was precociously gifted. He first performed in public when he was nine years old and organized his own orchestra when he was 12. When he was 17, he composed his first masterpiece, the overture to *A Midsummer Night's Dream*. In 1829 he made the first of several visits to England and Scotland and was inspired to write his *Hebrides Overture*. Later he visited Italy and France where he met BERLIOZ, LISZT and CHOPIN. He settled in Germany as an established conductor and, with SCHUMANN, founded the Leipzig Conservatorium. In 1846 he triumphantly conducted the first performance of his *Elijah* oratorio at the Birmingham Festival but by now his health was failing and he died the following year.

Mendelssohn combined classical technique and romantic expressiveness. He appreciated his phenomenal gifts (he was also a better than average writer and painter). He was liked by fellow composers, as well as by the public at large, and he did much to 'popularize' serious music. He pioneered the revival of J.S. BACH with a performance of the ST MATTHEW PASSION in 1829.

Mendelssohn's principal works include: 5 symphonies (for example, the SCOTTISH, REFORMATION and

Italian symphonies); overtures (for example, *The Hebrides* (FINGAL'S CAVE), *Calm Sea and Prosperous Voyage*); oratorios (e.g. *St Paul*, *Elijah*, *Christus*); and numerous pieces for organ, piano and chamber orchestra.

meno (It.) 'Less', so *meno mosso* means 'slower' (less moved).

Menotti, Gian Carlo (1911–) An Italian-born composer who emigrated to the USA in 1928. He is best known for his operas, for example, *Amelia goes to the Ball*, *The Telephone*, *The Saint of Bleeker Street* and *Help, help, the Globolinks*. He has also written ballets and various pieces for orchestra.

Menuhin, Yehudi (1916–) An American-born violinist and conductor who settled in England after the Second World War. He was a child prodigy and achieved international fame. He also has a worldwide reputation as a conductor, especially of chamber music. In 1963 he founded the Menuhin School of Music for musically gifted children. He was knighted in 1965.

Mer, La (The Sea) Three symphonic sketches for orchestra by DEBUSSY, inspired by the sea (1905).

Merbecke or **Marbeck, John** (1510–85) An English composer and organist who was the first person to set the English (as distinct from the Latin) liturgy to music.

'Mercury' Symphony The unexplained nickname for HAYDN's symphony no. 43. in E (*c.*1771).

Merry Widow, The (*Die Lustige Witwe*) An operetta by LEHÁR to a libretto by V. Léon and L. Stein. The story is one of romance and diplomatic intrigue. It was first performed in 1905.

Merry Wives of Windsor, The (*Die Lustigen Weiber von Windsor*) An opera by NICOLAI to a libretto by S.H. Mosenthal (after Shakespeare). It was first performed in 1849.

Messiaen, Olivier Eugène Prosper Charles (1908–92) French composer and organist. In his formative years he was influenced by Indian music; and also by birdsong, which he wrote down in musical notation. He has subsequently used birdsong in many of his pieces. He was imprisoned in a concentration camp by the Nazis during the Second World War, when he wrote *Quartet for the End of Time*. He is one of the most influential of all modern composers and he has made use of a wide range of influences, such as ancient Greek music. His principal works include: *Nativité du Seigneur*, *L'Ascension* (for organ); *Turangalîla-symphonie* (for orchestra); *La Transfiguration de Notre Seigneur Jésus-Christ* (for solo instruments, chorus and orchestra); *Visions de l'Amen* (for piano); and many pieces for miscellaneous instruments.

Messiah An oratorio by HANDEL to text taken from the Bible. It includes the famous HALLELUJAH CHORUS. It was composed within a month and was first performed in 1742.

mesto (It.) 'Sad'.

metallophone An instrument that is similar to a XYLO-PHONE but has metal bars (usually bronze).

metronome An instrument that produces regular beats and can therefore be used to indicate the pace at which a piece of music should be played. The first clockwork metronome was patented by MAELZEL in 1816 and had a metal rod that swung backwards and forwards on a stand. The speed of ticking could be altered by sliding a weight up or down the rod. Electronic metronomes are also manufactured today.

Metropolitan Opera House, New York The home of the prestigious Metropolitan Opera Company which was formed in 1883. The opera house is part of the Lincoln Center for the Performing Arts and is affectionately called 'The Met.'

Meyerbeer, Giacomo (1791–1864) A German-born composer who visited Italy and wrote operas in the style of ROSSINI. His best known works, written for the Paris Opéra, include *Robert le Diable*, *Les Huguenots* and *L'Africaine*.

mezzo (It.) Literally 'half', so *mezzo-soprano* means a voice between soprano and contralto.

mf An abbreviation of *mezzo forte*, (It.) meaning moderately loud.

m.g. An abbreviation of *main gauche*, (Fr.) meaning 'left hand'.

microtones INTERVALS that are smaller than a SEMITONE in length, for example, the quarter-tone.

Midsummer Marriage, The An opera by TIPPETT, who also wrote the libretto. Like *The* MAGIC FLUTE *of* MOZART, the opera tells two parallel stories concerning two pairs of lovers (Mark and Jenifer, Bell and Jack), who have to undergo trials before they can be finally united. It contains the well-known *Ritual Dances*, and was first performed in 1955.

Midsummer Night's Dream, A 1 An overture to Shakespeare's play by MENDELSSOHN (1826), to which he later added incidental music. **2** Incidental music to Shakespeare's play by ORFF (1939). **3** An opera by BRITTEN which uses text from Shakespeare's play (1960).

Mikado, The An operetta by GILBERT and SULLIVAN. It is set in Japan and is subtitled *The town of Titipu*. It is probably the most famous of the 'Savoy operas' and it played for 672 nights after its first performance in 1885.

Mikrokomos A collection of 153 short piano pieces by BARTOK, providing graded pieces for the teaching of technique. It is rich in invention.

Milhaud, Darius (1892–1974) A French composer and pianist, of Jewish ancestry, who became a member of the group known as '*Les* SIX'. He was an extremely prolific composer and experimented with many different types of music from jazz to Latin-American and electronic. His work includes the ballets *The Creation of the World* and *The Ox on the Roof*, the operas *Cristophe Colomb* and *David*, and the orchestral piece *Saudades do Brasil*.

military band A band in the armed forces that plays military music, usually for marching. There are many different types of military band, and the number of players can vary. Most bands comprise a mixture of brass, woodwind and percussion instruments.

'Military' Symphony HAYDN's symphony no.100 in G (1794). It is so called because it employs 'military' instruments (such as cymbals and bass drum, which

171

were not used in the orchestra of the time) and has a solo trumpet call in the second movement.

minim A note, formerly the shortest in time-value, with half the value of a SEMIBREVE; the equivalent of a half-note in in US terminology.

minstrel A professional entertainer or musician of the medieval times. Such people were often employed by a royal court or aristocratic family.

minuet A French rural dance in 3/4 time that was popular during the 17th and 18th cents. It remained popular and was incorporated into classical sonatas and symphonies as a regular movement.

'Minute' Waltz The nickname of CHOPIN's waltz in D flat (1847) which, if played very fast, should last only a minute.

mirliton (Fr.) Any wind instrument in which a thin membrane is made to vibrate and make a noise when the player blows, hums or sings into it. It is now known as the KAZOO.

mirror music Any piece of music that sounds the same when played backwards.

Miserere (Lat.) Short for *Miserere mei Deus* (Have mercy upon me, O God), the first line of the 51st Psalm. It has been set to music by several composers, including VERDI.

Missa (Lat.) 'Mass', so *missa brevis* means 'short mass', and *missa cantata* means 'sung mass'.

misterioso (It.) 'Mysteriously'.

misura (It.) 'Measure'; equivalent to a BAR.

Mitridate, Re di Ponte An opera seria by MOZART to a libretto by V.A. Cigna-Santi (after Racine). Mozart wrote it when he was 14 and it was first performed in 1770.

Mixolydian mode 1 The set of notes, in ancient Greek music, which are the equivalent of the white notes on a piano from B to B. **2** In church music of the Middle Ages onwards, the equivalent of the white notes on a piano from G to G.

mixture An organ stop that brings into play a number of pipes that produce HARMONICS above the pitch corresponding to the actual key which is played.

moderato (It.) 'Moderate' (in terms of speed).

modes The various sets of notes or SCALES which were used by musicians until the concept of the KEY was accepted (*c.*1650). Modes were originally used by the ancient Greeks and were adapted by medieval composers, especially for church music. Modes were based on what are now the white notes of the piano.

modulation The gradual changing of key during the course of a part of a composition by means of a series of harmonic progressions.

Moeran, Ernest John (1894–1950) An English composer of Irish ancestry. His compositions include a symphony, violin and cello concertos, miscellaneous orchestral pieces, songs, and works for chamber orchestra.

moll (Ger.) 'Minor' (as opposed to major, *dur*).

molto (It.) 'Very', so *allegro molto* means 'very fast'.

Moments Musicaux A set of six short piano pieces by SCHUBERT. The same title has also been used by many lesser composers for piano works.

monody A type of accompanied solo song which was developed during the late 16th and early 17th cents. It contained dramatic and expressive embellishments and devices, and consequently had an influence on opera.

monothematic A piece of music that is developed from a single musical idea.

Monteverdi (Monteverde), Claudio Giovanni Antonio (1567–1643) An Italian composer from Cremona working in Mantua and Venice, who was ordained a priest in 1632. He composed many religious works (e.g. Masses, Vespers, Magnificats) but also numerous secular works, especially madrigals, operas and ballets. Unfortunately, only 3 of his 12 operas survive in their complete state (ORFEO, *Il ritorno d'Ulisse in patria* and *L'*INCORONAZIONE DE POPPEA). Monteverdi's role in the development of music has been to compared to Shakespeare's in literature; he injected a new imagination into every form of music he worked with.

Moore, Douglas Stuart (1893–1969) An American composer and teacher. His works include operas (e.g. *The Devil and Daniel Webster*, *The Ballad of Baby Doe*), and orchestral and choral pieces.

morbido (It.) 'Soft' or 'gentle'.

morceau (Fr.) A 'piece' (of music).

mordent A musical ornament whereby one note rapidly alternates with another one degree below it; this is indicated by a sign over the note.

morendo (It.) 'Dying', i.e. decreasing in volume.

moresca (It.) A sword dance dating from the 15th and

16th cents. which represents battles between the Moors and the Christians. It was the origin of the English morris dance. It has been included in operas, often to a marching rhythm.

Morley, Thomas (1557–*c.*1602) An English composer who was given the patent to print song-books by Elizabeth I. As well as publishing his own works, he also published works of his contemporaries and educational booklets. He is considered to be the father of the English madrigal and he also wrote ballets and pieces for the lute.

Morton, Ferdinand ('Jelly Roll') (1885–1941) A Black American jazz pianist, singer and composer who helped to establish jazz as a genuine art form.

mosso (It.) 'Moved', so *più mosso* means 'more moved', i.e. quicker.

motet A musical setting of sacred words for solo voices or choir, with or without accompaniment. The first motets were composed in the 13th cent.

Mother Goose (*Ma mère l'oye*) A suite of five pieces for piano duet by RAVEL. It was based on fairy stories and was later produced as a ballet (1912).

motif (motive) A small group of notes which create a melody or rhythm, for example the first four notes of BEETHOVEN's 5th symphony form a motif.

motion The upward or downward progress of a melody.

moto (It.) 'Motion', so *con moto* means 'with motion' or quickly.

motto theme A short theme that recurs during the course of a composition. In this way, it dominates the piece, and is usually used to create dramatic effect.

'Mourning' Symphony The nickname for HAYDN's symphony no. 44 in E minor (1771). It is so called because Haydn requested the slow movement to be played at his own funeral.

mouth organ *see* harmonica.

movement A self-contained section of a larger instrumental composition, such as a symphony.

Mozart, Wolfgang Amadeus (1756–91) An Austrian composer, keyboard player, violinist, violist and conductor. He was born in Salzburg and was taught music by his father, Leopold, who was a violinist, composer and writer himself. The young Mozart was an infant prodigy and composed his first pieces for harpsichord when he was five. In 1762 Leopold took his son and daughter, Maria Anna, on a tour of Munich, Vienna and Pressburg where the children gave virtuoso harpsichord performances. By this time, Wolfgang could also play the violin, although he had received no formal instruction. The following year, Mozart went on an extended European tour which took in Paris and London, which is where he met J.C. BACH and wrote his first three symphonies. In 1768 he composed his first operas, *La finta semplice* and *Bastien und Bastienne*. In Vienna, Mozart met HAYDN, who was one of the few of his contemporaries with a true appreciation of his genius, for, despite his precocious gifts, he found it difficult to achieve patronage. Between 1773 and 1777 he spent most of his time in Salzburg with occasional visits to Vienna, Munich and Paris. For a time, he entered the service of the Archbishop of

Salzburg, but this was not a success and in 1781, after a sojourn in Paris, he moved to Vienna where he married the singer, Constanze Weber. In Vienna Mozart earned a living as a freelance composer, teacher and performer but he was perpetually in financial difficulties. However, it was during his last years in Vienna that he composed many of his greatest pieces, including the symphonies that have been nicknamed HAFFNER, LINZ and JUPITER, and the operas COSÌ FAN TUTTE, *The* MARRIAGE OF FIGARO and *The* MAGIC FLUTE (which was influenced by his interest in Freemasonry). He never finished his last work *The* REQUIEM, and died, most probably of typhoid, in 1791. The theory that he was poisoned by his rival SALIERI has never been proved.

Mozart was influenced by the works of J.C. and C.P.E. BACH, HANDEL, HAYDN and GLUCK, amongst others, but his own contribution to nearly all musical forms was colossal. He helped to establish the classical style of composition, especially with his operas, symphonies and piano concertos, which are considered to be among the greatest ever written. His work could be dramatic, witty, light-hearted or profound, and his influence on other composers is incalculable.

His principal compositions include: the operas, IDOMENEO, *The Marriage of Figaro*, DON GIOVANNI, *Così fan tutte* and *The Magic Flute*; 41 symphonies; 27 piano concertos; 23 string quartets; 17 piano sonatas; and 18 Masses.

Mozart and Salieri An opera by RIMSKY-KORSAKOV which is essentially a setting of Pushkin's dramatic poem of the supposed fatal poisoning of MOZART by SALIERI. It was first performed in 1898.

mp Abbrev. for *mezzo piano* (It.), meaning 'half-soft'.

M.S. (m.s.) Abbrev. for *mano sinistra* (It.), meaning 'left hand'.

muffled drum A drum with a piece of cloth or towelling draped over the vibrating surfaces. It produces a sombre tone when struck, and is usually associated with funeral music.

Mundy, John (*c*.1566–1630) An English organist and composer who was taught by his composer father, William. His works include madrigals and pieces for viols.

musette (Fr.) 1 A type of bagpipe popular at the French court in the 17th and 18th cents. 2 An air in 2/4, 3/4 or 6/8 time that imitates drone of the bagpipe.

Musical Joke, A *see* Musikalischer Spass, Ein.

Musgrave, Thea (1928–) A Scottish composer who is best known for her operas (for example, *The Decision*, *The Voice of Ariadne*), and her ballets *Beauty and the Beast* and *A Tale for Thieves*. She has also written choral and orchestral works.

musica ficta (Lat.) Literally, 'feigned music'; it is a term for ACCIDENTALS used in MODE music.

musical box A clockwork MECHANICAL INSTRUMENT in which a drum studded with small pins plays a tune by plucking the teeth of a metal comb.

musical A type of play or film in which music plays an important part and the actors occasionally sing, for example, *My Fair Lady*, *West Side Story*.

musical comedy A term used between 1890 and 1930 to describe a humorous play with light music and singing in it.

Musikalischer Spass, Ein (A Musical Joke) A miniature symphony in F by MOZART for two horns and strings. It is a satire on popular music of the time.

musicology The scientific study of music.

musique concrète A term coined by the French composer Pierre Schaffer in 1948 to describe a type of music in which taped sounds are distorted or manipulated by the composer. The term ELECTRONIC MUSIC is now more generally used.

Mussorgsky (Musorgsky), Modest Petrovich (1839–81) A Russian composer who gave up a military career to write music. Although he came from a wealthy family, he regularly lived in a state of poverty, largely on account of his chronic alcoholism. Due to his affliction, he left much of his music unfinished but has nevertheless been hailed as a composer of genius. Ironically, many of his pieces were tampered with after his death by composers who could not, or did not, recognize his talent for invention. For example, RIMSKY-KORSAKOV revised his opera *Boris Godunov*. He was a member of 'The FIVE', and his best known works include the operas BORIS GODUNOV and *Sorochintsy Fair* (unfinished), the piano piece PICTURES AT AN EXHIBITION, and many songs.

mutation stops Organ stops that produce sound – usually a HARMONIC – which is different from the normal or octave pitch corresponding to the key which is depressed.

mute Any device used to soften to reduce the normal volume, or alter the tone, of an instrument. With bowed instruments, a small clamp is slotted onto the bridge; in brass instruments a hand or bung is pushed into the bell; in the piano the soft (left) piano is pressed; and with drums, cloths are placed over the skins, or sponge-headed drumsticks are used.

Muti, Riccardo (1941–) An Italian conductor with an international reputation.

My Country *see* Má Vlast.

N

Nachtmusik (Ger.) Literally, 'night music', i.e music suitable for performing in the evening, or suggestive of night.

naker The medieval English name for a small kettledrum (often with snares) of Arabic origin, from which TIMPANI developed. It was always used in pairs.

Nardini, Pietro (1722–93) An Italian violinist and composer. He was admired as one of the greatest violinists of his day. His works include six string quartets as well as sonatas for violin and piano.

Nares, James (1715–83) An English organist and composer, who is best known for his church music and songs.

national anthem A song or hymn which is adopted by a country and sung or played at official occasions.

nationalism A late 19th-cent. and early 20th-cent. movement in which a number of composers (notably

'The FIVE' in Russia, and SMETANA, GRIEG, ELGAR and SIBELIUS) set out to write work which would express their national identity, often by reference to folk music and by evocation of landscape. It was in part a reaction to the dominance of German music.

natural A note which is neither sharpened nor flattened. (See Appendix for symbol.)

neck The narrow projecting part of a stringed instrument that supports the finger-board; at the end of the neck lies the peg-box which secures the strings and enables them to be tuned.

neo-classicism A 20th-cent. musical movement which reacted against the overtly romantic forms of the late 19th cent. Composers who adhered to the philosophy (in particular STRAVINSKY, HINDEMITH, POULENC and PROKOFIEV) attempted to create new works with the balance and restraint found in the work of 18th-cent. composers, especially BACH.

neume A sign used in musical notation from the 7th to 14th cent. It gave an indication of pitch.

New World Symphony *see* From the New World.

Nibelung's Ring, The *see* Ring of the Nibelung, The.

Nicolai, Carl Otto Ehrenfried (1810–49) A German composer and conductor whose most famous work is the comic opera *The* MERRY WIVES OF WINDSOR. He also wrote other operas, two symphonies and some church music.

Nielsen, Carl August (1865–1931) A Danish composer, violinist and conductor who produced works of a strong individuality. For many years his music was not appreciated outside Denmark, but after the Second

World War he was widely recognized as being inventive and original. His works include the opera *Saul and David*, six symphonies, many choral pieces, and music for chamber orchestra, piano and organ.

niente (It.) 'Nothing'; used in *quasi niente* ('almost nothing'), indicating a very soft tone.

Nightingale, The An opera by STRAVINSKY, who also wrote the libretto in conjunction with S. Mitusov (after the fairytale by Hans Andersen). It was first performed in 1914. Stravinsky based his symphonic poem *The Song of the Nightingale* on the opera; this piece was also used as ballet music.

Nights in the Gardens of Spain (*Noches en los Jardines de España*) Three symphonic impressions for piano and orchestra by FALLA (1909–15).

Nilsson, Birgit (1918–) A Swedish soprano of international repute who is particularly famous for her role as Brünnhilde in WAGNER's operatic cycle The RING OF THE NIBELUNG.

ninth An INTERVAL of nine notes, in which both the first and last notes are counted.

nobile, nobilmente (It.) 'Noble, nobly'.

Noches en los Jardines de España *see* Nights in the Gardens of Spain.

nocturne Literally, a 'night piece', i.e. a piece of music, often meditative in character and suggesting the quietness of night. The form was invented by John FIELD and later perfected by CHOPIN.

Nocturnes The titles of certain pieces of music (nocturnes) by FIELD and CHOPIN, and also the title of three orchestral pieces by DEBUSSY.

noire (Fr.) Crochet.

nomenclature *see* notation.

nonet A group of nine instruments, or a piece of music for such a group.

Nono, Luigi (1924–) An Italian composer who was influenced by WEBERN and is considered a champion of 'modern' music. He has devout left-wing opinions which have influenced his output. His most influential works include the opera *Intolleranza 1960* (with live and taped music, and live and filmed action), and *On the Bridge of Hiroshima*, a piece for voices and orchestra.

Norman, Jessye (1945–) A Black American opera singer who is one of the most impressive sopranos of the post-Second World War era. With her magnificent voice and sensitivity of interpretation, she has been outstanding in many diverse roles.

nota cambiata *see* changing note.

notation (nomenclature) The symbols used in written music to indicate the pitch and rhythm of notes.

note 1 A sound which has a defined pitch and duration. **2** A symbol for such a sound. **3** The key of a piano or other keyboard instrument.

Noveletten (Ger.) Literally, 'short stories'; it was a title used by SCHUMANN for a set of piano pieces that 'told a story'.

Novello, Ivan (1893–1951) A British composer, playwright and actor, who was particularly celebrated for his revues and musicals. He wrote the famous First World War song 'Keep the Home Fires Burning'.

Novello, Vincent (1781–1861) A London-based editor,

organist and composer who founded the firm of Novello which published works by MOZART, HAYDN, BEETHOVEN and PURCELL and therefore helped to publicize serious music in England. His son, Joseph Alfred, continued in his father's footsteps, and his daughter, Clara Anastasia, became a celebrated soprano.

Nozze di Figaro, Le *see* Marriage of Figaro, The.

nuance A subtle change of speed, tone etc.

Nunc Dimittis (Lat.) The Song of Simeon, 'Lord, now lettest Thy Thou servant depart in peace', which is sung at both Roman Catholic and Anglican evening services. It has been set to music by numerous composers.

nut 1 The part of the bow of a stringed instrument which holds the horsehair and which incorporates a screw that tightens the tension of the hairs. **2** The hardwood ridge at the peg-box end of a stringed instrument's finger-board that raises the strings above the level of the finger-board.

Nutcracker, The A ballet by TCHAIKOVSKY based on a tale by Hoffmann. It relates the story of Klara, who is given a nutcracker one Christmas; when she sleeps that night, she is taken on a magical tour of the Kingdom of Sweets by a prince. It was first performed in 1892.

O

o When placed over a note in a musical score for strings, indicates that the note must be played on an open string or as a harmonic.

obbligato (It.) 'Obligatory'; a term that refers to a part which cannot be dispensed with in a performance (some parts can be optional). However, some 19th-cent. composers used the word to mean the exact opposite, i.e. a part that was optional.

Oberon An opera by WEBER to a libretto written by J.R. Planché. It is subtitled *The Elf-King's Oath* and relates a story in which the king of fairies, Oberon, vows never to be reconciled with his wife, Titania, until he has found a pair of perfect lovers. It was first performed in 1826.

Oberwerk (Ger.) A swell organ. *See* organ.

oblique motion Two parallel melody lines, or parts: one moves up or down the scale while the other stays on a consistent note.

oboe A WOODWIND instrument with a conical bore and a double reed. The instrument has a history dating back to ancient Egyptian times. SHAWMS evolved from these Egyptian predecessors and became known as 'hautbois' (high-wood) instruments in the 17th and 18th cents. The modern oboe (the word is a corruption of 'hautbois') dates from the 18th cent. The established variations of the instrument are: the oboe (treble), the COR ANGLAIS (alto), the BASSOON (tenor), and the double bassoon (bass).

Obrecht (Hobrecht), Jacob (1450–1505) A Flemish

composer who travelled extensively in Europe and was one of the foremost musicians of his era. He is remembered for writing 24 Masses, 22 motets and many songs.

ocarina A small, egg-shaped wind instrument, often made of clay, which is played in a way similar to a RECORDER. It was invented in the mid-19th cent. and is still made, mainly as a toy.

Ockeghem (Okeghem, Ockenheim), Johannes (Jan) (c.1430–c.1495) A Flemish composer of considerable originality, who achieved fame with his motets, Masses and songs.

octave 1 An INTERVAL of eight notes, inclusive of the top and bottom notes, e.g. C to C.

octet A group of eight instruments, or a piece for such a group.

octobass A huge kind of three-stringed double bass, some 4 m in height, which incorporated pedal-operated levers to stop the immensely thick strings. It was invented by J.B. Vuillaume in Paris in 1849, but proved impractical.

Ode for St Cecilia's Day 1 The title of four choral works by PURCELL. **2** The title of a choral setting of Dryden's poem by HANDEL.

Oedipus Rex An 'opera-oratorio' by STRAVINSKY to a Latin text by J. Daniélou (a translation of Cocteau's play after Sophocles). It was first performed in 1927.

oeuvre (Fr.) A 'work' (OPUS).

Offenbach, Jacques (1819–80) A German-French composer, conductor and cellist. The son of a Jewish

CANTOR, he wrote outstandingly tuneful light music. Of his 90 operettas, ORPHEUS IN THE UNDERWORLD and *The* TALES OF HOFFMANN are the most famous.

offertory An ANTIPHON sung (or music played on the organ) while the priest prepares the bread and wine at a communion service.

Ogdon, John (1937–1989) An English pianist and composer who was a member of the 'MANCHESTER SCHOOL'. He had a formidable repertoire as a pianist and composed many pieces for the instrument.

Oistrakh, David (1908–74) A Russian violinist who only gained international recognition after the Second World War. His son Igor (1931–) is also a celebrated violinist and a conductor.

Okeghem, Johannes *see* Ockeghem, Johannes.

Ondes Martenot (Ondes Musicales) An electronic instrument patented by Maurice Martenot in 1922. It was used by such composers as MESSIAEN.

On Hearing the First Cuckoo in Spring An orchestral piece by DELIUS, first performed in 1913.

On Wenlock Edge A cycle of six settings by VAUGHAN WILLIAMS of poems from Housman's 'A Shropshire Lad'.

op. Abbrev. for OPUS.

open harmony *see* harmony.

open string Any string on an instrument that is allowed to vibrate along its entire length without being stopped.

opera A dramatic work in which all, or most of the text is sung to orchestral accompaniment. The word stands for *opera in musica* (It.), meaning a 'musical work'.

Opera is a formidable musical form and has a history dating back to the 17th cent. It demands a LIBRETTO, an ORCHESTRA, singers, an ample stage, and, only too often, considerable funds to produce. A 'comic opera' is essentially an opera that includes spoken words, usually has easily-accessible music, and involves comic situations leading to a happy resolution.

opéra-bouffe (Fr.) A comic opera, i.e. an opera with lightweight music and a lightweight libretto.

opera buffa (It.) *see* opéra-bouffe.

opéra-comique (Fr.) A comic opera. *See* opera; opéra-bouffe.

opera seria (It.) 'Serious opera', as usually applied to work of the 17th and 18th cents.

operetta A short opera or, more usually, a term taken to mean an opera with some spoken dialogue, and a romantic plot with a happy ending.

ophicleide The largest member of the now redundant key-bugle family (bugles with keys).

opus (Lat.) 'Work'; a term used by composers (or their cataloguers) to indicate the chronological order of their works. It is usually abbreviated to Op. and is followed by the catalogued number of the work.

oratorio The musical setting of a religious or epic LIBRETTO for soloists, chorus and orchestra, performed without the theatrical effects of stage and costumes etc.

orchestra A group of instruments and their players. A standard, modern orchestra contains four families of instruments: strings, woodwind, brass and percussion. The exact number of players within each section can vary and extra instruments can be called for by a particular score.

orchestration The art of writing and arranging music for an orchestra.

Orfeo, L' (The Story of Orpheus) An opera by MONTE-VERDI to a libretto by A. Striggio. It tells the familiar story of Orpheus, who ventures into the underworld to retrieve his love, Euridice. It was first performed in 1607.

Orff, Carl (1895–1982) A German composer and teacher. He was passionately involved in education and wrote many pieces especially for children (e.g. *Schulwerk*). His most famous piece is CARMINA BU-RANA, which was written as a 'scenic-cantata' to be performed on the stage with dancers etc. However, it is now usually performed as a traditional concert work. His other works include the operas *The Moon*, *The Clever Girl*, *Antigone* and *Oedipus the Tyrant*.

organ A keyboard wind instrument, played with the hands and feet, in which pressurized air is forced through pipes to sound notes. Pitch is determined by the length of the pipe. There are essentially two types of pipe; flue pipes, which are blown like a whistle, and reed pipes in which air is blown over vibrating strips of metal. Flue pipes can be 'stopped' (blocked off at one end) to produce a sound an octave lower than when open. There are a number of keyboards on an organ, one of which is operated by the feet (pedal board). Those operated by the hands are called manuals and there are four common categories: the solo (used for playing solo melodies), the swell (on which notes can be made to sound louder or softer), the great (the manual that opens up all the most powerful pipes), and the choir (which operates the softer sounding pipes). In addition there are a number of 'stops' (buttons or levers) that can alter the pitch or tone of specific pipes. The organ dates back to before the time of Christ and has gone through many stages of evolution. Electronic organs have been invented and these tend to produce sounds rather different from those in which pumped air is actually used.

organistrum *see* hurdy-gurdy.

Ormandy, Eugene (1899–85) A Hungarian-born conductor who was a child prodigy on the violin. He moved to the USA in 1921 and has conducted many of the world's leading orchestras.

ornaments and graces Embellishments to the notes of a melody, indicated by symbols or small notes. They were used frequently in the 17th and 18th cents.

Orpheus 1 A symphonic poem by LISZT (1854). **2** A ballet by STRAVINSKY, first performed in 1948.

Orpheus in the Underworld (*Orphée aux enfers*) An operetta by OFFENBACH to a libretto by H. Crémieux and L. Halévy. The classic story is used to satirize 19th-cent. society. It was first performed in 1858.

oscillator An electronic instrument that converts electrical energy into audible sound.

ossia (It.) 'Or'; used to indicate an alternative passage of music.

ostinato (It.) 'Obstinate'; a short phrase or other pattern that is repeated over and over again during the course of a composition.

Otello (Othello) **1** An opera by VERDI to a libretto by A. Boito (after Shakespeare). It was first performed in 1887. **2** An opera by ROSSINI to a libretto by F.B. di Salsa (after Shakespeare), first performed in 1816.

ottava (It.) Octave.

overtones *see* harmonics.

overture A piece of music that introduces an an opera, oratorio, ballet or other major work. However, a CONCERT OVERTURE is often an independent piece, written for performance in a concert hall.

P

p 1 Abbrev. for *piano* (It.), meaning 'soft'. **2** Abbrev. for 'pedal' (organ).

Pachelbel, Johann (1653–1706) A German organist and composer who wrote motets, concertos and cantatas, and is now mainly known for his canon and gigue in D major.

Paderewski, Ignacy Jan (1860–1941) A Polish pianist, composer and statesman. He was perhaps the most fêted pianist of his era, renowned particularly for his playing of CHOPIN. In 1919 he became prime minister of Poland. He composed the opera *Manru*, a symphony and many songs.

Paganini, Niccoló (1782–1840) An Italian violinist and composer. He learned to play the violin from his father and went on to become the most famous virtuoso violinist of all time. He delighted in composing complicated and difficult pieces for himself and he may have refused to play some other composers' works because they offered no challenge to his virtuosity. In addition to being an extrovert performer he was also a capable composer, who wrote five violin concertos and several pieces for the guitar.

Palestrina, Giovanni Pierluigi da (*c*.1525–94) An Italian polyphonic composer who wrote noted Masses (for example, *Missa Papae Marcelli*), motets, and other religious works.

pandora A plucked stringed instrument of the CITTERN family. It was particularly popular in England during the 16th cent.

panpipes A set of graduated pipes, stopped at the lower end, which are bound together by thongs. Each pipe makes a single note and sound is produced by blowing across the open end. They are popular instruments in South America and parts of Eastern Europe.

pantonality *see* atonal.

Panufnik, Andrzej (1914–) A Polish composer and conductor who settled in England in 1954. He became a conductor of international repute and composed several noted pieces, including the ballet *Miss Julie*, and the orchestral pieces *Sinfonia rustica* and *Sinfonia sacra*.

Papillons (Butterflies) Twelve short piano pieces by SCHUMANN (1832).

parameter A 20th-cent. term used to describe aspects of sound that can be varied but which nevertheless impose a limit. It is particularly applied to electronic music with regard to volume etc.

Paris Opéra The most important opera house in France, usually just referred to as the 'Opéra'; its official title is the 'Academie de Musique'. It was opened in 1671.

Paris Symphonies A set of six symphonies by HAYDN which were commissioned by the 'Concert de la Loge Olympique', a Masonic concert society based in Paris.

Paris Symphony The title given to MOZART's symphony no. 31 in D. It was composed while Mozart was in Paris (1778).

Parker, Charlie ('Bird') (1920–55) A Black American jazz saxophonist and composer. He helped to create the jazz style of BEBOP and gained his nickname because he was a frequent performer at the Birdland Jazz Club in New York. He is reckoned to be one of the most creative of all saxophonists. Drug addiction caused his early death.

Parker, Horatio, William (1863–1919) An American organist and composer. He wrote several oratorios (such as *Hora Novissima*), two operas, choral works, and pieces for piano and organ.

Parry, (Charles) Hubert (Hastings) (1848–1918) An English composer, teacher and musical historian who is remembered for his choral works (for example, *Blest Pair of Sirens*, *Ode on St Cecilia's Day*), motets (such as *Songs of Farewell*), and many orchestral works. However, his most famous piece of all was his setting of Blake's 'Jerusalem'. He was an eminent teacher, being at various times a director of the Royal College of Music and a professor of music at Oxford

Parsifal

University. He did much to revive the musical life of late 19th-cent. England. He was knighted in 1898 and made a baronet in 1903.

Parsifal An opera by WAGNER, who also wrote the libretto. The story concerns Parsifal, who wins back the magic spear that can heal the wounds of Amfortas, ruler of the knights of the Holy Grail, from the evil magician, Klingsor. It was first performed in 1882.

part A voice or instrument in a group of performers, or a piece of music for it.

Partch, Harry (1901–1974) A self-taught American composer who experimented with musical ideas and invented his own instruments. Many of his instruments were virtual sculptures and he became a famous, if somewhat eccentric, performer of highly individualistic music.

parte (It.) 'Part', so *colla parte* means 'with the part'.

part-song A composition for unaccompanied voices in which the highest part usually sings the melody while the lower parts sing accompanying harmonies.

passacaglia (It.) A type of slow and stately dance originating in Spain, for which keyboard music was written in the 17th cent. It has come to mean a work in which such a theme recurs again and again.

passage work A piece of music that provides an opportunity for virtuoso playing.

passamezzo (It.) 'Half-step'; a quick Italian dance in duple time that became popular throughout Europe in the late 16th cent.

passepied (It.) A French dance in triple time, like a

quick MINUET, that is thought to have originated in Brittany. It was incorporated into French ballets of the mid-17th cent.

passing note A note that is dissonant with the prevailing harmony but which is nevertheless useful in making the transition from one chord or key to another.

Passion music The setting to music of the story of Christ's Passion (the story of the crucifixion taken from the gospels), for example, BACH's ST JOHN PASSION and ST MATTHEW PASSION.

pasticchio (It.) Literally, 'pie', a dramatic entertainment that contains a selection of pieces from various composers' works.

pastorale 1 A vocal or instrumental movement or composition in compound triple time which suggests a rural subject; it usually has long bass notes that imitate the sounds of the bagpipe drone. **2** A stage entertainment based on a pastoral (idealized rural) subject.

Pastoral Symphony 1 BEETHOVEN's symphony no. 6 in F (1808). It is so called because it incorporates country sounds (such as a cuckoo, nightingale) and each of the five movements has an evocative title. **2** VAUGHAN WILLIAM's 3rd symphony (1922/1955). **3** The name given to an orchestral movement in HANDEL's MESSIAH. **4** The name given to an instrumental section in BACH's CHRISTMAS ORATORIO.

'Pathetic' Sonata *see* Sonate Pathétique.

'Pathetic' Symphony *see* Symphonie Pathétique.

Patience A comic opera by GILBERT and SULLIVAN. It is a satire on contemporary aestheticism and pokes fun at the likes of Oscar Wilde. It was first performed in 1881.

patter song A kind of comic song which has a string of tongue-twisting syllables and is usually sung quickly to minimal accompaniment. It is often found in opera.

pausa (It.) 'Rest'.

pause A symbol over a note or rest to indicate that this should be held for longer than its written value. (See Appendix for symbol.)

pavan, pavane A stately court dance, normally in slow duple time, which was occasionally incorporated into instrumental music in the 16th cent.

Pavane pour une Infante défunte (Pavane for a dead Infanta) A piano piece by RAVEL (1899), who also wrote the orchestral version (1912). The name was chosen simply for its sonorous qualities.

Pavarotti, Luciano (1935–) An Italian tenor and one of the most famous of the modern era. He has sung in all the world's major opera houses.

pavillon (Fr.) Literally, a 'tent', so, with reference to the shape, the bell of a brass instrument.

peal A set of church bells or, as a verb, to ring a set of church bells.

Pearl-Fishers, The (*Les pêcheurs de perles*) An opera by BIZET to a libretto by E. Cormon and M. Carré. It is set in ancient Ceylon and tells how Leila, who has taken a vow of chastity, is loved by two men, Zurga and Nadir. It was first performed in 1863.

Pears, Peter (1910–86) An English tenor. He was closely associated with BRITTEN, who wrote parts with his voice in mind. He was also famed for singing pieces by BACH and SCHUBERT. He was knighted in 1978.

Pearsall, Robert Lucas de (1795–1856) A English composer who revived the polyphonic style and who is most famous for his madrigals, part-songs and religious pieces.

pedal The part of an instrument's mechanism that is operated by the feet, such as piano pedals.

Peer Gynt 1 Incidental piano music by GRIEG for the original production of Ibsen's play (1878). Grieg later arranged the work into two orchestral suites. **2** Incidental music for Ibsen's play by Saeverud. **3** An opera by EGK, who also wrote the libretto (after Ibsen) (1938).

peg-box The part of a stringed instrument which houses the pegs that anchor and tune the strings.

Pélleas et Mélisande 1 An opera by DEBUSSY based on the play by Maeterlinck. It tells the story of two lovers and a jealous husband. It was first performed in 1902. **2** Incidental music to Maeterlinck's play by FAURE (1898). **3** Incidental music to Maeterlinck's play by SIBELIUS (1905). **4** A symphonic poem by SCHOENBERG (1903).

Penderecki, Krzysztof (1933–) A Polish composer. He has experimented with all manner of unconventional sounds (for example, rustling paper, wood being sawn, clacking typewriters etc.) and has on occasion asked singers to whistle and hiss. Nevertheless, his music is easily accessible and his works have proved popular. His compositions include the operas *The Devils of Loudon* and *Paradise Lost*, pieces for chorus and orchestra (such as *St Luke Passion*), and many orchestral works.

penny-whistle *see* tin whistle.

pentatonic scale A scale composed of five notes in an octave. It is found in various types of folk music from Scottish to Chinese.

Pepusch, Johann Christoph (1667–1752) A German-born composer, conductor, organist and teacher who settled in London in 1700. He became an expert in music theory and ancient music. His works include odes, motets, masques, cantatas and he wrote the overture to John Gay's BEGGAR'S OPERA.

percussion instruments The family of instruments that produce sound when struck or shaken, for example, maracas, drums, triangle.

perdendosi (It.) 'Losing itself', i.e. dying away (of sound).

perfect interval *see* interval.

Pergolesi, Giovanni Battista (1710–36) An Italian composer, violinist and organist who became famous for his comic INTERMEZZOS, *La serva padrona* and *Livietta e Tracollo*. He also wrote church music and sonatas. Many pieces have been wrongly attributed to him.

Peri, Jacopo (1561–1633) An Italian composer and singer. He is credited with writing the music for *Eurydice* (1600), the first opera for which the complete music is extant. He wrote other operas as well as madrigals and ballets, but little of his work survives.

Perlman, Itzhak (1945–) An Israeli violinist who has been a soloist with many famous orchestras.

Pérotin (*c.*1160–1220) A French composer, one of the first to be known by name. He wrote church music and motets.

perpetuum mobile (Lat.) 'Perpetually in motion', i.e. a short piece of music with a repetitive note-pattern that is played quickly without any pauses.

pesante (It.) 'Heavy', 'ponderous' or 'solid'.

Peter and the Wolf A musical story for children told by a narrator with accompanying orchestral music by PROKOFIEV. It was first performed in 1936.

Peter Grimes An opera by BRITTEN to a libretto written by M. Slater (after George Crabbe's poem 'The Borough'). The story concerns Peter Grimes, a fisherman, who is a misfit and refuses help when he needs it.

Petrassi, Goffredo (1904–) A progressive Italian composer whose works include the operas *The Tapestry* and *Death in the Air*, ballets, and orchestral and choral pieces.

Petrushka A ballet with music by STRAVINSKY. The story concerns a puppet who comes to life. It was first performed in 1911.

Phantasie (Ger.) *see* fantasia.

philharmonic (Gr.) Literally, 'music loving'; an adjective used in the titles of many orchestras, societies etc.

Philosopher, The The nickname given to HAYDN's symphony no. 22 in E flat (1764). It may be so called because of the slow, reflective opening movement.

phrase A short melodic section of a composition, of no fixed length, although it is often four bars long.

piacere (It.) 'Pleasure', so *a piacere* means 'at [the performer's] pleasure'.

piacevole (It.) 'Pleasantly'.

piangevole (It.) 'Sadly'.

piano 1 (It.) 'Soft'. **2** The commom abbreviated form of PIANOFORTE.

piano accordion *see* accordion.

pianoforte (piano) A keyboard instrument which was invented by Bartolomeo Cristofori in Florence in 1709, and for which important works were being written by the end of the 18th cent. Most modern instruments usually have 88 keys and a compass of 7⅓ octaves, although it is possible to find larger versions. The keys operate hammers which strike strings at the back of the instrument. These strings can run vertically (upright piano) or horizontally (grand piano). Most pianos have one string for the very lowest notes, two parallel strings for the middle register notes and three strings for the highest notes. Normally, when a note is played, a damper deadens the strings when the key returns to its normal position, but a sustaining (right) pedal suspends the action of the dampers and allows the note to coninue sounding. The soft (left) pedal mutes the sound produced, either by moving the hammers closer to the strings so that their action is diminished, or by moving the hammers sideways so that only one or two strings are struck. On some pianos, a third, sostenuto pedal, allows selected notes to continue sounding while others are dampened.

pianissimo (It.) 'Very quiet'.

pibroch (Gaelic) A type of Scottish bagpipe music with the form of theme and variations.

Piccinni, Niccoló (1728–1800) An Italian composer who was also a notable opera producer. He had a famous competitive feud with GLUCK. He wrote some 120 operas including IPHIGENIE EN TAURIDE, for which settings were commissioned from both Piccinni and GLUCK, *Pénélope* and *La buona figola*.

piccolo A small flute with a pitch an octave higher than a concert flute. It is used in orchestras and military bands.

pick A common expression for plucking the strings on a guitar.

Pictures at an Exhibition A piano suite by MUSSORGSKY (1874), which represents ten pictures at a memorial exhibition of the artist V.A. Hartmann. Several composers, including RAVEL, have arranged the work for orchestra.

Pierrot Lunaire A melodrama for voice and instruments by SCHOENBERG. It is a setting of 21 poems by Albert Giraud, translated from French into German by O.E Hartleben. It was first performed in 1912.

Pijper, Willem (1894–1947) A Dutch composer, pianist and author. He is often considered to be the father of modern Dutch music and his works include three symphonies, numerous pieces of chamber music and the opera *Halewijn*.

Pilgrim's Progress, The An opera by Ralph VAUGHAN WILLIAMS, who also wrote the libretto (after Bunyan). It was first performed in 1951.

pipe A hollow cylinder in which vibrating air produces sound. On many instruments, the effective length of the pipe can be altered to produce a range of notes by means of holes that are opened or closed by the fingers.

pipe organ An American term for a real organ, as opposed to a CABINET ORGAN.

Pirates of Penzance, The A comic opera by GILBERT and SULLIVAN, subtitled 'The Slave of Duty'. It tells of how Frederic, a novice pirate, is torn between loyalty to his band and his duty as citizen. It was first performed in 1879.

Piston, Walter (1894–1976) An American composer, teacher and author who became professor of music at Harvard University in 1944. His works, in traditional tonal style, include the ballet *The Incredible Flautist*, eight symphonies and many pieces of chamber music.

pistons The valves on brass instruments that allow players to sound different notes.

pitch The height or depth of a sound that determines its position on a scale.

più (It.) 'More', so *più allegro* means 'faster'.

pizz. An abbreviation of PIZZICATO.

Pizzetti, Ildebrando (1880–1968) An Italian composer and an important academic. He is best known for his operas, for example *Deborah e Jaele*, *Vianna Lupa*, *Murder in the Cathedral*. His other works include orchestral pieces and compositions for piano.

pizzicato (It.) 'Plucked' (with specific reference to using the fingers to pluck the strings on a bowed instrument).

plainsong The collection of ancient melodies to which parts of Roman Catholic services have been sung for centuries. The best known type is the GREGORIAN CHANT. Plainsong is usually unaccompanied and sung in unison. It is also in free rhythm, i.e. it does not have bars but follows the prose rhythm of the psalm or prayer.

Planets, The A suite for orchestra, organ and female chorus by HOLST. It was first performed in 1918.

plectrum A small piece of horn, plastic or wood which is used to pluck the strings of guitars etc.

Pleyel, Ignaz Joseph (1757–1831) An Austrian pianist, violinist and composer who founded a piano-manufacturing company in Paris. His compositions, which include 29 symphonies, piano sonatas and songs, were admired by HAYDN and MOZART.

poco (It.) 'Little' or 'slightly', so *poco diminuendo* means 'getting slightly softer'.

poi (It.) 'Then', so *scherzo da capo, poi la coda* means 'repeat the scherzo, then play the coda'.

point The tip of a bow; the opposite end to the part that is held (heel).

point d'orgue (Fr.) 'Organ point'. It can indicate a harmonic pedal (a note sustained under changing harmonies); the sign for a pause; or a cadenza in a concerto.

pointillism A term borrowed from a style of late 19th-cent. painting used to describe a style of music in which notes seem to be isolated as 'dots' rather than as sequential parts of a melody. It is applied to the works of certain 20th-cent. composers, such as WEBERN.

polacca (It.) *see* polonaise.

polka A round dance in quick 2/4 time from Czecho-slovakia. It became popular throughout Europe in the mid-19th cent.

polonaise (Fr.) A stately ballroom dance of Polish origins in moderately fast 3/4 time. It was used by CHOPIN in 16 strongly patriotic piano pieces.

polyphony (Gk.) Literally, 'many sounds', i.e. a type of music in which two or more parts have independent melodic lines, arranged in COUNTERPOINT.

polytonality The use of two or more keys at the same time.

Pomp and Circumstance A set of five military marches for orchestra by ELGAR. A.C. Benson's words, 'Land of Hope and Glory', were later set to the finale of the first march for the *Coronation Ode* which was sung at Edward VII's coronation in 1902.

ponticello (It.) 'Bridge' (of a stringed instrument).

pop music Short for 'popular' music, i.e. 20th-cent. music specifically composed to have instant appeal to young people. There are many types of pop music, with influences ranging from jazz and folk to rock and reggae.

Porgy and Bess An opera by GERSHWIN to a libretto by D. Hayward and Ira Gershwin. It tells the story of a crippled man, Porgy, who longs for Bess but cannot have her because she belongs to a dock worker. It was first performed in 1935 with an all-Black cast.

portamento (It.) Literally, 'carrying'; an effect used in singing or on bowed instruments in which sound is smoothly 'carried' or slid from one note to the next without a break.

Porter, Cole (1892–1965) An American composer of musical shows famous for the numerous popular songs – often with extremely witty lyrics – which they contained. His shows include *Kiss me Kate* and *Anything Goes.*

position A term used in the playing of stringed instruments for where the left hand should be placed so that the fingers can play different sets of notes; for example, first position has the hand near the end of the strings, second position is slightly further along the finger-board.

posthorn A simple (valveless) brass instrument similar to a bugle, but usually coiled in a circular form.

postlude The closing section of a composition.

pot-pourri (Fr.) A medley of well-known tunes played at a concert.

Poulenc, Francis (1899–1963) A French composer and pianist who became a member of the group known as *Les* SIX. He was influenced by SATIE and was friendly with the poets Cocteau and Apollinaire, some of whose works he set to music. His early works were witty and often satirical, while his later pieces were more serious. His works include the operas *Les Mamelles de Tirésias* and *Dialogues des Carmélites*, ballets (such as *Les Biches*), concertos, chamber music, choral works, and compositions for piano.

pp (PP) An abbreviation for PIANISSIMO, very soft; *ppp* means even softer.

'Prague' Symphony The nickname for MOZART's symphony no. 38 in D. It is so called because it was first performed in Prague in 1787. It is unusual in that it only has three (and not the more usual four) movements.

precentor The official in charge of music, or the leader of the singing, at a cathedral, monastery, etc.

precipitato, precipitoso (It.) 'Precipitately', hence also impetuously.

prelude An introductory piece of music or a self-contained piano piece in one movement.

Prélude à l'après-midi d'un faune (Prelude to the 'Afternoon of a Faun') An orchestral piece by DEBUSSY to illustrate the poem by Mallarmé. It was first performed in 1894. Nijinsky later based a ballet on the piece.

Préludes, Les A symphonic poem by LISZT which was inspired by Lamartine's work *Nouvelles Méditations poétiques*. It was first performed in 1894.

presto (It.) 'Lively'; *prestissimo* indicates the fastest speed of which a performer is capable.

Previn, André (1929–) A German-born conductor, pianist and composer who has done much to make serious music more accessible to the public at large. He moved to the USA at the start of the Second World War and composed film music for which he won four Oscars. He also became a highly respected jazz pianist. He has conducted many of the world's leading orchestras and his compositions include concertos for violin, sitar and guitar, and many pieces for piano.

prima donna (It.) The 'first lady', i.e. the most important female singer in an opera.

primo (It.) 'First', as the first or top part of a piano duet (the lower part being termed *secondo*, second).

Prince Igor An unfinished opera by BORODIN, who also wrote the libretto (it was later finished by RIMSKY-KORSAKOV and GLAZUNOV). It tells the story of Prince

Igor who gets captured by the Polovtsians but escapes. It was first performed in 1890.

Princess Ida A comic opera by GILBERT and SULLIVAN which has the subtitle 'Castle Adamant'). It tells the story of Princess Ida who starts a women's university. It was first performed in 1884.

principal 1 The leader of a section of an orchestra (for example, principal horn). **2** A singer who takes leading parts in an opera company, but not the main ones (for example, a principal tenor).

principal subject The first subject in a SONATA FORM or a RONDO.

Prix de Rome (Fr.) An annual prize awarded by the French Government to artists of various disciplines (including music) who were sent to study in Rome for four years. BERLIOZ, GOUNOD, BIZET and DEBUSSY were all winners, but RAVEL failed after many attempts. It was first awarded in 1803, and was discontinued in 1968.

programme music Music which attempts to tell a story or evoke an image. The term was first used by LISZT to describe his symphonic poems. Parts of BEETHOVEN'S PASTORAL SYMPHONY can be described as programme music.

Prokofiev, Sergey Sergeyvich (1891–1953) A Russian composer whose mother was a pianist. She encouraged her young son's obvious talents and he composed his first opera when he was nine. He studied under RIMSKY-KORSAKOV and soon became known as a modernist composer. After the Revolution he left Russia and travelled all over the world, living in

London, Paris, Japan and the USA at various times. He returned to the Soviet Union in 1934 and lived in Moscow until his death.

Prokofiev's early works were marked by violent rhythms and dissonant sounds but when he returned to Moscow his compositions mellowed; his music was not much liked by the Soviet authorities. His principal compositions include: the operas *Magdalen*, *The Gambler*, LOVE OF THREE ORANGES, *Betrothal in a Monastery* and *War and Peace*; the ballets *Romeo and Juliet* and *Cinderella*; 7 symphonies; choral pieces; and the children's (instructional) entertainment, PETER AND THE WOLF, for narrator and orchestra.

Promenade Concerts An annual season of concerts given in London's Royal Albert Hall. The 'Proms' were instituted in 1895 by Robert Newman and were conducted until 1944 by Sir Henry Wood. Cheap tickets are available for standing-room; people do not, however, walk about. Several cities around the world (such as Boston, Mass.) have similar concert seasons.

Prometheus 1 A ballet with music by BEETHOVEN (1800). **2** A symphonic poem by LISZT (1850). **3** A tone poem for orchestra by SKYRABIN (1819). **4** The title of song settings of Goethe's poem by SCHUBERT, WOLF and others.

psalm A poem (song) in the Old Testament's Book of Psalms.

psalmody The singing of psalms to music or the musical setting of a psalm.

psalter A book of psalms and psalm-tunes.

psaltery A medieval stringed instrument, similar to the

DULCIMER except that the strings are plucked and not struck. It is usually trapezium-shaped and is usually played horizontally.

Puccini, Giacomo Antonio Domenico Michele Secondo Maria (1858–1924) An Italian opera composer who came from a musical family. His works are often considered more superficial than his illustrious predecessor, VERDI, but his dramatic flair and talent for melody and orchestration have made many of his operas perennial favourites. His main works include: LA BOHEME, TOSCA, MADAM BUTTERFLY, TURANDOT, MANON LESCAUT and *Edgar*.

pulse *see* beat.

Pult (Ger.) 'Desk', i.e. the music stand that two orchestral players share.

punta (It.) 'Point'; so *a punta d'arco* means 'at the point of the bow', indicating that only the tip of the bow should be used to play the strings.

Purcell, Henry (1659–95) An English composer and organist who started his musical career as a choirboy. In 1677 he was appointed 'composer to the King's violins'. He became the organist at Wesminster Abbey in 1679 and started to publish works that he wrote for pleasure rather than for a patron. He particularly excelled at writing music for stage plays; in all, he wrote incidental music to some 40 stage productions. By the time he died, he was recognized as being one of the most important of all English composers and his works are still appreciated to this day for their brilliant originality. His principal compositions include: the opera DIDO AND AENEAS; music for plays *King Arthur*,

The Fairy Queen, *The Indian Queen* and *The Tempest*;
odes (17 for the royal family, four for St Cecilia's day);
numerous songs and cantatas; chamber music; and
many keyboard pieces. His brother, Daniel, was also
an able musician. He, too, wrote music for the theatre
in addition to odes and songs.

Q

quadrille A French dance that was particularly fashionable in the early 19th cent. It comprised five sections in
alternating 6/8 and 2/4 time.

quadruplet A group of four notes of equal value played
in the time of three.

quadruple time (common time) The time of four
crotchets (quarter notes) in a bar; it is indicated by the
time-signature 4/4 or C.

Quantz, Johann Joachim (1697–1773) A German composer and flautist. He was a virtuoso performer and
after touring Europe he entered the service of
Frederick the Great, who recognized his talent. He
composed some 300 flute concertos and many other
works for the instrument. He also wrote an important
treatise on flute playing.

quarter note (US) *see* crotchet

quarter tone Half a semitone, which is the smallest
interval traditionally used in Western music.

quartet A group of four performers or a composition
for such a group.

quasi (It.) Literally, 'as if' or 'nearly'; so *quasi niente* means 'almost nothing', or as softly as possible.

quaver A note which is half the length of a crotchet and the eighth of a semibreve (whole note).

Queen of France, The The nickname given to HAYDN's symphony no. 85 in B flat (1785). It is supposed to have been a favourite of Marie Antoinette.

Quilter, Roger (1877–1953) An English composer who studied in Germany for a time. He is best known for his songs. His work also includes the light opera *Julia*, and the orchestral work *A Children's Overture*.

quintet A group of five performers, or a piece of music for such a group.

quintuple time Five beats, usually crotchets, in a bar, i.e. 5/4 time.

quodlibet (Lat.) 'What you will'; a term used to describe a collection of tunes that are cleverly woven together to create an amusing entertainment.

R

Rachmaninov, Sergei Vassilievich (1873–1943) A Russian composer and pianist. He established himself as a virtuoso pianist from an early age and after graduating from the Moscow conservatory, he embarked upon a series of concert tours. As well as playing the piano, he also conducted and composed; his early works were influenced by TCHAIKOVSKY. After the Revolution, he left Russia and emigrated to the USA. Rachmaninov was essentially a romantic and many of his works express a powerful emotional energy. His principal compositions include: 3 operas (such as *The Miserly Knight*); 3 symphonies; pieces for piano and orchestra (such as *Rhapsody on a theme by Paganini*); choral pieces; numerous piano pieces; and songs.

racket (rackett, ranket) A woodwind instrument with a double reed used between the late 16th and early 18th cents. It came in four sizes (soprano, tenor, bass, double bass) and created a distinctive buzzing sound.

raga A type of Indian scale or a type of melody based on such a scale. Each raga is associated with a mood and with particular times of the day and year.

rag A piece of RAGTIME music, notably as developed by Scott JOPLIN.

ragtime A style of syncopated popular dance music, dating from the late 19th cent. The combination of ragtime and the BLUES led to the development of jazz. Scott JOPLIN was a famous ragtime piano player.

'Raindrop' Prelude The nickname for CHOPIN's piano prelude in D flat. It is so called because the repeated note A flat resembles the sound of raindrops.

Rainier, Priaulx (1903–1986) A South African composer and violinist who won a scholarship to study in England and remained there for the rest of her life. Her works include orchestral pieces (e.g. *Sinfonia da Camera*), chamber music, compositions for piano, and many songs.

Rake's Progress, The An opera by STRAVINSKY to a libretto by W.H. Auden and C. Kallman. The story is derived from a series of Hogarth paintings. It was first performed in 1951.

Rakhmaninov *see* Rachmaninov, Sergei.

rallentando (It.) 'Slowing down'.

Rameau, Jean Philippe (1683–1764) A French composer, organist and harpsichordist. He spent the greater part of his early life as an organist in various major cities in France. However, during this period, he published an several influential textbook, the *Traité de l'harmonie*, and composed motets and cantatas. When he was 50, he started to write operas with Voltaire contributing several libretti. His major compositions include the operas *Hippolyte et Aricie*, *Castor et Pollux* and *Dardanus*; the opera-ballets *Les Indes galantes* and *Les Fêtes d'Hébé*; pieces of chamber music; church music and trio sonatas; and works for harpsichord.

rap A term for an influential type of pop music of the late 20th cent. which has a pulsating rhythm, and in which lyrics for songs are usually spoken to the beat and not sung.

Rape of Lucretia, The A chamber opera by BRITTEN to a libretto by R. Duncan (after Obey's play *Le Viol de Lucrèce*). The story is set in ancient Rome and tells the tragic tale of Lucretia, who killed herself after being raped by Tarquin. It was first performed in 1946.

rattle A type of percussion instrument which traditionally consists of a hollowed out gourd filled with seeds which rattle when shaken. An alternative type of rattle is a contraption in which a strip of wood, held in a frame, strikes against a cog-wheel as the frame is twirled round. It is occasionally required as a percussion instrument in orchestras.

Rattle, Simon (1955–) An English conductor of international standing and principal conductor of the City of Birmingham Symphony Orchestra. He is especially noted for his interpretation of 20th-cent. music

Ravel, Maurice (1875–1937) A French composer and pianist. He was born in the Basque region of the South of France but was brought up in Paris. By the time he was 20, he had evolved his own style of composition but his unconventional harmonies were not well liked by traditional academicians and he failed four times to win the coveted PRIX DE ROME. Ravel was labelled an 'impressionist' early in his career, but later he drew on many different sources (such as jazz, folk music, Eastern music) while at the same time being influenced by the works of LISZT and RIMSKY-KORSAKOV. As well as being a versatile and talented composer for the piano, he was also a master of orchestration. His principal works include: the ballets DAPHNIS ET CHLOE and MA MERE L'OYE; the operas *L'Heure espagnole*, *L'Enfant et les sortilèges*; pieces for orchestra (such as *Bolero*); chamber music; many pieces for piano; and numerous songs.

Ravenscroft, Thomas (*c*.1590–*c*.1633) An English composer and publisher of many collections of rounds, catches, canons and popular songs of the time. He also composed instrumental works.

Rawsthorne, Alan (1905–71) An English composer and pianist who was trained as a dentist before turning to music. His works include 3 symphonies, 2 piano concertos, 3 string quartets, pieces of chamber music, and many songs.

Razor Quartet The name given to HAYDN's string quartet in F minor and major (published 1789). The story goes that when Haydn was visited by the English music publisher, John Bland, he said he would give his 'best quartet for a good razor'. When Bland obliged, Haydn repaid him with a quartet.

re (ray) In the TONIC SOL-FA, the second note of the major scale.

rebec (rebeck) A small instrument with a pear-shaped body and usually three strings, which were played with a bow. It developed from the Arabian *rebâb* and was used in Europe from the 16th cent.

rebop *see* bebop.

recapitulation *see* sonata form.

recit. An abbreviation of RECITANDO or RECITATIVE.

recital A public concert given by just one or two people, e.g. a singer with piano accompaniment.

recitando (It.) 'Reciting', i.e. speaking rather than singing.

recitative A way of singing (usually on a fixed note) in which the rhythm and lilt is taken from the words and there is no tune as such. It is commonly used in opera and oratorio.

reciting note In PLAINSONG, the note on which the first few words of each verse of a psalm are sung.

recorder A straight, end-blown flute, as opposed to a side-blown (concert) flute. Notes can be played by opening or closing eight holes in the instrument with the fingers. Recorders come in consorts (families): descant, treble, tenor and bass.

reed The small part found in many blown instruments

that vibrates when air is blown across it and actually creates the sound. It is usually made of cane or metal. In single-reed instruments (for example, clarinet, saxophone), the reed vibrates against the instrument itself; in double-reed instruments (for example, cor anglais, bassoon), two reeds vibrate against each other; in free-reed instruments (for example, harmonium, concertina), a metal reed vibrates freely within a slot.

reed-organ The generic term for a number of instruments which have no pipes and use free reeds to produce their notes. Examples are the accordion and the harmonium.

reed-pipe An organ pipe with a metal reed in the mouthpiece which vibrates when air is passed over it.

reel A Celtic dance, usually in quick 4/4 time and in regular four-bar phrases.

'Reformation' Symphony The title given by MENDELSSOHN to his symphony no. 5 in D (1830). It was composed for the tercentenary of Luther's founding of the German Reformed Church at Augsburg. However, it was not performed then because of opposition from the Roman Catholic Church.

regal A portable REED-ORGAN of the 16th and 17th cents.

Reger, Max (1873–1916) A German composer, pianist, organist, conductor and teacher. He was opposed to PROGRAMME MUSIC and claimed to be a progressive composer, while in fact he was musically a conservative. He was an undoubted master at developing

COUNTERPOINT and complex harmonies. He made a name for himself as an organist while touring Europe and Russia. His works include many pieces for organ and piano, several orchestral pieces, and compositions for chamber orchestra.

reggae A type of Jamaican pop music with a heavy and pronounced rhythm and strongly accented upbeat.

register 1 A set of organ pipes which are controlled by a single stop. **2** A part of a singer's vocal COMPASS, e.g. chest register, head register etc. The term is also applied to certain instruments, for example, the Chalumeau register of the clarinet.

Reich, Steve (1936–) An American composer, a pupil of MILHAUD, whose work is marked by the use of repetition progressing through gradual change, and shows the influence of non-European music. His compositions include *Music for Eighteen Musicians* and *Music for Large Ensemble*.

Reinhardt, Jean-Baptiste ('Django') (1910–53) A Belgian jazz guitarist of gypsy origin who, with Stephane GRAPELLI, led the quintet the Hot Club de France (1934–9). He lost the use of two fingers in a fire when aged 18, which caused him to develop his highly individual technique and style.

related keys *see* modulation.

relative major, relative minor Terms used to describe the connection between a major key and a minor key that share the same key signature, for example A minor is the relative key of C major.

répétiteur (Fr.) A person hired to teach musicians or singers, particularly opera singers, their parts.

replica (It.) 'Repeat', so *senza replica* means 'without repetition'.

reprise A musical repetition; it is often found in musical comedies when songs heard in one act are repeated in another.

Requiem A Mass for the dead in the Roman Catholic Church, so called because of the opening words *Requiem aeternam dona eis, Domine* (Grant them eternal rest, O Lord).

resolution A term for a process in harmony by which a piece moves from discord to concord.

Respighi, Ottorino (1879–1936) An Italian composer, violinist, conductor, pianist and teacher. He studied composition with RIMSKY-KORSAKOV, who influenced him greatly, and then taught composition himself in Rome. His works include operas (such as *Belfagor*); a ballet (*La Boutique fantastique*, which was adapted from music by ROSSINI); orchestral compositions, notably *The Fountains of Rome* and *The Pines of Rome*; and pieces for voice and orchestra.

responses The plainsong replies of a choir or congregation to solo chants sung by a priest.

'Resurrection' Symphony The nickname for MAHLER's symphony no. 2 (1894). It is so called because it ends with a choral setting of Klopstock's poem '*Auferstehen*' which means 'resurrection'.

rest A silence.

resultant tone *see* combination tone.

retardation A SUSPENSION in which a discordant note is resolved upwards by one step rather than downwards.

retrograde motion A term for music that is played backwards.

Reubke, Julius (1834–58) A German pianist and composer who studied under LISZT. He is best known for his organ sonata *The Ninety-fourth Psalm*.

reveille (pronounced 'revally') A bugle call used by the British Army to awaken soldiers.

'Revolutionary' Étude The nickname for CHOPIN's étude in C minor. He wrote the piece when he heard that Warsaw had been invaded by the Russians.

Reznìček, Emil Nikolaus von (1860–1945) An Austrian composer and conductor who worked in Germany. His works include operas (for example, *Donna Diana*, *Till Eulenspiegel*), 4 symphonies, choral pieces, and many songs.

rf, rfz Abbreviations for RINFORZANDO.

R.H. Abbrev. for 'right hand'.

rhapsody The title commonly given by 19th and 20th cent. composers to an instrumental composition in one continuous movement. Rhapsodies are often based on folk tunes, and are nationalistic or heroic in tone.

Rhapsody in Blue A work for piano and orchestra by GERSHWIN. It was the first 'serious' work to include jazz idioms and was first performed in 1924.

Rheingold, Das *see* Ring des Nibelungen, Der.

'Rhenish' Symphony The name given to SCHUMANN's symphony no. 3 in E (1850) because it was composed after he visited Cologne on the River Rhine.

rhythm The aspect of music that is concerned with time. In notation, rhythm is determined by the way in

219

which notes are grouped together into bars, the number and type of beats in a bar (as governed by the time signature), and the type of emphasis (accent) that is given to the beats. Along with melody and harmony, it is one of the essential characteristics of music.

rhythm and blues A type of popular music that combines elements of blues and jazz. It developed in the USA and was widely accepted by white audiences and pop musicians. ROCK 'N' ROLL evolved from rhythm and blues.

rhythm-names *see* time-names.

rhythm section The name given to the percussion and double bass section of a jazz band; it provides the all-important beat.

rigaudon (rigadoon) A jaunty dance from the South of France that has two or four beats to the bar. It was used in French ballets and operas, and it became popular in England in the late 17th cent.

Rigoletto An opera by VERDI to a libretto by F.M. Piave (based on Victor Hugo's play *Le Roi s'amuse*). It tells the story of Rigoletto, a hunch-backed jester at the court of the Duke of Mantua, who unwittingly has his daughter, Gilda, killed instead of her lover, the Duke. It contains possibly the most famous of all operatic arias, 'La donna è mobile'.

rigoroso (It.) 'Rigorously', i.e. in exact time.

Riley, Terry (1935–) An American composer and saxophonist. He is best known for his unconventional compositions which only take on a comprehensible form during rehearsals. He usually performs his own works and uses assorted electronic equipment. His works include *Poppy Nogood and the Phantom Band* and *Rainbow in Curved Air*.

Rimsky-Korsakov, Nikolay Andreyevich (1844–1908) An influential Russian composer. He was born into a wealthy family who gave him a conventional education. He joined the Russian Navy for a time but became increasingly interested in music. He was encouraged by BALAKIREV to write a symphony which was first performed in 1865. Thereafter, he took composing seriously and became a leading member of the group known as 'THE FIVE'. He was also made a professor of music at the St Petersburg Conservatory, a post that he held until his death, apart from a short period when he supported the 1905 revolution.

Rimsky-Korsakov's music is typically Russian and he freely used local history, folk tunes, legends and myths as sources of inspiration. His principal compositions include: 16 operas (for example, *The* SNOW MAIDEN, *The Tsar's Bride*, *The Golden Cockerel*; 3 symphonies; numerous orchestral pieces (such as SHEHERAZADE); many pieces for chamber orchestra; and over 80 songs. He also wrote an autobiography, *My Musical Life*.

rinforzando (It.) Literally, 'reinforcing', i.e. a sudden strong accent on a note or chord.

Ring des Nibelungen, Der (The Ring of the Nibelung) A cycle of four operas by WAGNER, who also wrote the libretti. The operas are: *Das Rheingold* (The Rhine Gold), *Die Walküre* (The Valkyrie), *Siegfried* and *Götterdämmerung* (Twilight of the Gods). The story told in the operas is based upon a convoluted Norse myth concerning the conflict between power and love. The entire cycle was first performed in 1876.

ripieno (It.) Literally, 'full'; a term used to describe passages that are to be played by the whole Baroque orchestra, rather than only a soloist.

Rise and Fall of the City of Mahagonny, The An opera by Kurt WEILL to a libretto by Bertolt Brecht. It is a biting satire on capitalism and was first performed in 1930.

risoluto (It.) 'Resolute' or 'in a resolute manner'.

rit. An abbreviation of RITARDANDO.

ritardando (It.) 'Becoming gradually slower'.

ritenuto (It.) 'Held back' (in tempo), i.e. slower.

Rite of Spring, The (*Le Sacre du printemps*) A ballet with music by STRAVINSKY. It concerns the sacrifice of a virgin. When it was first performed in 1913, it caused an uproar, as much for the strident music as for the story line.

ritmo, ritmico 'Rhythm, rhythmic'.

ritornello (It.) Literally, a 'small repetition'. **1** A short passage for the whole orchestra in a Baroque aria or concerto, during which the soloist is silent. **2** A short instrumental piece, played between scenes in early opera.

rock A type of pop music that evolved from ROCK 'N' ROLL in the USA during the 1960s. It mixes COUNTRY AND WESTERN with RHYTHM AND BLUES and is usually played loudly on electric instruments. Revered exponents include bands such as the Rolling Stones and the Who.

rock 'n' roll A type of pop music, with a strong, catchy rhythm, that evolved in the USA during the 1950s and is often associated with 'jiving' (fast dancing that requires nimble footwork). Chuck Berry, Little Richard and Elvis Presley were some of its greatest early exponents.

rococo The highly decorative, florid style of architecture and painting typical of the 18th cent. Music from the same period is sometimes similarly termed.

Rodgers, Richard (1902–80) An American composer of musicals. With Lorenz Hart as his librettist, he created such shows as *The Boys from Syracuse* and *Pal Joey*; with Oscar HAMMERSTEIN as librettist, he wrote *Oklahoma* and *South Pacific*, both of which were turned into memorable films.

Rodrigo, Joaquin (1902–) A Spanish composer who was blind from the age of three but composed many outstanding works, such as *Concierto de Aranjuez* (for guitar and orchestra) and *Concierto heroico* (for piano and orchestra).

Roman, Johan Helmich (1694–1758) A Swedish composer. He initially made a name for himself as an oboe player and violinist but, after studying in England, turned to composition. He is often referred to as the 'father of Swedish music' and he wrote some 20 symphonies and many violin and piano sonatas.

romantic music Music dating from the so-called Romantic Era, i.e. *c.*1820–*c.*1920. During this phase music tended to be more poetic, subjective and individualistic than in the previous 'Classical Era'. Lyricism, drama and often nationalistic feeling were characteristic of romantic music.

Romberg, Andreas Jakob (1767–1821) A German violinist and composer. His works include operas, choral works and symphonies. His cousin, Bernhard, also became a notable composer.

Rondine, La (The Swallow) A comic opera by PUCCINI to a libretto by G. Adami. It was first performed in 1917.

rondo A form of instrumental music which incorporates a recurring theme, either in an independent piece or (more usually) as part of a movement. It usually starts with a lively tune (the 'subject'), which is repeated at intervals throughout the movement. Intervening sections are called EPISODES and these may or may not be in different keys from the subject. Rondo forms often occur in the final movements of symphonies, sonatas and concertos.

root The lowest ('fundamental' or 'generating') note of a chord. Hence, for example, the chord C-E-G has a root of C.

Rosenkavalier, Der (The Knight of the Rose) An opera by Richard STRAUSS to a libretto by Hugo von Hofmannsthal. The story concerns the love life of Octavian (the Rosenkavalier), the bearer of a love token. It was first performed in 1911.

rosin A hard resin that is applied to the hair of bows used to play violins etc. It causes increased friction between the hairs of the bow and the strings.

Rossini, Gioacchino Antonio (1792–1868) An Italian composer both of whose parents were musical. He wrote his first opera, *La Cambiale di matrimono* (The Marriage Contract) in 1810. In 1815 he went to

Naples, where he composed some of his greatest operas, including OTELLO and *La Cenerentola*. In 1823 he elected to live in Paris where he became director of the Théâtre Italien. He went back to Italy in 1830, but returned to Paris before his death. His major works were operas (38 in all) which include *The Italian Girl in Algiers*, *The* BARBER OF SEVILLE, WILLIAM TELL and *The* THIEVING MAGPIE. However, he also wrote songs, piano pieces and instrumental quartets.

Rostropovich, Mstislav Leopoldovich (1927–) A Russian cellist and pianist. He was possibly the greatest cellist of the 20th cent. and many composers, notably PROKOFIEV, BRITTEN and SHOSTAKOVICH, wrote pieces for him. He is also a conductor of international repute.

Rouget de Lisle, Claude Joseph (1760–1836) A French royalist soldier and composer who is best remembered for writing the words and music for the MARSEILLAISE.

round *see* canon.

round dance A dance in which partners start opposite each other and subsequently form a ring.

Roussel, Albert (1869–1937) A French composer who was influenced by Chinese and Indian music. His highly individualistic works include four symphonies, the opera-ballet *Padmâvati*), ballets (such as *Bacchus and Ariadne*), chamber music, and many songs.

Royal Albert Hall A purpose-built, domed concert hall in central London at the southern edge of Hyde Park, renowned for its good acoustics. Conceived by Prince Albert, it was built in his memory following his death in 1861, and was opened in 1871.

Royal Festival Hall A concert hall in London which was opened in 1951 as part of the Festival of Britain.

rubato (It.) Literally, 'robbed', i.e. the taking of time from one note or passage and passing it on to another note or passage.

Rubbra, (Charles) Edmund (1901–86) An English composer who studied under VAUGHAN WILLIAMS and HOLST. His works include 10 symphonies, concertos, Masses, motets, and modern-day madrigals.

Rubinstein, Anton Gregoryevich (1821–94) A Russian virtuoso pianist and composer who flew against the wind by composing Western as opposed to Russian (nationalistic) music. Most of his works have not survived the test of time, but his songs and piano pieces are still occasionally performed.

Rubinstein, Artur (1887–1982) A Polish-born pianist who became an American citizen in 1946. He was one of greatest interpreters of piano music of the 20th cent. and was especially noted for his performance of works by BRAHMS, CHOPIN, BEETHOVEN, SCHUBERT and SCHUMANN.

Ruddigore A comic opera by GILBERT and SULLIVAN, subtitled 'The Witch's Curse'. It parodies of Victorian melodrama, and was first performed in 1887.

Ruggles, Carl (1876–1971) An American composer and painter who experimented with various forms of music and helped to establish an 'American' style of 'modern' composition. His works include *Angels* (for muted trumpets and trombones), and various pieces for assorted intruments. *Sun-Treader* is his most notable work.

Rule Britannia A patriotic English song with words (possibly) by James Thomson and music by ARNE, first performed in a MASQUE called *Alfred* in 1740.

rumba A sexually suggestive and fast Afro-Cuban dance in syncopated 2/4 time.

Russian Quartets The title given to a set of six string quartets by HAYDN (1781), who dedicated them to Grand Duke Paul of Russia.

S

sackbut An instrument of the 15th cent., similar to the TROMBONE, but smaller.

Sacre du Printemps, Le *see* Rite of Spring, The.

Sadler's Wells A theatre in London, dating originally from the 17th cent., which was famed for its opera, ballet and dance companies. The opera company became the English National Opera in 1974.

'St Anthony' Variation A work by BRAHMS, (in two forms, for orchestra and for two pianos), first performed in 1873. It is also known as *Variations on a Theme by Haydn* (the 'St Anthony' Chorale).

St John Passion The accepted name for BACH's *Passion according to St John*, a setting of the Passion for solo voices, chorus and orchestra. It was first performed in 1723.

St Matthew Passion The accepted name for BACH's *Passion according to St Matthew*, a large-scale setting of the Passion for solo voices, chorus and orchestra. It was first performed in 1729.

Saint-Saëns, Charles Camille (1835–1921) A French composer and pianist who gave his first recital when aged 10. He was a prolific composer but his works have often been written off as superficial, despite their popularity. His output includes operas (e.g. SAMSON AND DELILAH), several symphonies, pieces for piano duet and orchestra (such as CARNIVAL OF ANIMALS), and many works for individual piano.

Saite (Ger.) A 'string'.

Salieri, Antonio (1750–1825) An Italian composer, conductor and teacher. He taught BEETHOVEN, LISZT and SCHUBERT at various times but is, rightly or wrongly, more often remembered for his jealousy of MOZART. His works include some 40 operas, and many pieces of church and piano music.

Salome An opera by Richard STRAUSS with a libretto taken from a translation of Oscar Wilde's drama. It was first performed in 1910.

Salomon, Johann Peter (1745–1815) A German-born violinist and composer who settled in England. He became an influential advocate of HAYDN and MOZART. He organized Haydn's visits to England and commissioned several works from the great composer, whose London Symphonies are sometimes called the 'Salomon' Symphonies. He was a notable concert promoter.

saltando (It.) Literally, 'leaping', i.e. an instruction to the string player to bounce the bow lightly off the string.

saltarello A festive Italian folk dance in 3/4 or 6/8 time.

Salvatore, Carlo *see* Cherubini, (Maria) Luigi.

Salzburg Festival An annual festival of music and drama, established in 1920 to celebrate the works of MOZART (who was born in Salzburg). Today many other composers' works are also performed.

samba A Brazilian carnival dance, in 2/4 time but with syncopated rhythms.

samisen *see* shamisen.

Sammartini (San Martini), Giovanni Battista (*c.*1698–1775) An important Italian composer and organist who may have instructed GLUCK. He composed a large body of work, including operas, symphonies, violin concertos, and over 200 chamber works. His brother, Giuseppe, was also a famous composer of the time.

Samson and Delilah (*Samson et Dalila*) An opera by SAINT-SAENS to a libretto by F. Lemaire. It retells the biblical story and was first performed in 1877.

sämtlich (Ger.) 'Complete', as in *sämtliche Werke*, the 'complete works'.

San Carlo, Teatro di One of Italy's leading opera houses, in Naples. It was built in 1737.

Sanctus (Lat.) 'Holy, holy, holy'; a part of the ordinary of Mass in the Roman Catholic Church. It has been set to music by many composers.

Sándor, György (1912–) A Hungarian-born pianist who has lived in the USA since 1939. He specializes in performing works by BARTOK and PROKOFIEV.

sarabande (Fr.) A slow dance in 3/2 or 3/4 time which came to Italy from Spain.

Sargent, (Harold) Malcolm (Watts) (1895–1967) An immensely popular English conductor who began as a pianist and composer. He will always be remembered for his performances as conductor-in-chief of the London PROMENADE CONCERTS for 16 years. He was knighted in 1947.

Satie, Erik Alfred Leslie (1866–1925) A French composer and pianist whose mother was Scottish. For a time he worked as a café pianist. He became an accepted member of Parisian 'Left Bank' society, and met DEBUSSY, Picasso, Cocteau and Diaghilev. He was regarded with some suspicion by contemporary critics, being at once witty and serious – characteristics reflected in his compositions, which include three ballets (e.g. *Parade*), operettas, and many piano pieces, often with ironic titles.

Satz (Ger.) A 'movement' or 'piece of music'.

sautillé (Fr.) *see* saltando.

Sax, Adolphe (1814–94) A Belgian instrument maker who invented the SAXOPHONE and SAXHORN.

saxhorn A family of bugle-like brass instruments patented by Adolphe SAX in 1845. They were innovative in that they had valves, as opposed to the keys normally associated with the bugle family.

saxophone A family of instruments patented by Adolphe SAX in 1846 which, although made of brass, actually belong to the WOODWIND group because they are REED instruments. Saxophones come in many different sizes (e.g. soprano, tenor) and are commonly used in jazz bands as well as orchestras.

Scala, La (Teatro alla Scala) Milan's, and Italy's, premier opera house, which was opened in 1778.

Scala di Seta, La *see* Silken Ladder, The.

230

scales An ordered sequence of notes that ascend or descend in pitch. The most frequently used scales in European music are the 'major' and 'minor' scales, which use tones (whole notes) and semitones (half-notes) as steps of progression.

Scarlatti, Alessandro (1660–1725) An Italian composer who was instrumental in developing opera when it was in its formative years. In all he composed some 115 operas (e.g. *Mitridate Eupatore*) of which only 70 or so survive. He also wrote 150 oratorios and hundreds of cantatas. Although few of his pieces are performed today, virtually all operas owe something to his inspiring inventiveness.

Scarlatti, (Guiseppe) Domenico (1685–1757) An Italian composer and harpsichordist who was the son of Alessandro SCARLATTI. He devised new techniques of playing keyboard instruments and was as influential as his father. He wrote some 550 pieces (*essercizi*) for the harpsichord.

scat singing A type of singing used in jazz in which nonsense sounds rather than words are sung.

scherzetto (It.) A short SCHERZO.

scherzo (It.) Literally, a 'joke', i.e. a cheerful, quick piece of music, either vocal or instrumental. The third movement (of four) in many symphonies, sonatas etc. often takes the form of a scherzo.

Schmidt, Franz (1874–1939) An Austrian composer, cellist, organist and pianist. His works include two operas, the oratorio *The Book of the Seven Seals*, four symphonies, and chamber music.

schnell (Ger.) 'Quick'.

231

Schoenberg, Arnold (1874–1951) An Austrian composer who was one of the most influential of the 20th cent. Although he learned the violin as a child, he was largely self-taught as a composer. His early works were influenced by BRAHMS and WAGNER. Between the turn of the century and 1920 he taught music in both Berlin and Vienna but continued to compose in an increasingly experimental and 'expressionistic' style. By 1910 he had (temporarily) abandoned the use of key signatures and was interested in exploring the most fundamental basics of music. In the mid-1920s he perfected the concept of TWELVE-NOTE MUSIC, which gave him more freedom to manoeuvre when composing. In 1933 he fled from the Nazi regime (he was Jewish) and emigrated to the USA, where he continued to teach. During this phase of his life he returned to more traditional forms of music but continued to pour out compositions as fruitfully as ever.

Schoenberg's lyrical yet complex music was not always popular (it still is not universally appreciated), but few would deny his influence; he explored the boundaries of serious music and created a wake in which others (e.g. WEBERN) followed. His principal compositions include: the monodrama *Erwartung*, for soprano and orchestra; the operas *Die glückliche Hand*, *Von Heute auf Morgen* and *Moses und Aron* (unfinished); orchestral works (such as *Pelleas und Melisande*); piano and violin concertos; chamber music; and many vocal works, including PIERROT LUNAIRE for SPRECHGESANG.

Schottische (Ger.) Literally, 'Scottish'; a round dance, similar to the POLKA, that was popular in the 19th cent. It is not in fact Scottish, but is so called because it is what those on the Continent thought a Scottish dance should be like.

Schrammel quartet A Viennese ensemble usually comprising two violins, a guitar and an accordion, or the music composed for such an ensemble. It takes its name from Joseph Schrammel (1850–93), who wrote waltzes for such a group.

Schreker, Franz (1878–1934) An Austrian avantegarde composer and conductor whose works include operas (e.g. *Der ferne Klang*), orchestral pieces, and songs.

Schubert, Franz Peter (1797–1828) An Austrian composer who was the son of a musically-minded school teacher. He learned the piano, organ and violin and became a chorister at the Imperial Chapel in Vienna. He composed his first songs when he was 14 and received composition lessons from SALIERI after leaving school at the age of 16. After teaching for four years in his father's school he devoted his life to music. He lived a Bohemian lifestyle in Vienna, living largely off the generosity of friends. In 1822 he caught syphilis. He died of typhoid at the age of 31.

Schubert is famous for his songs, some 600 in all, but he also composed operas (e.g. *Alfonso and Estrella*), nine symphonies (including the GREAT C MAJOR SYMPHONY and the 'UNFINISHED' SYMPHONY), chamber music (including the TROUT QUINTET), piano music, and Masses.

Schuman, William Howard (1910–) An American composer of distinctively American music. His works include nine symphonies, concertos for piano and violin, ballets, and the opera *The Mighty Casey*, which is about a baseball player.

Schumann, Clara Josephine (née Wieck) (1819–96) A German pianist and composer who married Robert SCHUMANN in 1840. She became famous for playing work by her husband after he died, but she was also a talented composer of piano music herself.

Schumann, Robert (Alexander) (1810–56) A German composer who was the son of bookseller and publisher. He learned to play the piano when he was young, but was sent to law school in Leipzig by his mother after his father's death. He gave up law in favour of music in 1830 but was devastated two years later when damage to his right hand prevented him from becoming a concert pianist. Instead, he concentrated on composing. In 1840 he married Clara Wieck, the daughter of his former teacher, despite the opposition of her father, and during this happy stage of his life he composed many of his greatest works. In 1844 he had a mental breakdown and he and his wife moved to Dresden. He later became a conductor in Düsseldorf, but in 1854 he attempted to commit suicide. He spent the last years of his life in a mental asylum. His principal works include: the opera *Genoveva*; choral pieces (such as *Paradise and the Peri*); four symphonies; concertos for piano and cello; chamber music; piano pieces (such as PAPILLONS); and more than 250 songs.

Schütz, Heinrich (1585–1672) A German composer and organist who was possibly the greatest German composer of his era. His works include many religious pieces which married Lutheran philosophy to contemporary Italian musical styles, e.g. *Twelve Sacred Songs*, *Christmas Oratorio*, as well as three impressive Passions.

Schwarzkopf, Elisabeth (1915–) A German soprano who is recognized as being one of the great singers of the 20th cent. She had a very wide repertoire, which included in particular MOZART, Richard STRAUSS and WOLF.

scordatura (It.) 'Mis-tuning', i.e. tuning stringed instruments to abnormal notes, so as to produce special effects.

score Music written down in such a way that it indicates all the parts for all the performers, i.e. the whole composition.

scoring The writing of a SCORE.

Scotch snap The name for a rhythm which leaps from a short note to a longer note. It is found in many Scottish folk tunes.

'Scottish' ('Scotch') Symphony MENDELSSOHN's symphony No. 3 in A minor (completed in 1842). It was inspired by a visit to Scotland and was dedicated to Queen Victoria.

Scott, Cyril Meir (1879–1970) An English composer and poet who was nicknamed 'the English Debussy'. His works include the opera *The Alchemist*, many pieces for piano, and several orchestral compositions.

scraper A percussion instrument in which sound is

produced by scraping a stick over a series of notches cut into a piece of wood or bone.

Scriabin *see* Skryabin.

scroll The decorative end of the PEG-BOX of a violin (or other stringed instrument), which may be carved into a curl resembling a scroll, or an animal head.

Segovia, Andrés (1893–1987) A Spanish guitarist of lasting fame. He was responsible for reviving interest in the guitar as a serious 'classical' instrument and was honoured by many composers (such as VILLA-LOBOS) writing pieces especially for him. He also composed works for the guitar himself.

segue (It.) 'Follows', i.e. a direction to start playing the following movement without a break.

seguidilla A Spanish dance in 3/8 or 3/4 time in the style of the BOLERO, but much faster.

semibreve A 'half of a BREVE'; the note with the longest time-value normally used in modern Western notation. In US notation, this is called a whole note.

semiquaver A note with half the time-value of a quaver, and a sixteenth the time-value of a semibreve. In US notation, this is called a sixteenth-note.

semitone 'Half a TONE'; the smallest INTERVAL regularly used in modern Western music.

semplice (It.) 'In a simple manner'.

sentence *see* phrase.

senza (It.) 'Without', so *senza sordino* means 'without mute' (in music for strings).

septet A group of seven performers or a piece of music written for such a group.

septuplet A group of seven notes of equal time-value to be played in the time of four or six.

sequence 1 The repetition of a short passage of music in a different pitch. **2** A form of hymn in Latin used in the Roman Catholic Mass, such as DIES IRAE and STABAT MATER.

serenade 1 A love song, traditionally sung in the evening and usually accompanied by a guitar or mandolin. **2** A DIVERTIMENTO performed during an evening entertainment.

serenata (It.) An 18th-cent. form of secular CANTATA or a short opera composed for a patron.

serialism A method of composition developed by SCHOENBERG in which all semitones are treated as equal, i.e. tonal values are eliminated. *See* twelve-note music.

serpent An obsolete bass woodwind instrument with several curves in it (hence its name). It was used during the 16th cent. in church orchestras and military bands.

Sessions, Roger (1896–1985) An American composer whose talent was recognized early: he wrote his first opera when he was 13 and went to Harvard University a year later. He absorbed all types of music into his own compositions and was a champion of 'modern' music. His works include operas (e.g. *The Trial of Lucullus*), symphonies, chamber music and pieces for piano.

seventh An INTERVAL in which two notes are seven steps apart (including the first and last), for example F to E.

sevillana A Spanish folk dance originally from the city of Seville. It is similar to the SEGUIDILLA.

sextet A group of six performers or a piece of music written for such a group.

sextolet *see* sextuplet.

sextuplet A group of six notes to be performed in the time of four notes.

sforzando (It.) 'Forcing', i.e. a strong accent placed on a note or chord.

shake An alternative term for TRILL.

shamisen A Japanese long-necked lute with three strings. It has no frets and is plucked with a plectrum.

shanai A double reed instrument from India, similar to a SHAWM.

Shankar, Ravi (1920–) An Indian sitar player who, more than anyone, has been responsible for popularizing the instrument (and Indian music) in the West. He regularly tours the world giving recitals.

shanty A song, with a pronounced rhythm, that was sung by sailors to help them coordinate their actions in the days of sailing ships. Shanties usually follow a format in which solo verses are followed by a chorus.

sharp The sign which raises the pitch of the line or space on which it stands on a stave by a semitone.

Sharp, Cecil James (1859–1924) A pioneer collector of English and American folk music who founded the English Folk Dance Society. His endeavours spurred a revival of interest in folk song and dance.

shawm (shawn) A double-reed woodwind instrument that dates from the 13th cent. It was developed from

Middle Eastern instruments and produced a coarse, shrill sound. It was a forerunner of the OBOE.

Sheherazade A symphonic suite by RIMSKY-KORSAKOV (1888), based on stories from the *Arabian Nights*.

Shéhérazade (Fr.) A set of three songs with orchestra by RAVEL (1903).

sheng A sophisticated Chinese mouth organ, dating back some 3000 years.

Shield, William (1748–1829) An English composer whose works include some 50 operas (e.g. *Rosina*), songs, and trio sonatas.

shofar (shophar) An ancient Jewish wind instrument, made from a ram's horn, which is still used in synagogues.

shop ballad *see* ballad.

Shostakovich, Dmitri (1906–75) A Russian composer who wrote his first symphony for his graduation from the St Petersburg (Leningrad) Conservatory. This work established him as an important composer. Many of his subsequent works were reviled by the Soviet authorities. He responded by writing his ironic 5th symphony, 'a Soviet artist's reply to just criticism', which was duly officially praised as a masterpiece. He was in Leningrad as the city was besieged by the Germans in 1941 and during this time wrote the LENINGRAD SYMPHONY, which became an anthem for liberty. After the demise of Stalin in 1953, Shostakovich was more able to explore an individual style of composition, (including some TWELVE-NOTE MUSIC) although the bulk of his work adopts classical idioms. His works include operas (for example, *The Nose*,

Lady Macbeth of Mtsensk), ballets (such as *The Age of Gold*), 15 symphonies, chamber music and theatre scores.

Sibelius, Jean (1865–1957) A Finnish composer and undoubtedly the most famous of all Finnish musicians. He started to compose when he was 10. He began to study law but reverted to music. Always interested in folklore, he based many of his compositions around Finnish epics and legends. After the turn of the century his pieces became more abstract, but in 1929 he gave up composing altogether, either because he was ill or because he was not satisfied with his output. Sibelius's works have always had popular appeal, mainly because they are comparatively accessible. His works include 15 symphonies, symphonic poems (for example, FINLANDIA, *En Saga*), a violin concerto, theatre music (such as *The Tempest*), choral works, chamber music, and many pieces for piano.

siciliano A slow dance from Sicily in 6/8 or 12/8 time, with a characteristic lilting rhythm.

side drum, (snare drum) A cylindrically shaped drum that is the smallest usually used in an orchestra. Snares, made of gut or sprung metal are stretched across the bottom parchment and vibrate against it when the upper membrane of parchment is struck; this gives the drum its characteristic rattling sound. The snares can be released so that a more hollow sound is produced.

Siegfried *see* Ring des Nibelungen.

Siegfried Idyll A work for orchestra by WAGNER which incorporates themes from the opera *Siegfried*.

signature *see* key signature; time signature.

signature tune A few bars of catchy music that are associated with a performer or broadcast show.

Signor Bruschino, Il A comic opera by ROSSINI to a libretto by Foppa. It is famous largely because of its overture in which the violinists are instructed to tap their music stands. It was first performed in 1813.

Silken Ladder, The (*La Scala di Seta*) An opera by ROSSINI to a libretto by G. Rossi. The ladder in question leads a lover to his beloved. It was first performed in 1812.

similar motion The simultaneous progression of two or more parts in the same direction.

simile (It.) 'Like' or 'similar', i.e. a direction to continue in the same vein that has already been indicated.

simple interval Any INTERVAL which is an octave or less. Compare compound interval.

simple time *see* compound time.

Sinding, Christian (1856–1941) A Norwegian composer and pianist who studied in Leipzig. His works include operas, four symphonies and many songs. However, he is best remembered for his piano piece *The Rustle of Spring*.

sine tone An electronically produced note that is entirely 'pure'.

sinfonia (It.) Literally, 'symphony', i.e. an instrumental piece. It is also a term used for a small orchestra.

sinfonietta A short symphony or a symphony for a small orchestra.

single chant *see* Anglican chant.

Singspiel (Ger.) Literally, 'sing-play', i.e. a comic opera in German with spoken dialogue replacing the sung RECITATIVE.

sinistro, sinistra (It.) 'Left', as in *mano sinistra,* meaning 'left hand'.

sistrum An ancient type of rattle in which loose wooden or metal discs are suspended on metal bars strung across a frame.

sitar A type of Indian lute which is believed to have originated in Persia. It has moveable metal frets and three to seven 'melody' strings; below these strings lie 12 or so 'sympathetic' strings which create a droning sound. The sitar is plucked with a long wire plectrum. It has a distinctive 'twangy' sound and is usually played in consort with the TABLA.

Six, Les (Fr.) 'The Six', the name given in 1920 to six young French composers by the poet and music critic H. Collet who, with another of their champions, Jean Cocteau, was passionately anti-WAGNER. The six were AURIC, Durey, HONEGGER, MILHAUD, POULENC, and Tailleferre. Subsequently a number of other composers became members of the group, but it ceased to have an effective function after 1925.

sixteenth-note (US) *see* semiquaver.

Skalkottas, Nikos (1904–49) Greek composer and violinist who was a disciple of SCHOENBERG but who later incorporated Greek folk music into his compositions. His works include *Greek Dances* for orchestra, much chamber music, and pieces for piano.

sketch A short piano or instrumental piece.

skiffle A type of pop music played in England during the 1950s. Skiffle bands relied on American idioms (e.g. BLUES) and attempted to become 'authentic' by incorporating home-made instruments (such as tea-chest basses) into their outfits.

Skryabin, Alexander Nikolaievich (1872–1915) A Russian composer and pianist. He was hailed as a talented pianist at an early age and played his own works on European concert tours. His work was initially influenced by CHOPIN and LISZT, but from 1905 it became increasingly mystical. His works include symphonies and orchestral pieces (e.g. *The Divine Poem*, *Poem of Ecstasy*), and many piano sonatas.

slancio, con (It.) 'With impetus'.

Slavonic Dances Two sets of dances by DVORAK, inspired by folk music. They were originally composed as piano duets but were later orchestrated.

Slavonic Rhapsodies Three orchestral compositions by DVORAK.

Sleeping Beauty, The A ballet by TCHAIKOVSKY, originally choreographed by Petipa. It was first performed in 1890.

sleigh bells Small metal bells with steel balls inside which are mounted together in groups to produce a richly textured jingling sound. They are traditionally hung on sleighs, but are occasionally used in orchestras to create special effects.

slide trombone *see* trombone.

slide trumpet An early form of trumpet which had a slide similar to that used in the TROMBONE. It became obsolete when the valve TRUMPET was invented.

slur A curved line that is placed over or under a group of notes to indicate that they are to be played, or sung, smoothly, that is, with one stroke of the bow (violin music) or in one breath (singing).

Smetana, Bedřich (1824–84) A Czech composer who studied in Prague, the city where he later taught until 1856. He worked for a time as a composer and teacher in Sweden, but in 1863 he returned to Prague where he wrote his most famous work, the opera *The* BARTERED BRIDE, and also composed MA VLAST (My Country), his greatest instrumental piece. In the later 1870s Smetana became stone deaf, but he continued to write music. Smetana's work was strongly nationalistic and he is considered the father of Czech music. His works include nine operas (the last, *Viola*, was unfinished), piano pieces, chamber music, and symphonic poems (such as *Richard III*).

Smith, Bessie (1895–1937) A Black American jazz singer who earned the title 'Empress of the Blues' for the emotional intensity of her singing. She made many recordings with such people as Louis ARMSTRONG.

Smith, John Stafford (1750–1836) An English composer and organist. One of his major achievements was to collect and publish old English music dating back to the 12th cent. He also wrote church music and songs, including *Anacreon in Heaven*, the tune of which was adapted for the American national anthem, *The Star-Spangled Banner*.

smorzando (It.) 'Fading' or 'dying away', i.e. the music is to become softer and slower.

Smyth, Ethel Mary (1858–1944) An English composer

and writer who studied music in Germany. She was an active supporter of the women's suffrage movement and was jailed in England in 1911. Her works include operas (such as *The Wreckers*, *The Boatswain's Mate*), chamber music, and choral works. She also wrote an acclaimed autobiography, and was made a D.B.E in 1922.

snare drum *see* side drum.

Snow Maiden, The An opera by RIMSKY-KORSAKOV, who also wrote the libretto. The story tells of the Snow Maiden who falls in love but melts in the spring sunshine. It was first performed in 1882.

soave (It.) 'Soft' or 'gentle'.

soca music A type of powerful, rhythmic dance music from the English-speaking islands of the Caribbean. It evolved from soul (hence SO) and calypso (CA).

soft pedal *see* piano.

soh In the TONIC SOL-FA, the fifth note (or DOMINANT) of the major scale.

solemnis (Lat.) 'Solemn', as in *Missa Solemnis*, 'Solemn Mass'.

solenne (It.) 'Solemn'.

solennelle (Fr.) 'Solemn'.

sol-fa *see* tonic sol-fa.

solfeggio (It.) A type of singing exercise in which the names of the notes are sung. *See* tonic sol-fa.

solo (It.) 'Alone', i.e. a piece to be performed by one person, with or without accompaniment.

solo organ A manual on an ORGAN with strong, distinctive stops, used for individual effect.

Solti, Georg (1912–) A Hungarian-born conductor

who has worked with many of the world's leading orchestras, including the London Philharmonic Orchestra and, since 1969, the Chicago Symphony Orchestra. He is especially famous for conducting works by WAGNER, MAHLER and ELGAR. He was knighted in 1972.

sonata Originally a term for any instrumental piece to distinguish it from a sung piece or CANTATA. However, during the 17th cent. Two distinct forms of sonata arose: the *sonata da camera* (chamber sonata), in which dance movements were played by two or three stringed instruments with a keyboard accompaniment, and the *sonata da chiesa* (church sonata) which was similar but more serious. In the 18th cent. the sonata came to be a piece in several contrasting movements for keyboard only or for keyboard and one solo instrument.

sonata form A method of arranging and constructing music that is commonly used (since *c.*1750) for symphonies, sonatas, concertos etc. There are three sections to sonata form: the 'exposition' (in which the subject or subjects are introduced), the 'development' (in which the subject(s) are expanded and developed), and the 'recapitulation' (in which the exposition, usually modified in some way, is repeated).

sonata-rondo form A type of RONDO, popular with such composers as BEETHOVEN, which is a combination of rondo and SONATA FORM.

Sonate Pathétique BEETHOVEN's piano sonata in C minor. The title *pathétique* means 'with emotion'.

Sondheim, Stephen (1930–) An American composer

and lyric-writer. He wrote the lyrics for the musical *West Side Story*, and his own compositions include the shows *Company*, *Sweeney Todd* and *A Little Night Music*.

sonatina A short sonata.

song cycle A set of songs which have a common theme or have words by a single poet. SCHUBERT, SCHUMANN and MAHLER wrote notable song cycles.

song form *see* ternary form

Song of the Earth, The (*Das Lied von der Erde*) A song cycle by MAHLER, for mezzo-soprano, tenor and orchestra, first performed in 1908. The words are a translation of ancient Chinese poems.

Songs of a Wayfarer (*Lieder eines Fahrenden Gesellen*) A set of four songs for contalto or baritone and orchestra by MAHLER, composed 1883–5. Mahler also wrote the words which concern the feelings of a man rejected in love.

Songs without Words (*Lieder ohne Worte*) A collection of 48 piano pieces in eight books by MENDELSSOHN, composed 1832–45.

sopra (It.) 'Above', so *come sopra* means 'as above'.

soprano The highest pitch of human voice, with a range of about two octaves above approximately middle C. The term is also applied to some instruments, such as soprano saxophone (the highest pitched saxophone).

sordino (It.) 'Mute'.

Sorcerer, The A comic opera by GILBERT and SULLIVAN. It was first performed in 1877.

Sorcerer's Apprentice, The (*L'Apprenti sorcier*) A tone poem by DUKAS (1897), based on a ballad by Goethe. The story is about a sorcerer's apprentice who casts a spell in his master's absence, then discovers that he does not know how to reverse it.

sospirando (It.) 'Sighing'.

sostenuto (It.) 'Sustained'.

sotto (It.) 'Below', as in *sotto voce*, which literally means 'under the voice' or whispered.

soul music A type of emotionally-charged music developed by black musicians in America. 'Soul', as it is usually called, derives from BLUES and GOSPEL music with the addition of rock rhythms.

sound hole The opening in the belly (upper surface) of a stringed instrument, e.g the f-shaped holes in a violin or the round hole in a guitar.

soundpost A piece of wood connecting the belly (upper surface) of a stringed instrument (such as a violin) to the back. It helps to distribute vibrations through the body of the instrument.

Sousa, John Philip (1854–1932) An American bandmaster and composer who formed a successful military-style band that toured the world giving concerts. He composed many marches (such as *The Stars and Stripes Forever*). The giant tuba, the 'sousaphone', which encircles the player's body, was especially designed for his band.

sousaphone *see* Sousa, John Philip.

special effects A non-specific term used of any extraordinary noises or sounds that may be required of an orchestra, or part of an orchestra, to satisfy the demands of a composer, such as cow bells etc.

species A discipline used in teaching strict COUNTER-POINT, developed by FUX, who listed five rhythmic patterns, or 'species', in which one voice part could be combined with another.

spinet A type of small harpsichord.

spirito (It.) 'Spirit', so *con spirito* means 'with spirit'.

spiritual A type of religious folk song or hymn that was developed by black (and white) Americans in the 18th and 19th cent. Spirituals are characterized by strong syncopated rhythms and simple melodies. They were superseded by GOSPEL music.

Spohr, Ludwig (Louis) (1784–1859) A German violinist, composer, conductor and teacher. He toured Europe giving concerts and was among the first conductors to use a BATON. His works include 9 symphonies, 10 operas (e.g. *Faust*), and numerous miscellaneous pieces for violin, piano and harp.

Spontini, Gasparo Luigi Pacifico (1774–1851) An Italian composer whose best known works include the spectacular operas *La Vestale* and *Fernand Cortez*

Sprechgesang (Ger.) Literally, 'speech-song', i.e. a type of singing that is half speech. It was used by SCHOENBERG in his song cycle PIERROT LUNAIRE.

Spring Sonata The title given to BEETHOVEN's sonata in F for violin (1801).

Spring Symphony 1 The title of SCHUMANN's symphony no. 1 in B flat (1841). **2** A song-symphony for three solo singers, mixed chorus, boys' choir and orchestra by BRITTEN (1949).

Stabat Mater (Lat.) 'His Mother stood', the initial

249

words of a verse from the Gospel account of the Crucifixion. It was set to music by, for example, PALESTRINA. Later settings include those by HAYDN, SCHUBERT and ROSSINI, amongst others.

staccato (It.) 'Detached', i.e. notes should be shortened and played with brief intervals between them.

staff *see* stave.

Stamitz, Karl (1745–1801) A German-born violinist and composer of Czech descent. His works include 70 symphonies, a symphony for two orchestras, and two operas. His father, Johann, and brother, Anton, were also noted musicians.

Stanford, Charles Villiers (1852–1924) An Irish-born composer, and also an influential teacher (VAUGHAN WILLIAMS and BLISS were among his pupils). He was knighted in 1901. Little of his music is now performed, but he is remembered for his opera *Shamus O'Brien*, and his 3rd (*Irish*) symphony. His church music is still heard. He was knighted in 1901.

Stanley, John (1713–86) An English composer and famous organist, blind from early childhood. His works include concertos for strings, pieces for flute, and compositions for organ.

Star-Spangled Banner, The The song officially adopted as the US national anthem in 1931. The words were written by Francis Scott Key in 1814 to a tune by John Stafford SMITH.

stave (staff) A set of horizontal lines (usually five) on which music is written. Each line, and the gaps between them, represent a different pitch.

steel drum A percussion instrument ('pan') made by

West Indian musicians (particularly from Trinidad) out of discarded oil drums. Each drum can be tuned to play a range of notes by beating and heat-treating different sections of the 'head', i.e. the top of the drum.

Steinway & Sons A firm of piano manufacturers founded by Heinrich Steinweg (Henry Steinway) in New York in 1853. A London branch opened in 1875.

stem The line, or 'tail', attached to the head of all notes smaller than a semibreve.

Stern, Isaac (1920–) A Russian-born violinist who has lived in the USA since childhood. He made his first public appearance (in the USA) at the age of 15 and has remained a premier solo performer ever since.

stesso (It.) 'Same', so *lo stesso tempo* means 'the same speed'.

Stockhausen, Karlheinz (1928–) A German composer who was a pupil of MESSIAEN and MILHAUD. He became interested in electronic music and has influenced many composers. Such music is now a recognized art form. Stockhausen has challenged the concepts of established formulae (for example with *Gruppen*, a piece for three orchestras and three conductors) and has frequently been considered outrageous by traditionalists. The element of chance is incorporated into his compositions, and luck, as much as anything else, makes a performance succeed or fail. His works include pieces for piano (usually electrically amplified), pieces that are largely allowed to flow with the performers' own whims (such as *Mantra*), and hundreds of experimental compositions (such as *Carré* for four orchestras and choruses).

stomp A BLUES composition in which the beat is literally stamped on the floor.

stop A handle or knob on an organ that admits or prevents air from reaching certain pipes and which can therefore be used to modify the potential output of the MANUALS and PEDALS.

stopping On stringed instruments, the placing of fingers on a string to shorten its effective length and raise its pitch.

Storace, Stephen (1763–96) An English composer who travelled Europe (meeting MOZART in the process). His works include operas (such as *No Song, no Supper*), chamber music and songs.

Stradella, Alessandro (1642–82) An Italian composer, singer and violinist who was eventually murdered (at the second attempt) for eloping with a nobleman's mistress. His works include six oratorios, and assorted sonatas and concertos.

Stradivari, Antonio (1644–1737) An Italian violin-maker whose instruments are unsurpassed for the quality of their sound. He was taught the craft by AMATI and founded his own business in Cremona.

Stradivarius *see* Stradivari.

strathspey *see* reel.

Strauss, Johann 'the elder' (1804–49) An Austrian conductor and composer whose works include various waltzes and other pieces.

Strauss, Johann 'the younger' (1825–99) An Austrian violinist, conductor and composer of light music, especially Viennese waltzes. He formed his own orchestra which performed successfully throughout Europe. He composed 16 operettas (e.g. *Die Fledermaus*), and hundreds of dances including the famous BLUE DANUBE waltz.

Strauss, Joseph (1827–70) An Austrian composer and younger brother of Johann STRAUSS 'the younger'. He also composed dance music.

Strauss, Eduard (1835–1916) An Austrian composer and the youngest brother of Johann STRAUSS 'the younger'. He, too, composed waltzes.

Strauss, Richard (1864–1949) A German composer who was the son of a distinguished horn player. He started composing when he was six and wrote his first symphony when he was 16. He combined composition with an international career as a conductor. His compositions essentially comprise three types: symphonic poems, operas, and songs. His work was initially influenced by LISZT and WAGNER and he was seen by many as Wagner's successor. His first opera, SALOME, caused controversy and his second, ELEKTRA, was equally sensational. Later, influenced perhaps by his main librettist, Hofmannsthal, he concentrated on more joyous music. This resulted in *Der* ROSENKAVALIER and *Arabella*. He wrote particularly notably for the female voice, and also for the horn. His works include: operas (e.g. *Daphne*, *Capriccio*, *Die Liebe der Danae*, orchestral poems (e.g. ALSO SPRACH ZARATHUSTRA, DON QUIXOTE), songs (e.g. FOUR LAST SONGS), and two horn concertos.

Stravinsky, Igor Feodorovich (1882–1971) A Russian

composer whose father was a bass singer. For a time he studied under RIMSKY-KORSAKOV and was influenced by Russian music and also by that of DEBUSSY. Diaghilev commissioned his first masterpiece, the ballet *The* FIREBIRD, and he later wrote PETRUSHKA and *The* RITE OF SPRING for Diaghilev's ballet company. In 1914 he left Russia and, after spending time in France, emigrated to the USA (becoming a US citizen in 1945). On leaving his native land, he left behind his innate nationalism and started to experiment with traditional forms of music that he had not been entirely familiar with, such as neo-classical music. While living in the USA he adopted SERIALISM, evolving it to his own technique. Stravinsky greatly furthered the cause, and acceptability, of 'modern' music and his place in history is assured. His principal compositions include the ballets *Petrushka*, *The Rite of Spring* and *Agon*; the orchestral pieces *Fireworks* and DUMBARTON OAKS; choral works; and assorted pieces for miscellaneous instruments.

Streichquartett (Ger.) 'String quartet'.

strepitoso (It.) 'Boisterously'.

stretto 'Close together', i.e. a quickening of tempo.

stringendo (It.) 'Tightening', i.e. increasing tension, often with accelerated tempo.

string quartet A group of four performers who use stringed instruments (two violins, viola and cello); or a piece of music written for such a group.

strings A general term for the stringed instruments of the violin family.

Stroh violin A violin made of metal (invented by

Charles Stroh in 1901) which incorporates a trumpet bell and does not have a normal violin body.

Stück (Ger.) 'Piece'.

subdominant The fourth note of the major or minor scale.

subito (It.) 'Suddenly', as in *piano subito*, meaning 'suddenly soft'.

subject A musical theme (a substantial group of notes) on which a composition (or part of a composition) is constructed, for example, the first and second subjects in the exposition in SONATA FORM; the subject in a FUGUE; also the leading voice (first part) of a fugue.

submediant The sixth note of the major or minor scale.

subsidiary theme Any THEME that is less important than the main theme(s) of a composition.

suite A collection of short pieces that combine to form an effective overall composition; the Baroque suite was a set of (stylized) dances.

Suk, Josef (1874–1935) A Czech composer, violinist and viola player who was the son-in-law of DVORAK. He composed two symphonies and, amongst other works, symphonic poems.

sul, sull' (It.) 'On' or 'over', so *sul ponticello* means 'over the bridge' (in violin bowing).

Sullivan, Arthur Seymour (1842–1900) An English composer, organist and conductor who wrote many successful light operas to libretti by W.S. GILBERT. This partnership produced some of the most popular comic operas of all time, including H.M.S. PINAFORE,

The PIRATES OF PENZANCE, *The* MIKADO, RUDDIGORE, *The* YEOMAN OF THE GUARD and *The* GOLDOLIERS. However, Sullivan also wrote serious operatic music (e.g. *Ivanhoe*), ballet music, oratorios and church music. He was knighted in 1883.

Suppé, Franz von (1819–95) A Dalmatian-born composer and conductor of Belgian descent. He is best remembered for his satirical songs, his operettas and his overture *Poet and the Peasant*.

Surprise Symphony The name given to HAYDN's symphony no. 94 in G (1791). It is so called because the slow, opening movement is rudely interrupted by a sudden very hard drumbeat.

suspension A device used in harmony in which a note sounded in one chord is sustained while a subsequent chord is played (or sung), producing a dissonance which is then resolved.

sustaining pedal *see* piano.

Sutherland, Joan (1926–) An Australian soprano of international repute. She was made a D.B.E in 1979.

Svendsen, Johan Severin (1842–1911) A Norwegian composer, violinist and conductor. Having been a virtuoso violin player, he turned to composing while studying in Leipzig, where he was influenced by WAGNER. He wrote orchestral works, including two symphonies.

Swan Lake A ballet by TCHAIKOVSKY, which was originally choreographed by Petipa and Ivanov. It was first performed in 1877 and has subsequently become the best known of all ballets.

Sweelinck, Jan Pieterszoon (1562–1621) A Dutch composer, organist and harpsichordist. His important keyboard music was influenced by English composers. He himself became an influential teacher of Dutch and German composers.

swell organ A manual on an ORGAN. The notes played on this manual can become louder and softer by the opening and closing of the shutters on the swell box which encloses the pipes.

swing A type of American popular music of the 1935–45 era; it was played by big bands and had an insistent rhythm. Glenn Miller and his ensemble were influential in its development.

Sylphides, Les A ballet with music taken from piano pieces by CHOPIN. It was first performed (as a ballet) in 1909.

sympathetic strings Strings on certain instruments (such as the sitar) which are not actually plucked or bowed, but which are set in sympathetic vibration and produce a note without being touched, when the same note is played on a 'melody' string.

symphonic poem An orchestral composition, a form of PROGRAMME MUSIC, usually in one movement, which attempts to interpret or describe an emotion, idea, or story. The term was coined by LISZT.

Symphonie fantastique An orchestral work in five movements by BERLIOZ (1830). It was inspired by the composer's love for the actress Harriet Smithson.

symphony In essence a prolonged or extended SONATA for an orchestra. Most symphonies have four movements (sections) which, although interrelated, tend to have recognized forms, for example, a quick first movement, a slow second movement, a MINUET third movement, and a vibrant fourth movement (FINALE).

syncopation An alteration to the normal arrangement of accented beats in a bar. This is usually done by placing accents on beats or parts of a beat that do not normally carry an accent.

synthesizer An electronic instrument, operated by a keyboard and switches, that can generate and modify an extensive range of sound.

Szymanowski, Karol (1882–1937) A Polish composer who is considered the father of modern Polish music. After being influenced first by the German Romantic composers and then by DEBUSSY and STRAVINSKY, he turned to Polish folk music and his later works were in a nationalistic style. His works include operas (such as *King Roger*), the ballet *Harnasie*, four symphonies, and many pieces of chamber music.

T

tabla A pair of Indian drums, beaten by the hands, which are often used to accompany the SITAR in classical Indian music.

table An alternative name for the upper surface, or belly, of members of the violin family.

tabor An early type of snare drum.

tace (It.) 'Silent'.

Tafelmusik (Ger.) 'Table music', i.e. music sung during a banquet as an entertainment.

tail The stem attached to the head of a minim (half note), or a smaller note.

tail piece The piece of wood at the base of a violin to which the strings are attached.

tail pin The metal rod at the bottom of a cello or double bass which can be pulled out to adjust the height of the instrument above the floor.

Takt (Ger.) 'Time', so *im Takt* means 'in time'.

Tales of Hoffmann, The (*Les Contes d'Hoffmann*) An opera by OFFENBACH to a libretto by J. Barbier and M. Carré. It is based on three stories by E.T.A. Hoffmann which each recount love-affairs. Unfinished at the time of Offenbach's death, it was completed by E. Guiraud.

Tallis, Thomas (*c.*1505–85) An English composer and organist who is considered to be one of the most important and influential musicians of his era. His works include many religious pieces (e.g. motets, Masses, Magnificats), secular choral works, and compositions for keyboard.

talon (Fr.) The 'nut' or heel of a bow.

tambourin 1 A lively 18th-cent. piece in the style of a folk-dance from Provence, usually in 2/4 time. **2** A narrow drum played along with a pipe, as the accompaniment to dancing.

tambourine A small, shallow drum with a single skin fastened over a circular frame. Small metal cymbals (jingles) are slotted into the frame and rattle when the instrument is shaken or beaten by the hand.

tampon A type of drumstick which has a head at each end, held in the middle to produce a drum roll.

tam-tam A large bronze gong of Chinese origin.

Tancredi An opera by ROSSINI to a libretto by G. Rossi (after works by Tasso and Voltaire). It was first performed in 1813.

tango A Latin-American dance in moderately slow 2/4 time, originating from Argentina. It makes use of syncopated rhythms and became popular in Europe in the 1920s.

Tannhäuser (*Tannhäuser, und der Sängerkrieg auf Wartburg*, Tannhäuser and the Singing Contest at the Wartburg) An opera by WAGNER, who also wrote the libretto. The story concerns the two conflicting loves of Tannhäuser, a minstrel knight. It was first performed in 1845.

tanto (It.) 'So much', as in *allegro non tanto*, meaning 'quick, but not too quick'.

Tanz (Ger.) 'Dance'.

tap dance A dance in which the feet are used to tap out a rhythm. Tap dancing was made popular by Fred Astaire's performances in films during the 1930s. Special shoes with steel plates at the toe and heel are usually worn.

tarantella A very fast, wild folk dance from Southern Italy in 6/8 time, and gradually increasing in speed. CHOPIN used the form in a concert piece.

Tartini, Guiseppe (1692–1770) An Italian violinist, composer and teacher. He founded a famous violin school in Padua and wrote several treatises on violin playing and on acoustics in harmony. His works include many violin concertos, sonatas (such as *The Devil's Trill*), symphonies, and church music.

tasto (It.) The keyboard of a piano or the finger-board of a stringed instrument.

Taverner, John (*c*.1490–1545) An important English composer who taught at Oxford University and is best known for his religious works (chiefly Masses and Magnificats).

Tchaikovsky, Piotr Ilyich (1840–93) A Russian composer. His mother's death when he was 14 may have stimulated him to compose. After four years as a civil servant he enrolled at the St Petersburg Conservatory. He then moved to Moscow to teach and met members of 'The FIVE'. In 1877, after the success of his first piano concerto, he started a correspondence with Nadezhda von Meck that lasted for 15 years. She offered to sponsor him and this gave him the financial freedom to compose. In 1877 Tchaikovsky, in an apparent attempt to 'cure' his homosexuality, married Antonia Milyukova, but the marriage was such a disaster that he tried to kill himself after just 11 weeks. However, despite his problems, he continued to write music and the last years of his life were fruitful. He toured Europe and the USA as a conductor and won international praise. He died of cholera in St Petersburg after drinking unboiled water.

Tchaikovsky was the outstanding Russian composer of the 19th cent. Among his greatest works are his ballets where his theatrical flair is expressed most completely. Although he admired many Russian contemporaries and their works, the musicians that influenced him most were European, for example BIZET, SAINT-SAENS, MOZART. His principal works include the operas *Vakula the Smith*, EUGENE ONEDIN, *The Maid of Orleans* and *Yolanta*; the ballets SWAN LAKE, *The* SLEEPING BEAUTY and *The* NUTCRACKER; 6 symphonies; concertos for piano and violin; miscellaneous orchestral pieces; and many songs.

Te Deum laudamus (Lat.) 'We Praise Thee, O God'; a Christian hymn sung at Matins. Numerous composers (e.g. PURCELL, HANDEL, VERDI) have set it to music.

Te Kanawa, Kiri (1944–) A New Zealand soprano who is especially famous for roles in operas by VERDI, MOZART and Richard STRAUSS.

Telemann, Georg Philipp (1681–1767) A German composer. He taught himself music while studying law at Leipzig University. He became friendly with BACH and was hugely prolific. His works include 44 Passions, 40 operas, 600 French overtures and numerous pieces of chamber music.

temperament The way in which INTERVALS between notes have been 'tempered', or slightly altered, in Western music so that the slight discrepancy in seven octaves is distributed evenly over the range. In 'equal temperament' an octave is divided into 12 semitones, which means that, for example, D sharp is also E flat: this is a compromise, for strictly there is a marginal difference between D sharp and E flat.

tempo (It.) 'Time'. The time taken by a composition, therefore the speed at which it is performed, hence the pace of the beat. *A tempo* means 'in time'. Tempo can also mean a movement of a sonata or symphony, as in *il secondo tempo*, 'the second movement'.

ten. (It.) An abbreviation for TENUTO.

Tennstedt, Klaus (1926–) A German conductor and violinist. He has worked with many noted orchestras and is known for his interpretations of the works of MAHLER.

tenor 1 The highest adult male voice with a range an octave to either side of middle C. **2** As a prefix to the name of an instrument, it indicates the size between an alto member of the family and a bass, e.g. tenor saxophone. **3** The RECITING NOTE in psalm singing. **4** An obsolete term for a viola (tenor violin).

tenor drum A drum, frequently used in military bands, between a side drum and bass drum in size and pitch, and without snares.

tenuto (It.) 'Held'; a term which indicates that a note should be held for its full value, or in some cases, even longer.

ternary form A term applied to a piece of music that is divided into three self-contained parts, with the first and third sections bearing strong similarities.

ternary time *see* triple time.

terzett, terzetto (It.) *see* trio.

tessitura (It.) 'Texture'; a term that indicates whether the majority of notes in a piece are high up or low down in the range of a voice (or instrument).

tetrachord A group of four notes.

theme The melody, or other musical material, that forms the basis of a work or a movement and which may be varied or developed. It may return in one form or another throughout a composition.

Thieving Magpie, The (*La Gazza ladra*) An opera by

263

ROSSINI to a libretto by G. Gherardini. The story tells of a maid, Ninetta, who is sentenced to death for a theft; she is saved when a magpie is discovered to be the guilty party. It was first performed in 1817.

thirty-second note (US) A demisemiquaver.

Thomson, Virgil (1896–) An American composer and music critic of great originality. He lived in Paris for fifteen years, where he was influenced by the music of '*Les* SIX' and STRAVINSKY. His works include operas (e.g. *Four Saints in Three Acts*), ballets (e.g. *The Filling Station*), film music, chamber music, and many songs.

thorough bass *see* figured bass.

Threepenny Opera, The (*Die Dreigroschenoper*) An opera by Kurt WEILL to a text by Bertolt Brecht (plus some lyrics from Kipling and Villon). It is a reworking of *The* BEGGAR'S OPERA and was first performed in 1928.

Thus spoke Zoroaster *see* Also sprach Zarathustra.

thunder stick (bullroarer, whizzer) An instrument consisting of a flat piece of wood fastened to a piece of string. When the piece of wood is whirled around the head, it creates a roaring sound.

tie A curved line that joins two notes of the same pitch together, indicating that they should be played as one long note.

Till Eulenspiegel (full title: *Till Eulenspiegels lustige Streiche*, Till Eulenspiegel's Merry Pranks) A symphonic poem by Richard STRAUSS. It is based on a German folk tale of a famous rogue and was first performed in 1895.

timbre (Fr.) The quality of a tone, or the characteristic sound of an instrument.

time The rhythmic pattern (number of beats in a bar) of a piece of music, as indicated by the TIME SIGNATURE. Duple time has two beats in a bar, triple time has three beats in a bar, and so on.

time-names (rhythm-names) A French method of teaching time and rhythm in which beats are given names, such as 'ta', 'ta-té' etc.

time signature A sign placed at the beginning of a piece of music that indicates the number and value of beats in a bar. A time signature usually consists of two numbers, one placed above the other. The lower number defines the unit of measurement in relation to the semibreve (whole note); the top figure indicates the number of those units in a bar, for example, 3/4 indicates that there are three crotchets (quarter notes) in a bar.

timpani (kettledrums) The main orchestral percussion instruments, consisting of bowl-shaped shells over which the membrane is stretched. The shell is supported on a frame at the base of which, in 'pedal timpani', is the foot pedal that can alter the pitch of the drum as it is played. The drum can also be tuned by means of screws, which alter the tension of the membrane.

Tin Pan Alley The nickname given to West 28th Street, New York, where the popular-song publishing business used to be situated. It consequently became a slang expression for the popular music industry.

tin whistle (penny whistle) A metal whistle-flute,

similar to a RECORDER, but with six finger holes. It produces high-pitched sounds and is commonly used to play folk music.

Tippett, Michael Kemp (1905–) An English composer who started to play the piano when he was five and later went to the Royal College of Music. He was influenced by madrigals, blues and jazz. During the Second World War, he was imprisoned for his pacifist beliefs. He has written several important and impressive pieces, such as his oratorio *A Child of Our Time*. His output has not been huge but his pieces are invariably well crafted. They include operas (e.g. *King Priam*, *The Knot Garden*), 4 symphonies, many choral works, and chamber music. He was knighted in 1966.

toccata (It.) 'Touched'; a type of music for a keyboard instruments which is intended to show off a player's 'touch' or ability.

Tod und das Mädchen, Der *see* Death and the Maiden.

Tod und Verklärung, Der *see* Death and Transfiguration.

tonality The use of a KEY in a composition.

tone 1 An INTERVAL comprising two semitones, e.g. the interval between C and D. **2** (US) A musical note. **3** The quality of sound, e.g. good tone, sharp tone etc. **4** In PLAINSONG, a melody.

tone poem *see* symphonic poem.

tonguing In the playing of a wind instrument, this means interrupting the flow of breath with the tongue so that detached notes are played, or the first note of a phrase is distinguished.

tonic The first note of a major or minor scale.

tonic sol-fa A system of notation and sight-singing used in training, in which notes are sung to syllables. The notes of the major scale are: doh, re, me, fah, soh, la, te, doh (doh is always the TONIC, whatever the key). The system was pioneered in England by John Curwen in the mid-19th cent.

Tortelier, Paul (1914–90) A French cellist and composer, who played with many of the world's leading orchestras. His son, Jan Pascal Tortelier (1947–), is a noted vilionist and conductor.

Tosca An opera by PUCCINI to a libretto by G. Giacosa and L. Illica (based on Sardou's play *La Tosca*). The story tells how Tosca, a famous singer, agrees to succumb to Scarpia, the chief of police, if he spares the life of Cavaradossi, her lover. Amid much treachery, all three come to grief. It was first performed in 1900.

Toscanini, Arturo (1867–1957) An extremely famous Italian conductor who worked in both Europe and the USA. He had a reputation for being something of a disciplinarian and his performances were noted for their clarity and dynamism. His forte was Italian and German opera.

tosto (It.) 'Rapid', as in *più tosto*, 'quicker'.

trad jazz Literally, 'traditional jazz'; a term referring to the type of comparatively simple jazz with a strong melody, as played in New Orleans, which preceded the development of BEBOP.

Tragic Overture A concert overture by BRAHMS. It was first performed in 1881.

'Tragic' Symphony SCHUBERT's symphony no. 4 in C minor (1818). The composer named the work himself and it is, indeed, very serious in mood.

tranquillo (It.) 'Calm'.

transcription *see* arrangement.

transition 1 The changing from one key to another during the course of a composition. **2** A passage linking two sections of a piece, which often involves a change of key.

transposing instruments Instruments which sound notes different from those actually written down, for example, a piece of music in E flat for the B flat clarinet would actually be written in F.

transposition The changing of the pitch of a composition. Singers sometimes ask accompanists to transpose a song higher or lower so that it is better suited to their voice range.

Traviata, La (The woman who has been led astray) An opera by VERDI to a libretto by F.M. Piave (after Dumas's play *La Dame aux camélias*). The story concerns Violetta, a sickly courtesan, who falls in love with Alfredo whom she is requested to give up by his father. Alfredo insults her but is forgiven, and she dies in his arms.

treble The highest boy's voice.

tremolando (It.) 'Trembling'.

tremolo (It.) The rapid repetition of a single note, or the rapid alternation between two or more notes.

triad A chord of three notes which includes a third and a fifth.

Trial by Jury A comic opera by GILBERT and SULLIVAN.

It is the only one of their operettas which is sung throughout. It was first performed in 1875.

triangle A percussion instrument comprising a thin steel bar bent into a triangle but with one corner left unjoined. It is normally struck with a thin metal bar.

trill (shake) An ornament in which a note is rapidly alternated with the note above. It is used in both vocal and instrumental pieces.

trio 1 A group of three performers, or a piece of music written for such a group. **2** The middle section of a minuet, as found in sonatas, symphonies etc. It was originally a section scored for three parts.

triplet A group of three notes played in the time of two notes.

Tristan and Isolde An opera by WAGNER, who also wrote the libretto. The story is based on a tragic legend in which the two lovers drink a love potion, thinking it to be poison, which leads to disastrous consequences.

tritone An INTERVAL consisting of three whole tones.

Triumphes of Oriana, The A collection of 25 madrigals, edited by Thomas Morley and published in 1601. It is believed that they were written as a tribute to Queen Elizabeth I.

Trojans, The (*Les Troyens*) An opera in two parts (*The Taking of Troy* and *The Trojans at Carthage*) by BERLIOZ, who also wrote the libretto. The complete opera was first performed in 1890.

tromba marina A long, stringed instrument of the 15th

cent., also known as a 'sea-trumpet'. It consisted of a long, tapered box with one string mounted on top which was played with a bow; inside the box were some 20 sympathetic strings.

trombone A brass instrument that has changed little for 500 years. The body of the instrument has a cylindrical bore with a bell at one end and a mouthpiece at the other. A U-shaped slide is used for lengthening or shortening the tubing and therefore for sounding different notes. Tenor and bass trombones are often used in orchestras.

trope (Lat.) An addition of music or words to traditional PLAINSONG liturgy.

troppo (It.) 'Too much', as in *allegro non troppo*, meaning 'fast but not too fast'.

troubadours Poet-musicians of the early Middle Ages who originally came from the South of France and sang in the Provençal language.

Trout Quintet The popular name of SCHUBERT's quintet in A major for violin, viola, cello, double bass and piano (1819). The piece is so called because the 4th movement is a set of variations of his song *Die Forelle* (The Trout).

Trovatore, II (The Troubadour) An opera by VERDI to a libretto by S. Cammarano. The story tells of how Manrico, the son of a count, is kidnapped by gypsies when a child and becomes a troubadour. Later he falls in love with Leonora, who is also wooed by the Count di Luna. The count has Manrico put to death and then realizes that he has killed his own brother.

trumpet A brass instrument that has a cylindrical bore

with a funnel-shaped mouthpiece at one end and a bell (flared opening) at the other. The modern trumpet has three valves (operated by pistons) which bring into play extra lengths of tubing and are therefore used to change the pitch of the instrument. Trumpets are used in orchestras, jazz bands and military bands. Trumpet is also a generic term used to describe any number of very different wind instruments that are found all over the world.

Trumpet Voluntary A popular name for a piece that used to be wrongly attributed to PURCELL. It was composed by Jeremiah CLARKE and originally entitled *The Prince of Denmark's March*.

tuba A large brass instrument with a wide conical bore, a large cup-shaped mouthpiece, and a large bell which faces upwards. It can have between three and five valves and comes in three common sizes: tenor (EUPHONIUM), bass, and double bass. Tubas are found in orchestras and military bands.

tubular bells *see* bell.

Tuckwell, Barry (1931–) An Australian horn-player who has lived in Britain since 1951. He has played as a soloist with many leading chamber orchestras and has formed his own quintet, known as the Tuckwell Wing Quintet.

tuning The adjusting of the pitch of an instrument so that it corresponds to an agreed note, for example, an orchestra will usually have all its instruments tuned to the note of A.

tuning fork A two-pronged steel device which, when tapped, will sound a single, 'pure' note. It was invented by John Shore in 1711 and is used to tune instruments etc.

Turandot An opera by PUCCINI (completed after his death by Alfano) to a libretto by G. Adami and R. Simone (based on a play by Gozzi). Turandot is a Chinese princess who says she will marry any man who can answer three riddles, the penalty for failure being death. It was first performed in 1926.

tutti (It.) 'All'; in orchestral music, a *tutti* passage is one to be played by the whole orchestra.

twelve-note music (twelve-tone system) A method of composition formulated and advanced by SCHOENBERG. In the system, the twelve chromatic notes of an octave can only be used in specific orders called 'note rows'; no note can be repeated twice within a note row, and the rows must be used complete. In all, there are 48 ways in which a note row can be arranged (using inversion, retrograde motion and inverted retrograde motion) and it is with note rows that compositions are constructed.

Twilight of the Gods *see* Ring des Nibelungen, Der.

U

ukelele A small,,four-stringed guitar that was developed in Hawaii during the 19th cent. It was a popular music hall instrument during the 1920s.

Un Ballo in Maschera *see* Masked Ball, A.

'Unfinished' Symphony The title given to SCHUBERT's symphony no. 8 in B minor, written in 1822. He completed only two movements. Its first performance was in 1865, long after the composer's death.

unison The sounding of the same note or its octave by two or more voices or instruments.

up beat The upward movement of a conductor's baton or hand, indicating the unstressed (usually the last) beat in a bar.

upright *see* piano.

Urtext (Ger.) 'Original text'.

V

Valkyrie, The *see* Ring des Nibelungen, Der.

valse (Fr.) *see* waltz.

valve A device used on brass instruments (such as a trumpet) which, when depressed, increases the effective length of the tube, and thus alters the pitch being played.

Varèse, Edgard (1885–1965) A French-born experimental composer who was encouraged by DEBUSSY. He emigrated to the USA in 1916, where he was a champion of 'modern' music. He described his own music as 'organized sound' and he ignored the traditional conventions of melody and harmony. Towards the end of his life he experimented with electronic and taped music. His compositions include works for solo flute, percussionists, and *Déserts,* for orchestra and taped sounds.

variation The modification or development of a theme.

273

vaudeville (Fr.) Originally a type of popular, satirical song sung by Parisian street musicians. In the 18th cent. these songs (with new words) were incorporated into plays and the word came to mean the last song in an opera in which each character sang a verse. In the 19th cent. stage performances with songs and dances were called 'vaudevilles' and the Americans used the term to describe music hall shows.

Vaughan Williams, Ralph (1872–1958) An English composer who studied music in Germany, France and England. He became passionately interested in folk music and was for a time president of the English Folk Song and Dance Society. He also studied 16th-cent polyphonic music, which was the other great influence on his work. His music can be violent, jolly and mysterious, and he remains one of the most important English composers of the 20th cent. His works include 9 symphonies (e.g. *A London Symphony*, *Sea Symphony*, *Pastoral Symphony*), operas, (e.g. *Sir John in Love*, *The Poisoned Kiss*), ballets, (e.g. *Job*), choral works, piano music, and chamber music.

veloce (It.) 'Fast'.

Venite (Lat.) The first word of Psalm 95, *'Venite, exultemus Domino'* ('O come let us sing unto the Lord'), which is sung as a prelude to psalms at Anglican Matins.

Verdi, Giuseppe (1813–1901) An Italian composer of opera who started his musical career as an organist. A wealthy grocer, Antonio Barezzi, spotted his talent and paid for his private education in Milan (he later became Verdi's father-in-law). He became a musical director at Busseto, but returned to Milan in 1836 to write his first opera, *Oberto*, which was given its first performance at La Scala in 1839. The success of this work led to commissions. However, when his wife and two children died within a couple of years of each other, he vowed never to write music again. In 1841, however, he wrote *Nabucco*, which was performed in 1842 and was sufficiently successful to establish his reputation. He married again and continued to write a string of operas that guarantee his place in history as one of the greatest of opera composers. After his second wife, Giuseppina, died in 1897, his own health began to deteriorate and he eventually died of a stroke.

Verdi transformed Italian opera, which had traditionally favoured singers in preference to orchestras, by developing the importance of the orchestral element. His works include: 27 operas (e.g. MACBETH, RIGOLETTO, *Il* TROVATORE, *La* TRAVIATA, *Un Ballo in Maschera* (*A* MASKED BALL), DON CARLOS, AIDA, OTELLO and FALSTAFF); choral works (e.g. *Messa da Requiem*, *Te Deum*; chamber music; and many songs.

verismo (It.) 'Realism'; the term is used to describe a type of opera which was concerned with representing contemporary life of ordinary people in an honest and realistic way, e.g. MASCAGNI's *Cavalleria rusticana*.

Vespers The seventh of the Canonical Hours (services of the day) in the Roman Catholic Church. Many composers (such as MOZART) have written musical settings for the service.

vibraphone (vibes) An American instrument, similar to the GLOCKENSPIEL, which consists of a series of metal bars which are struck with mallets. Underneath the bars hang tubular resonators which contain small discs that can be made to spin by means of an electric motor. When the notes are sustained the spinning discs give the sound a pulsating quality.

vibrato (It.) Literally, 'shaking', i.e. a small but rapid variation in the pitch of a note.

Vickers, Jon (1926–) A Canadian tenor who is especially famous for his roles in WAGNER and VERDI operas.

Victoria, Tomás Luis de (*c*.1548–1611) An outstanding Spanish composer of polyphonic music, who was also a priest. He held various church positions in Rome before returning to Madrid. His works include motets, Masses, Magnificats and hymns.

Vienna State Opera One of the world's leading opera companies. Its famous conductors have included GLUCK, DONIZETTI, MAHLER, KARAJAN.

vierhändig (Ger.) 'Four-handed', i.e. a piano duet.

Village Romeo and Juliet, A An opera by DELIUS who also wrote the libretto. The story tells of two young lovers, the children of quarrelling landowners, who fulfil a suicide pact. It was first performed in 1907.

Villa-Lobos, Heitor (1887–1959) A Brazilian pianist and composer was was largely self-taught. His music was influenced by South American Indian music and Brazilian folk songs. His works include 12 symphonies, operas (e.g. *Yerma*, *Amazonas*), piano concertos, chamber music and pieces for the guitar.

villanella (It.) Literally, a 'rustic song', a popular part-song of the 17th cent.

viol A family of stringed instruments played with a bow which were widely used in the 16th and 17th cents. The instruments came in several sizes and designs, but they all usually had six strings and frets. Although they were similar in appearance to members of the violin family, they were constructed differently and gave a much softer sound.

viola Originally a general term for any bowed stringed instrument. However, it is now the name of the alto member of the violin family. It has four strings.

viola da braccio (It.) Literally, an 'arm viol'; a generic term for any stringed instrument played on the arm. It came to mean a violin or viola.

viola da gamba (It.) Literally, a 'leg viol', a term originally used of those members of the VIOL family played vertically between the legs or on the lap, but it came to be used exclusively for the bass viol.

viola d'amore (It.) Literally, a 'love viol', i.e. a tenor VIOL with seven strings (instead of six) and seven or fourteen sympathetic strings. It is so called because it had a particularly sweet tone.

violin A stringed instrument, played with a bow, which was introduced in the 16th cent. It was developed independently of the VIOL from the medieval fiddle. It has no frets and just four strings. The violin family includes the violin itself (treble), VIOLA (alto) and VIOLONCELLO or 'cello' (tenor). The DOUBLE BASS developed from the double bass VIOL, but it is now included in the violin family.

violoncello The tenor of the VIOLIN family, normally abbreviate to cello, dating from the 16th cent. It is held vertically between the legs of the seated player, and the TAIL PIN rests on the ground. It has four strings, which are played with a bow.

virginal A keyboard instrument dating from the 16th cent. in which the strings are plucked by quills. It was similar to the HARPSICHORD, except that it had an oblong body with strings running parallel to the keyboard. The word has also been used to describe any member of the harpsichord family.

vivace (It.) 'Lively'.

Vivaldi, Antonio (1675–1741) An Italian composer and violinist who was ordained as a priest in 1703. He taught music at a school for orphan girls in Venice and managed to travel extensively as well as write copious amounts of music. In 1740 he moved to Vienna and died in relative poverty. His music had an impact on BACH and was revived during the 19th century, his four concertos for violin, which are collectively known as *The* FOUR SEASONS, becoming especially popular. His works include some 450 concertos (200 of them for violin), 70 sonatas, 50 operas, and oratorios (such as *Judith*). He also wrote many religious pieces.

vivamente (It.) 'In a lively way'.

vivo (It.) 'Lively'.

vocal score *see* score.

voce (It.) 'Voice', as in *voce di petto*, 'chest voice'.

voice 1 The sound produced by human beings by the rush of air over the vocal chords, which are made to vibrate. There are three categories of adult male voice (bass, baritone and tenor); three female categories (contralto, mezzo-soprano and soprano); and two boy categories (treble and alto). **2** Parts in contrapuntal compositions are traditionally termed 'voices'.

volti subito (It.) 'Turn over quickly' (of a page).

voluntary 1 An improvised piece of instrumental music (16th cent.) **2** An organ solo (sometimes improvised) played before and after an Anglican service.

W

Wagenseil, Georg Christoph (1715–77) Austrian composer and keyboard player who was a pupil of FUX. He became a court composer in Vienna and his works include symphonies, concertos, oratorios and operas.

Wagner, (Wilhelm) Richard (1813–83) A German composer and conductor who was born in Leipzig but moved to Dresden in 1815 with his mother and stepfather. He became interested in opera while he was still young and after leaving Leipzig University became a conductor at various opera houses. He married Minna Planer in 1836 and lived in poverty in Paris for a time while he worked on his first two operas, *Rienzi* and *The* FLYING DUTCHMAN. They were accepted by the Dresden opera house and he was appointed an assistant conductor there in 1842. Six years later, he was obliged to flee Dresden because of his liberal sympathies for a minor uprising. He went to Zurich where he started to work on his epic cycle of operas, *Der* RING DES NIBELUNGEN. The *Ring* took some 25 years to complete and in the meantime, he wrote LOHENGRIN (produced at Weimar in 1850) and TRISTAN AND ISOLDE, complete in 1859, which may have been inspired by an illicit relationship with Mathilde Wesendonck. By 1864 Wagner was deeply in debt but was saved from imprisonment by an offer from Ludwig II (the 'mad king') to stay in Munich as his 'adviser'. *Tristan* finally had its first performance in Munich in 1865. Marital problems arose again when he had an affair with Cosima, the wife of his friend and conductor Hans von Bülow and the daughter of Liszt. After his wife died and Cosima had obtained a divorce, they were married in 1870.

The city of Bayreuth offered Wagner a site for an opera house in 1872 and the theatre, built with the help of Ludwig II, was opened four years later with the first complete performance of the *Ring*. In 1876 he began to work on PARSIFAL, which was produced at Bayreuth in 1882. The following year Wagner died of a heart attack while spending the winter in Venice.

Wagner's operas were designed as 'total art works', a synthesis of music, movement, poetry and the visual arts. In the *Ring* cycle, each character has a signature tune (*leitmotif*), which unifies the huge work and also helps to inform the audience of the visible action and the thoughts of the characters, as conveyed by the music. Wagner's intense, romantic pieces are some of the greatest of all operas and he is one of the giants in the history of music.

His operas include *Rienzi*, *The Flying Dutchman*, TANNHAUSER, *Lohengrin*, *Tristan and Isolde*, *The*

MASTERSINGERS OF NUREMBERG, *The Ring of the Nibelungen* (*The Rhine Gold*, *The Valkyrie*, *Siegfried*, *The Twilight of the Gods*), and PARSIFAL. In addition, he also wrote the SIEGFRIED IDYLL for orchestra, and some choral works.

Waldteufel, Emil (1837–1915) A French composer and pianist. He wrote many dances, mainly waltzes, which include *The Skater's Watz* and *España*.

Walton, William (Turner) (1902–1983) An English composer who learned the basics of music as a chorister but taught himself composition. He made his reputation with FACADE, a sequence of instrumental pieces to accompany poems by Edith Sitwell. He was initially influenced by '*Les* SIX' and jazz, but the majority of his later works were traditionally English. His works include two symphonies, operas (such as *Troilus and Cressida* and *The Bear*), oratorios (e.g. BELSHAZZAR'S FEAST), assorted concertos, chamber music, and music for films (for example *Hamlet* and *Henry V*).

waltz A dance in triple time. Waltzes evolved in Germany and Austria during the late 18th cent. and became particularly popular in Vienna.

Warlock, Peter (The pseudonym of Philip Heseltine) (1894–1930) An English composer and writer who was influenced by DELIUS (on whom he wrote a book) and Elizabethan music. He had an unstable personality that veered between aggressiveness and shyness. He eventually took his own life. His works include many songs and choral compositions (such as *The Curlew*), and orchestral pieces, including the *Capriol Suite*.

War Requiem, A An ambitious choral work by BRITTEN

for choirs, organ, solo voices and chamber orchestra. The piece consists of alternating settings of poems by Wilfred Owen and the Requiem Mass. It was first performed in 1962.

Water Music An orchestral suite by HANDEL. It is known that Handel composed music for a royal occasion on the Thames in 1717, and this is presumed to be the music.

Weber, Carl Maria Ernst von (1786–1826) A German composer, conductor and pianist who studied under Michael Haydn. He had various jobs as a conductor and in 1813 he went to Prague, where he was appointed conductor of the opera. In 1817 he was made conductor of the Dresden opera and he started work on *Der Freischütz*, his best known opera, which was performed in Berlin in 1821. He visited England in 1826 to conduct the first performance of OBERON but died shortly afterwards, of tuberculosis.

Weber is considered by many to be the creator of German romantic opera; using French opera as a framework, he introduced German themes. He had a colossal influence on subsequent composers up to, and including, WAGNER. His works include the operas *Abu Hassan*, *Freischütz*, *Euryanthe* and *Oberon*, 2 symphonies, concertos, 4 piano sonatas, and many songs.

Webern, Anton von (1883–1945) An Austrian composer who was a pupil of SCHOENBERG. With Schoenberg and Alban BERG, he formed a group known as the Second Viennese School, which was concerned with developing new forms of music. He adopted the TWELVE-NOTE SYSTEM and produced several, extremely short pieces that stripped music to its essentials, for instance, his *Six Bagatelles* for string quartet lasts precisely 3 minutes 37 seconds. Webern's influence on a new generation of composers was immense after he died and he was one of the most important developers of SERIALISM. His works include orchestral pieces (e.g. *Variation*), choral compositions, and pieces for voice and piano.

wedding march A tune played at the start or end of a wedding service. The two most famous wedding marches are MENDELSSOHN's 'Wedding March' from his incidental music to *A MIDSUMMER NIGHT'S DREAM* and WAGNER's 'Bridal Chorus' (familiar to most by its common title 'Here Comes the Bride') from the opera LOHENGRIN.

Weill, Kurt (1900–50) A German-born composer who was initially influenced by SCHOENBERG. His first success was *The* THREEPENNY OPERA (based on *The* BEGGAR'S OPERA), which he wrote in collaboration with Bertolt Brecht, and which was first performed in 1928. He began to adopt jazz idioms and this, coupled to the facts that his works were social satires and that he was a Jew, made him unwlecome in Nazi Germany. First he fled to Paris and then, in 1935, to the USA. While living in the USA, his music mellowed somewhat and he wrote several Broadway musicals. His works include the operas *The Threepenny Opera*, *Rise and Fall of the City of Mahagonny* and *Down in the Valley*; the musicals *Knickerbocker Holiday* and *Lost in the Stars*; orchestral pieces, and many songs.

Wesley, Samuel (1766–1837) An English organist and composer who was the son of the famous hymn writer, Charles Wesley. He is known for his many anthems (such as *The Wilderness*), church music, symphonies and organ pieces, and also as a noted promoter of the music of BACH.

whole note (US) A semibreve.

whole-tone scale A scale in which all the INTERVALS are whole-tones, i.e. two semitones.

Widor, Charles Marie Jean Albert (1845–1937) A French composer and organist who taught at the Paris Conservatoire. He is famous for his organ music. His works include operas, 10 organ 'symphonies' (his famous toccata comes from the fifth), piano concertos, and chamber music.

Wigmore Hall A concert hall in Wigmore St., London, famous for its chamber concerts and recitals. It was built in 1910.

Willaert, Adrian (*c.*1485–1562) An influential Flemish composer who went to live and work in Venice. His works include Masses, motets and various instrumental pieces.

Williamson, Malcolm (1931) An Australian composer who has lived and taught in Britain since 1950. He has written pieces especially for children. His works include operas (for example *Our Man in Havana*, *The Happy Prince* and *Julius Caesar Jones*), ballets, orchestral pieces, and songs.

William Tell An opera by ROSSINI to a libretto by V.J.E. de Jouy and H.L.F. Bis (based on Schiller's play). It tells the story of the Swiss, William Tell, who resists the invading Austrians. It was first performed in 1829.

Winterreise, Die ('The Winter Journey') A cycle of 24 songs by SCHUBERT, to words by W. Miller. The songs tell the story of a lovelorn young man.

Wolf, Hugo (1860–1903) An Austrian composer who had a fanatical respect for WAGNER. He worked fitfully, but had an extraordinary talent for writing songs. He ultimately went mad and died in an asylum. His works include many song cycles, two operas (e.g. *Der Corregidor*), and chamber music.

Wood, Henry Joseph (1869–1944) An English conductor who is famed for conducting the London PROMENADE CONCERTS from 1895 until 1940. He was responsible for introducing new music to British audiences and was internationally respected. He was knighted in 1911.

woodwind A term for a group of blown instruments that were traditionally made of wood (some of which are now made of metal), for example, flutes, oboes, clarinets and bassoons etc.

XYZ

Xenakis, Iannis (1922–) A Romanian-born, Greek composer who trained to be an architect in Paris. His interest in mathematics has greatly influenced his work and he uses computers while composing (though his works are usually scored in a traditional manner). His compositions include a ballet, *Kraanerg* (for orchestra and taped music), orchestral pieces (such as *Artées* for 10 instruments), and choral works.

xylophone A percussion instrument made up of hardwood bars arranged like a keyboard on a frame. It is played by striking the bars with mallets. Xylophones used in orchestras have steel resonators suspended beneath each bar.

Yeomen of the Guard, The A comic opera by GILBERT and SULLIVAN. The story is an escape saga set in the Tower of London. It was first performed in 1888.

Youmans, Vincent (1898–1946) An American composer who is best known for his musicals, e.g. *No! No! Nanette* and *Hit the Deck*.

Zadok the Priest The first of four anthems composed by HANDEL for the coronation of George II (1727). It is still performed at British coronations.

Zandonai, Riccardo (1883–1944) An Italian composer who composed operas in a VERISMO style. His operas include *Il grillo del Focolare* and *Francesca da Rimini*.

zarzuela A type of Spanish comic opera which has a satirical theme and includes dialogue. It usually comprises just one act.

Zauberflöte, Die *see* Magic Flute, The.

zimbalom *see* dulcimer.

zither The generic term for a range of stringed instruments. The European zither consists of a flat box which is strung with a variety of different kinds of string (up to 40). The player uses a plectrum to play melodies on one set of strings while the fingers on the other hand pluck a series of open strings to form a drone accompaniment.

Time values

- ○   semibreve (or whole note)
- ♩   minim (or half note)
- ♩   crotchet (or quarter note)
- ♪   quaver (or eight note)
- ♪   semiquaver (or sixteenth note)
- ♪   demisemiquaver (or thirty-second note)
- ♪   hemidemisemiquaver (or sixty-fourth note)

A dot following a note increases its value by a half.

Clefs

- treble clef
- bass clef
- soprano clef
- alto clef
- tenor clef

Accidentals

- ♯   sharp (raises note one semitone)
- ×   double sharp (raises note one tone)
- ♭   flat (lowers note one semitone)
- ♭♭   double flat (lowers note one tone)
- ♮   natural (restores the normal pitch after a sharp or flat)

The most commonly used time signatures

Simple duple:

- $\frac{2}{2}$ or ¢   two minim beats
- $\frac{2}{4}$ two crotchet beats
- $\frac{2}{8}$ two quaver beats

Compound duple:

- $\frac{6}{4}$ two dotted minim beats
- $\frac{6}{8}$ two dotted crotchet beats
- $\frac{6}{16}$ two dotted quaver beats

Simple triple:

- $\frac{3}{2}$ three minim beats

$\frac{3}{4}$	three crotchet beats
$\frac{3}{8}$	three quaver beats

Compound triple:

$\frac{9}{4}$	three dotted minim beats
$\frac{9}{8}$	three dotted crotchet beats
$\frac{9}{16}$	three dotted quaver beats

Simple quadruple:

$\frac{4}{2}$	four minim beats
$\frac{4}{4}$ or **C**	four crotchet beats
$\frac{4}{8}$	four quaver beats

Compound quadruple:

$\frac{12}{4}$	four dotted minim beats
$\frac{12}{8}$	four dotted crotchet beats
$\frac{12}{16}$	four dotted quaver beats

Dynamics

$<$	*crescendo*
$>$	*diminuendo*

Curved lines

♩♩	tie or bind; the two notes are played as one
♩♩	slur or legato; play smoothly (on a stringed instrument, in one bow)

Staccato marks and signs of accentuation

♩♩	*mezzo-staccato* (shortens note by about 1/4)
♩♩	*staccato* (shortens note by about 1/2)
♩♩	*staccatissimo* (shortens note by about 3/4)
♪	detached: accented
♪	attack

Miscellaneous

:‖	repeat preceding section
‖	end of section or piece
⌒	pause
𝄋	al segno, dal segno